IMAGES
of America

SHANDAKEN

I0806172

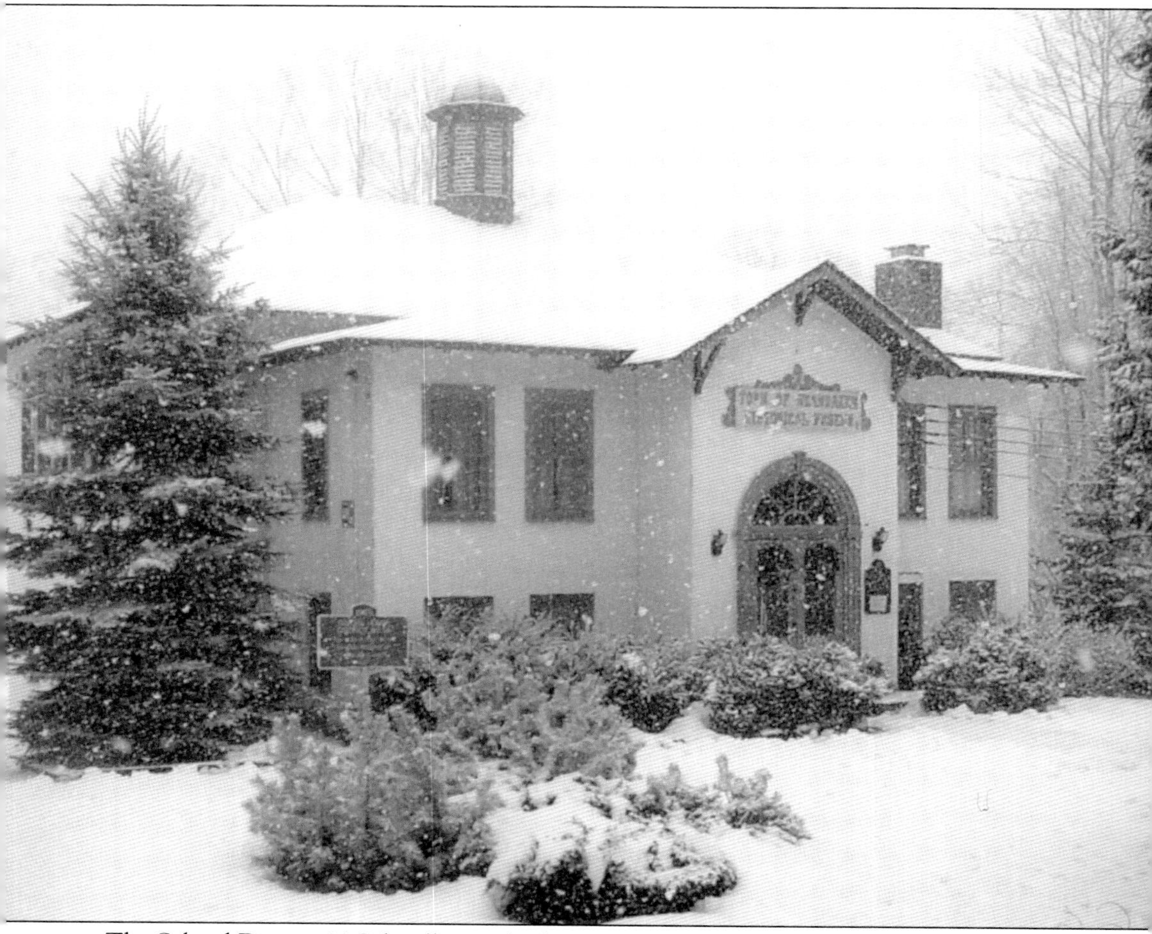

The School District 14 Schoolhouse, built in 1925, is listed on the National Register of Historic Places. Located at 26 Academy Street in Pine Hill, it is now home to the Town of Shandaken Historical Museum. (Courtesy of Ashley Bender.)

On the Cover: Students pose for a school portrait in front of the Phoenicia School in the spring of 1891. (Courtesy of the Town of Shandaken Historical Museum.)

IMAGES
of America

SHANDAKEN

Mary L. Herrmann

ARCADIA
PUBLISHING

ISBN 978-0-7385-7354-0

Published by Arcadia Publishing
Charleston, South Carolina

Printed in the United States of America

Library of Congress Control Number: 2010922401

For all general information, please contact Arcadia Publishing:
Telephone 843-853-2070
Fax 843-853-0044
E-mail sales@arcadiapublishing.com
For customer service and orders:
Toll-Free 1-888-313-2665

Visit us on the Internet at www.arcadiapublishing.com

To the people of Shandaken, past and present, especially the future inhabitants, as they are the ones history should be preserved for, so that they may appreciate the past and take care to make wise decisions in the future.

Contents

Acknowledgments

First and foremost, I would like to thank the Board of the Shandaken Historical Museum: Nancy Smith, June La Marca, Matthew Persons, Flavia DeMola, and Maureen Nagy and their predecessors for their hard work and dedication in preserving the history of our town. Their resolve to continue this selfless work despite personal and political obstacles so that history is recorded and saved for future generations is extraordinary and inspiring. It was no small task to start the collection and establish a museum to house it some 20-plus years ago. Without this dedication, countless documents and artifacts would be lost to time. Special thanks to Evelyn Bennett, longtime director of the museum, who put in countless hours caring for the collection. I would also like to thank Shandaken town supervisor Peter DeSclafani and Rose Dorn for their unwavering support and confidence in me.

To Rebekah Collinsworth and Arcadia Publishing for creating a market for publications such as this so the smaller, yet no less important, stories can be told.

Thank you to my husband, Joe, my children Joe, Ashley, Cody, and Sean, and my grandchildren Hailey and Ethan for all your love, trust, and support.

Unless noted, all the pictures in this book are courtesy of the Town of Shandaken Historical Museum.

INTRODUCTION

The first recorded settlers in Shandaken were Jacob Langjar (Longyear) and his wife, Maria Kockin, near Mount Pleasant in 1752. They were the lifelong tenants of Robert Livingston. They were soon joined by the Crispells, the Winnes, the Satterlees, the Meisners, the Furlows, the Markles, and the Hudlers. Their life was hard and not unlike the pioneers who settled the West. In fact, after a few generations, a party of Shandaken residents did go west to Grass Lakes, Michigan, and settled there also. Slowly more migrants came to the Catskill Mountain area, branching out from the colonies along the Hudson River that had already been developing for hundreds of years. They built their homes, raised their young, and started enterprises. The first innkeeper in Shandaken was Andrew Longyear; he did not cater to tourists so much as to the teamsters and travelers who depended on the wayside lodgings. They spent days completing what today would be the simplest of journeys.

Beginning in the early 1800s, tanning was the first industry to employ workers on a grand scale. When the hemlock—whose bark was used in the tanning process—were plentiful, barges brought hides up the Hudson and teamsters had the arduous task of bringing their heavily laden horse drawn wagons up the mountain trail to the tanneries. The bark was stripped from the trees and, except for those timbers sawn for planks to pave the turnpike, most of the grand hemlocks were left to decay. During the Civil War, leather was in high demand and tanning peaked. By the 1870s, the hemlock supply was depleted. Resourceful workers turned to hoop shaving as a source of income. This was also a means for the farmers to supplement their income in the winter months. Many former bark peelers and solitary mountain men spent long winters in small shacks slicing willowy, young growth into the strips that would bind barrels and crates. After a scant decade or two, with the invention of machines that were able to do the work of men more easily, this industry also became obsolete.

The bare mountains also gave up their treasure of bluestone for a while, and quarries became as common as farms. But, as if some nameless force was having a trial to bend the will of the mountain dwellers, the introduction of Portland cement would end yet another endeavor. Quarrying was no longer profitable by the beginning of the 1900s. The railroad had been built by this time and with it new commerce and business opportunities. Sawmills replaced the quarries as the hardwood trees, not having to compete with the majestic hemlocks that once covered the mountains, sprang up and afforded suitable wood for furniture making and lumber. It was reported that sawmills sprang up like mushrooms and stood at every accessible waterfall. While Chichester and Shandaken boasted larger chair factories (so-called because chairs were a predominant product), in the hamlets smaller furniture making shops began to cater to the tourist or boarder trade, as it was called back then. In addition to smaller pieces of furniture, they turned out napkin rings, bowls, vases, rolling pins, and such trinkets as the visitors desired from the native Catskill hardwoods.

An exhibit from the Shandaken Historical Museum on Industry poetically states, "The hard fact of the industrial collapse seems to fit the mood of our mountains. Our Catskills are a spot, not fitted for money making with its bustle and tense living; but ideal for remaking men amid the peace and loneliness of the outdoors. The Catskills remain, and probably forever will continue to be, a land of relaxation and romance."

The lawmakers of New York State created the State of New York Forest Preserve in 1885. The Catskill Park was created in April 1904. Today, in addition to the rules and regulations that governs these entities, the residents of Shandaken and the surrounding communities must also live with the limitations on development that protect the New York City watershed. In addition to providing recreation to half a million tourist annually, the region resources serve as the water supply for 10 million downstate neighbors. What some residents see as unfair and unwarranted burdens that restrict economic development, others regard as a blessing that will keep the pristine wilderness in trust for future generations.

A map of the school district dated 1900 shows a schoolhouse located every 2 miles. As transportation and roads improved several of these were combined until finally in 1960s the schools consolidated and Onteora Central School District was formed, combining the schools of not only Shandaken, but Woodstock and Olive also. Similarly, the local churches that once competed for standing in each hamlet joined their counterparts and shared resources.

Like church and school, community activities that served a civic function also fed the need for social interaction. Fire departments, citizens bands, social clubs, Grange organizations, and even Odd Fellows provided a necessary role in rural life. In these gatherings, citizens forged relationships, gained skills, and promoted civic pride. Parades and barbeques were counted on activities in the summer months. The local communities had Grange halls that were instrumental in working for a better life for rural people. Several hamlets had baseball teams who played in organized fashion with their wins and losses reported in the local press. Veterans and holidays were celebrated and revered with parades and ceremonies.

Shandaken is not unique in the American experience to have pride in the local who finds fame in the outside world, such as Basil Rowe, who was an aviation pioneer, or to be discovered by a notable personality such as Amelita Galli-Curci, who chose to reside here for a portion of her years. Such relationships bring a wholesome and validating presence to the authentic experience of living in a community that, to the outside observer, may appear to be a simple and inconsequential existence. Shandaken, like many small towns scattered across America, embodies a hardworking, proud populace that has sustained their existence by acknowledging the challenges to their survival and enduring in spite of them.

The railroad first came to Phoenicia in 1871 and a year later made its way up the grade to Pine Hill. Not having been granted permission to carve a tunnel through Belleayre Mountain, the railroad instead tackled the steep incline by constructing a double horseshoe curve at Pine Hill. The railroad desired passenger fares as well as freight revenue and helped to sponsor tourism in the mountains. Each hamlet had a station along the way and except for Phoenicia—home to the Empire State Railroad Museum—they have all been dismantled. At Phoenicia, the tracks veered north and a narrow-gauge line serviced Hunter. Passenger service to the mountain communities lasted a scant 80-plus years; passenger service was discontinued in 1954 and freight service ceased in 1976. Today a small privately run tourist train uses a minute section of track between Phoenicia and Mount Tremper/Mount Pleasant. Beginning with the commonality of automobile and improved roads in the earlier part of the century, and the airplane and air-conditioning later, tourism in the Catskills declined from the peak periods of her golden age. Capitalizing on the "ski trains" that brought crowds to Phoenicia beginning in the 1930s, in 1949 the State of New York opened Belleayre Ski Area to help the economy and bring business to the hamlets that "rolled up their sidewalks in the winters." Tourism remains a vital part of the local economy along with second-homeowners and commuters. The lack of commercial development due to the terrain, watershed protection, forest preserve, and parkland has resulted in a community whose historic past is abundantly evident. Here the landscape reveals a place where man, while living with nature, has, intentionally or not, left the surroundings as pristine and untouched by time as can be found in America.

Highmount was originally called Summit, referencing the crest of the mountain that the train reached before leaving Ulster County and descending into Delaware County. Pine Hill, just before Highmount as one heads west, was so named for the steep incline in the terrain at this location on the turnpike. The village of Pine Hill was incorporated in 1895, but the corporation was dissolved in 1986 and is now a hamlet of Shandaken. Smithville, having lost its identity after the straightening of State Route 28, was once as populated as any other hamlet. The graveyard on Matayas Road and the old Smithville School still remain as testaments of its existence.

Big Indian probably has the most romantic legend attached to the name. The story goes that Chief Winnisook, a seven-foot-tall American Indian, took a fancy to Gertrude Molyneaux who was married to Joe Bundy, a local settler. Bundy was a cruel husband and Winnisook persuaded Gertrude to run off with him. Ultimately during a raid, Bundy had a chance to exact his revenge and fired a fatal shot at Winnisook. The Big Indian took refuge in a hollow tree, where Gertrude later found his lifeless body. She buried him near the tree and remained there with her children. The burial plot is thought to be where the railroad tracks run through Big Indian by State Route 28 and Oliverea Road (County Route 47).

Oliverea and Slide, named after Slide Mountain—the highest peak at 4,220 feet, can be found further along Route 47. They both once boasted their own post offices and schoolhouses. While several smaller resorts still thrive in Oliverea, Slide is home of the Winnisook Club, a private cottage colony founded in 1890.

Shandaken, or Shandaken Center as the settlers knew it, is at the intersection of State Route 28 and County Route 42. Shandaken was home to the Whitney Chair Factory. North is Bushnellsville, so named for the Busnells, and east is Allaben, first called Elm Shade, then Fox Hollow, and finally named for Doctor Allaben. Between Allaben and Phoenicia, a spot where Shandaken Town Hall now stands was briefly known as Riseleys but when the post office was decommissioned so went the name.

In the beginning, Phoenicia rivaled Pine Hill as the largest hamlet in the township and by all accounts won out with the decline of the tourism market that peaked in the early part of the 1900s. While Belleayre Mountain has brought in winter guests, modern transportation offered traveler's opportunities to visit multitudes of localities and the Catskills never again experienced the tens of thousands of visitors who came in the early 1900s.

Chichester was named by the Chichester brothers, Frank and Samuel, who bought the valley and started the Chichester Chair Factory. Woodland, or Woodland Valley as it has come to be known, was aptly tagged for the forested charm that is lavishly conspicuous as one follows the winding road along the valley floor. Today, at road's end, a state-run campground keeps the area accessible to all. Mount Tremper and Mount Pleasant were first settled by the tenants of Robert Livingston who had purchased a portion of the Great Hardenberg Tract and attracted settlers to the area that had previously been used for hunting and fishing by the Native Americans.

By the end of the 19th century, most of the Catskill forests had been cut at least once, and only the highest unmanageable areas remained undisturbed. Recognizing the need to for regrowth of the forest to prevent detrimental runoff of silt, the upper slopes and summits were designated a State Forest Preserve in 1870. In 1904, the State of New York created the Adirondack and Catskill State Parks. The town of Shandaken is the only town completely within the borders of the Catskill Park. Several peaks have names associated with the early people places and natural world, including Belleayre, Tremper, Rose, Garfield, Wittenberg, Sheridan, Eagle, Big Indian, Fir, Spruce, Hemlock, and Panther Mountains.

John Burroughs was perhaps the most famous man of his time to be in awe of the mountain vistas of the Catskills. In his writings, he shared this reverence with the world. Slide Mountain, the tallest peak in all of the Catskills, inspired the poet and naturalist to write: "*Here the works of man dwindle, in the heart of the southern Catskills.*" A plaque commemorating both the man and the mountain graces the face of the summit rock in tribute to Burroughs and his vision. He was joined by scores of enthusiasts who came to holiday, hunt, fish, hike, and enjoy the wonders. The Hudson River painters came as far as Shandaken and Olive to capture the beauty. James

Dutcher of Oliverea was among the best of all mountain guides and brought all his boarders on hikes of Slide Mountain. In the 1870s he built a trail up the mountain from Winisook Lake, even building stone steps where needed. In 1891 the first public funds to be allocated by the New York State Legislature for Forest Preserve trail development were used to construct a "public path" to the summit of Slide Mountain. The present Burroughs Range Trail follows this route as it ascends Slide.

One

Early People and Places

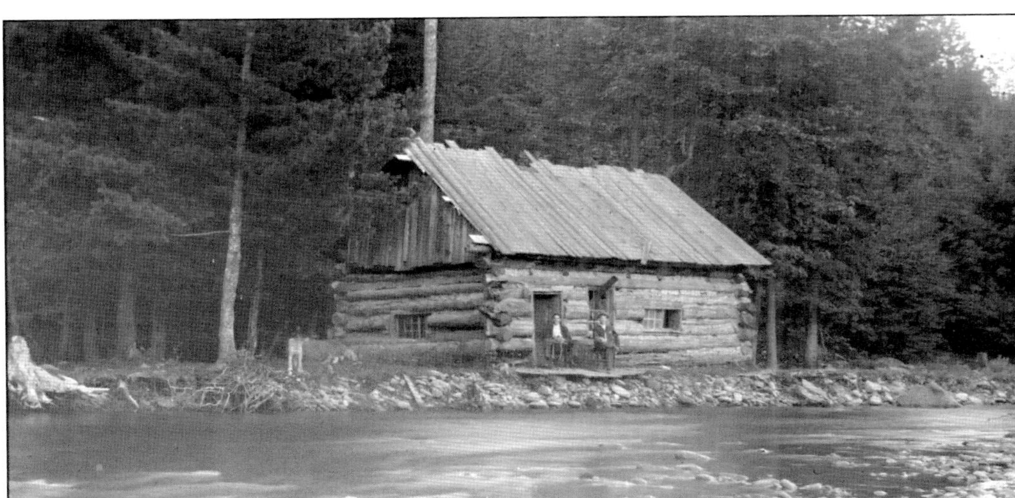

This rustic yet cozy log cabin was built on the banks of a stream, possibly in Woodland or along the Esopus in Shandaken. Although these men seem proud of their humble abode, settlers were often quick to replace their log cabins with wood framed dwellings to promote their prosperity. Such a building would undoubtedly been lost to a flood, regardless.

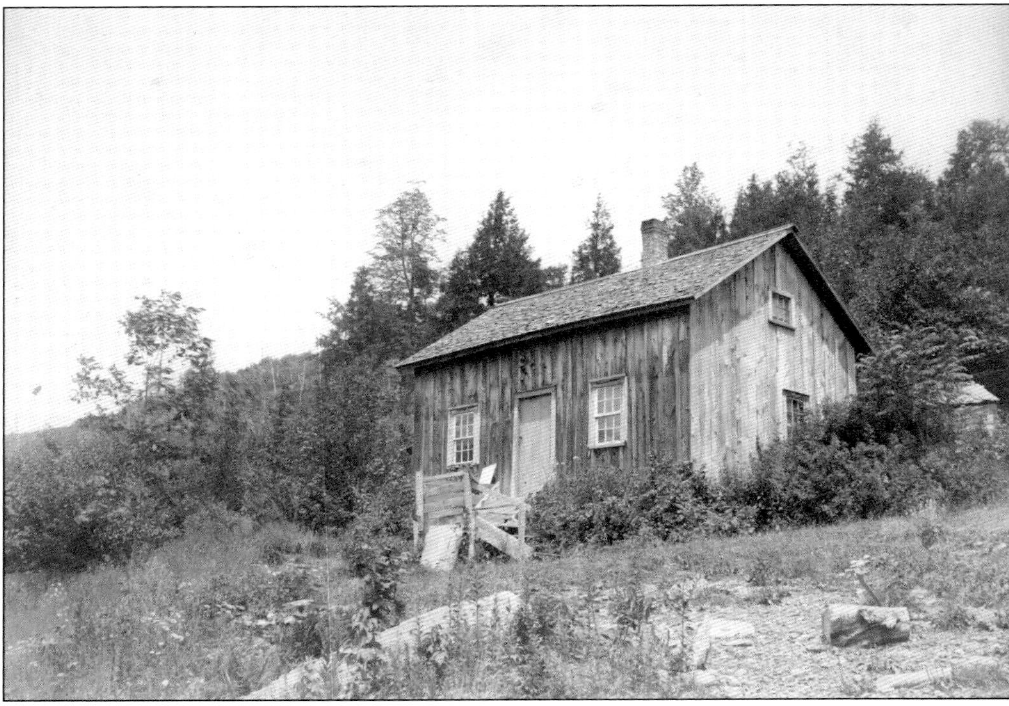

An early settler of Oliverea, Miles Parker was a member of the family that occupied this rustic abode. Parker was proprietor of many enterprises on the valley and was a very ingenious resident. The *Kingston Daily Leader* reported on December 30, 1896, "The wooden bridge erected across the Esopus by Miles Parker is a marvel of engineering by a backwoodsman."

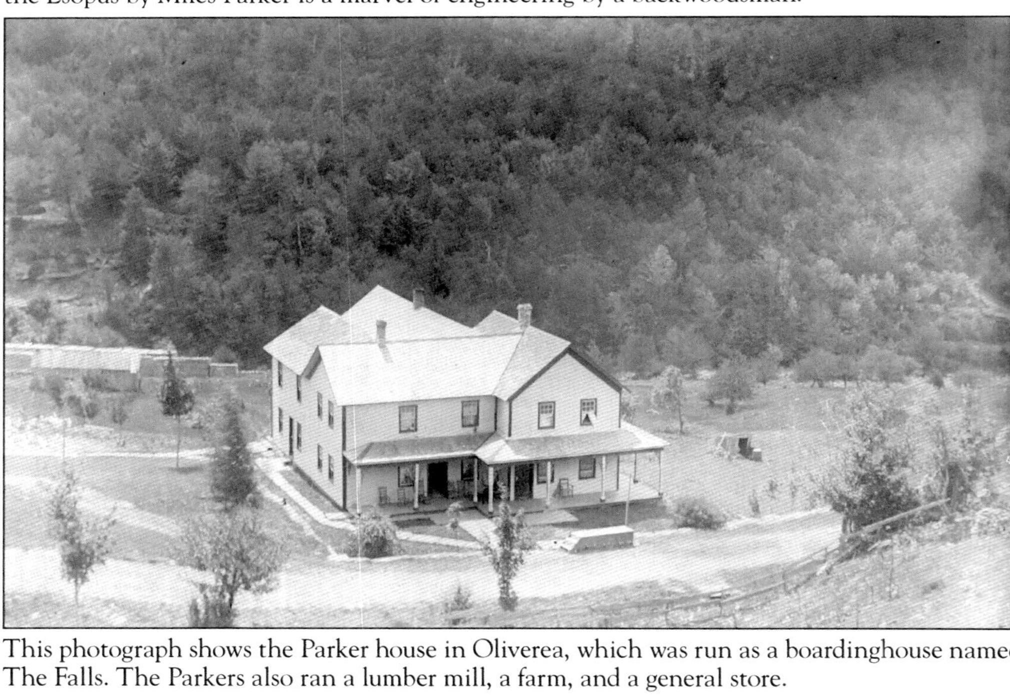

This photograph shows the Parker house in Oliverea, which was run as a boardinghouse named The Falls. The Parkers also ran a lumber mill, a farm, and a general store.

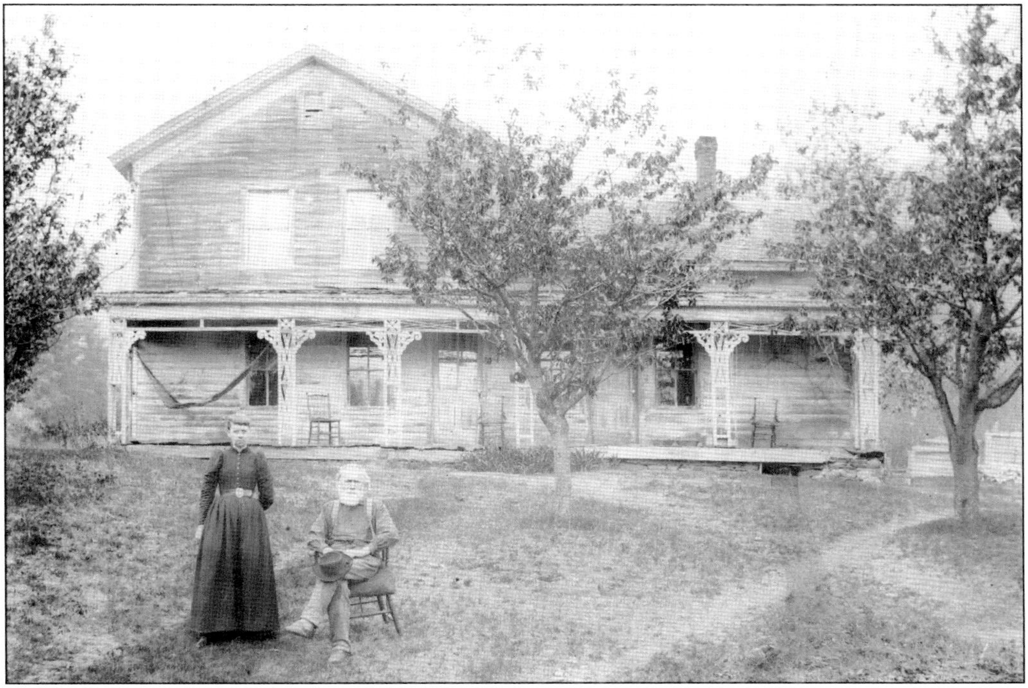

Lillie Barber Jamieson and Darius Rider pose in front of their homestead on old State Route 28 in Phoenicia around 1900.

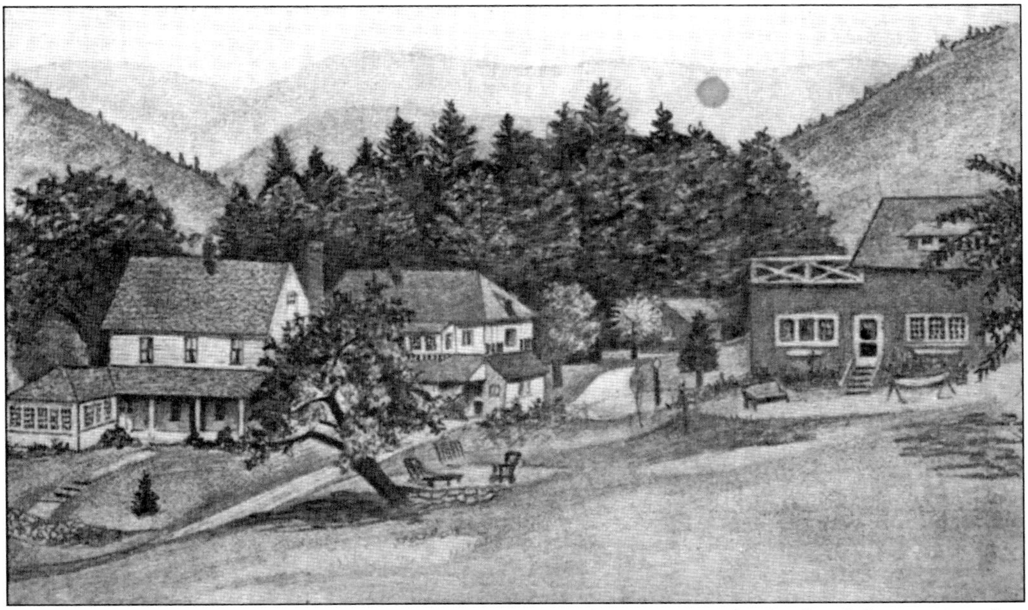

This is the old Will Larkin Farm in Woodland. Handwritten on the back of this card is this message: "Russ and I (Maynard) spent our first winter in Woodland here in 1921. I just bought 2 acres of land from John Lord for $40.00." Counted among the Larkin Farm's many visitors were John Burroughs, Thomas Edison, and Henry Ford. Later the Luries bought the property and ran it as a guesthouse.

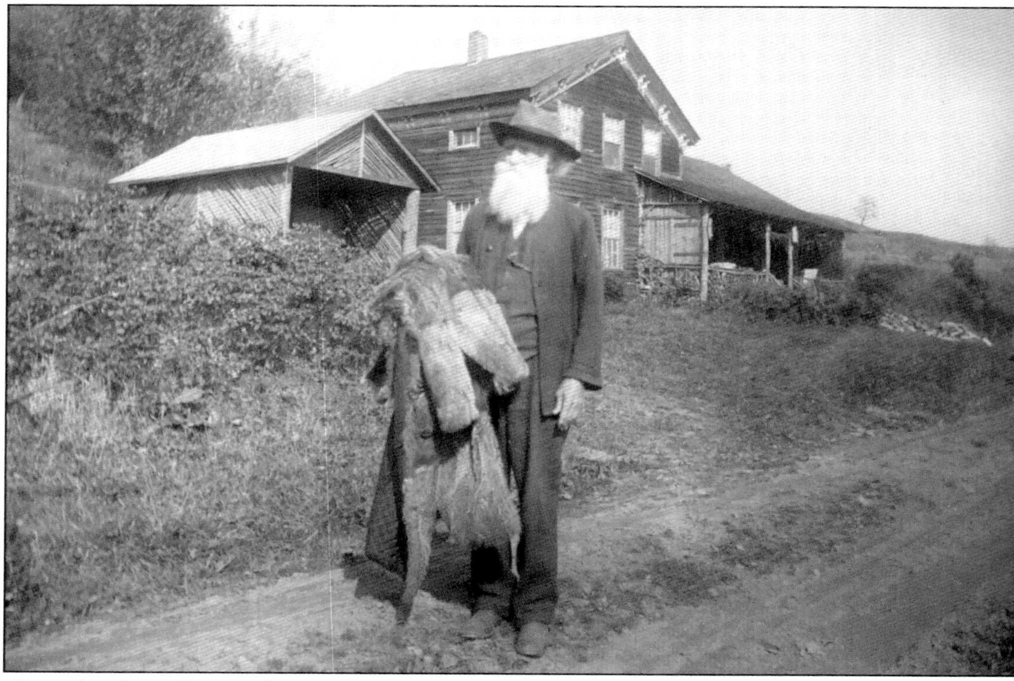

Naturalist John Burroughs is shown here in front of his beloved Woodchuck Hollow Lodge in Roxbury, New York. The acclaimed naturalist spent time at Roxmoor Colony in Woodland Valley. His writings were instrumental in presenting the Catskill Mountains to the general public. He had a special connection with Slide Mountain, and the Winnisook Club erected a monument to him there in 1923.

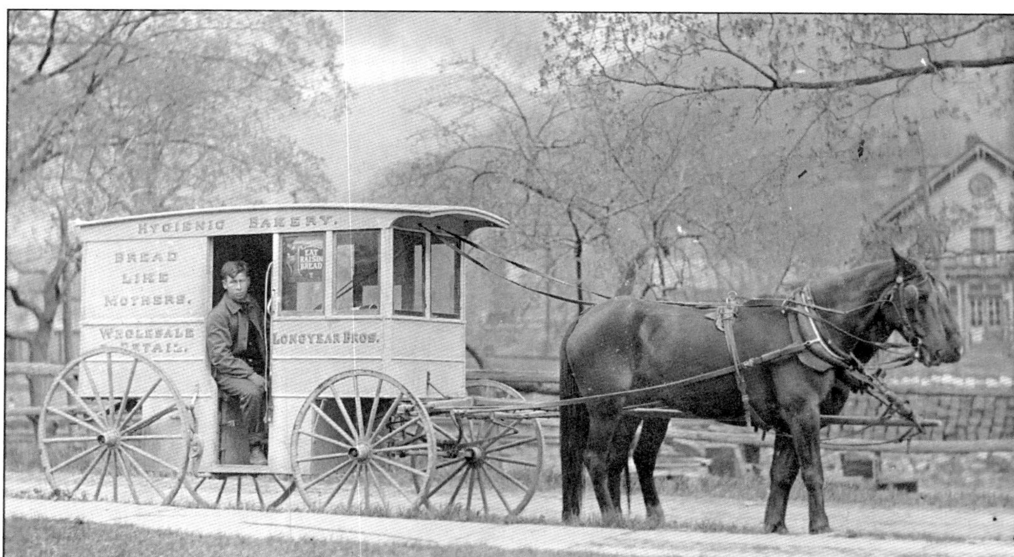

The Longyear family had many endeavors in the early days of Shandaken. Longyear family members are recorded as merchants, farmers, lumberers, quarrymen, and innkeepers. The shop was built in 1904 on Main Street in Phoenicia. Whether through marriage or sale of the business, the owner of the bakery was listed as J. H. Shurter in 1923.

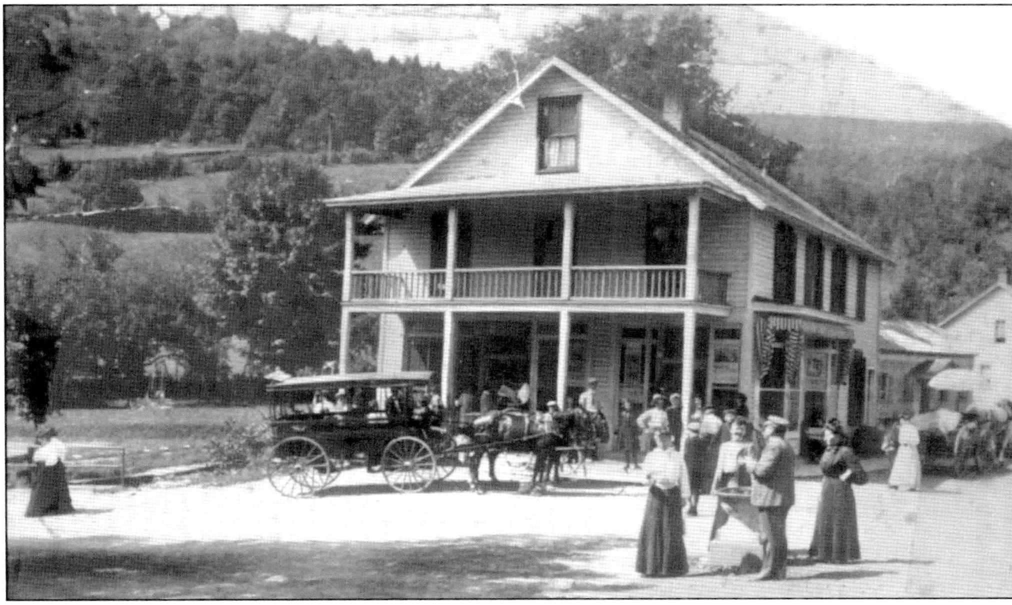

Ward Dunham owned the Corner Store, located at Main Street and Bonnieview Avenue in Pine Hill, at the time of this photograph. The post office was located in the building and the rig out front belonged to George Francis. It was used to taxi guests to and from the train depot. Notice the fountain in the middle of the road. The stream flows under the road to the left, and gravity must have driven the water to the fountain.

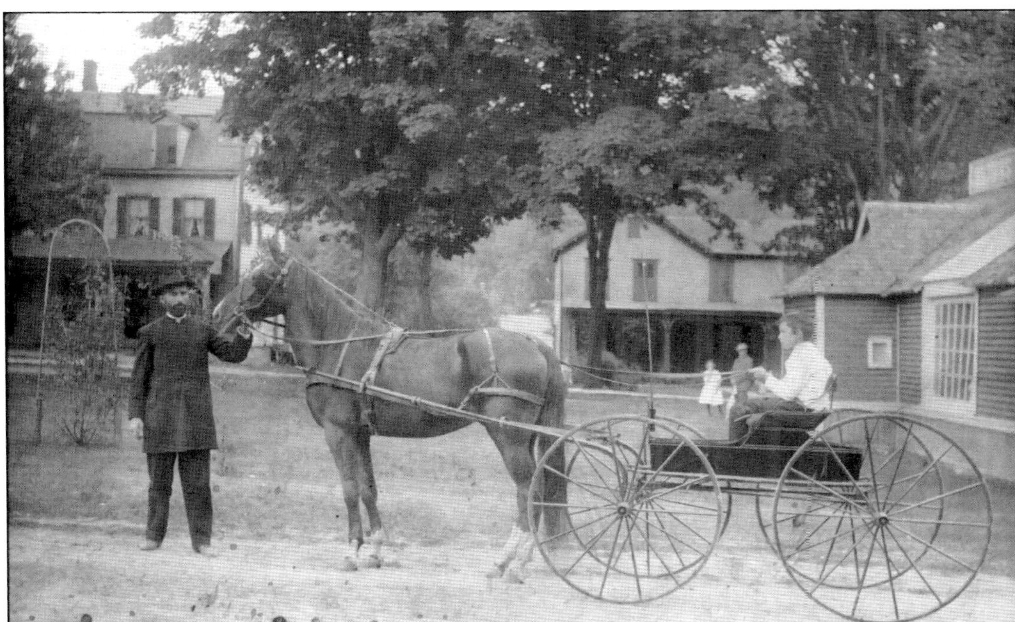

An unidentified man and boy seem proud of their horse and buggy in this portrait taken on Main Street in Pine Hill. The streets in Shandaken have not changed much since they were first laid out in the days of horse and wagons. With the exception of the straightening of State Route 28 and widening for modern automobiles, the town of Shandaken's footprint is virtually unchanged.

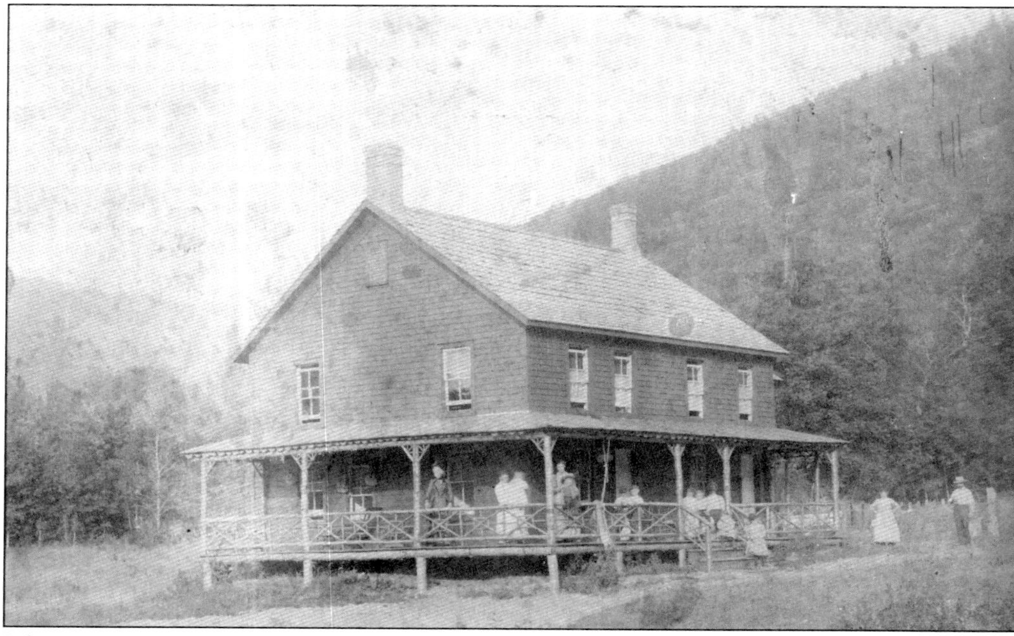

Like many structures in the town, Don Donahue's house began as this rustic version of a boardinghouse in the early 1900s. Now part of the former Budapest Hotel on State Route 28 in Big Indian, it and serves as a Baptist camp.

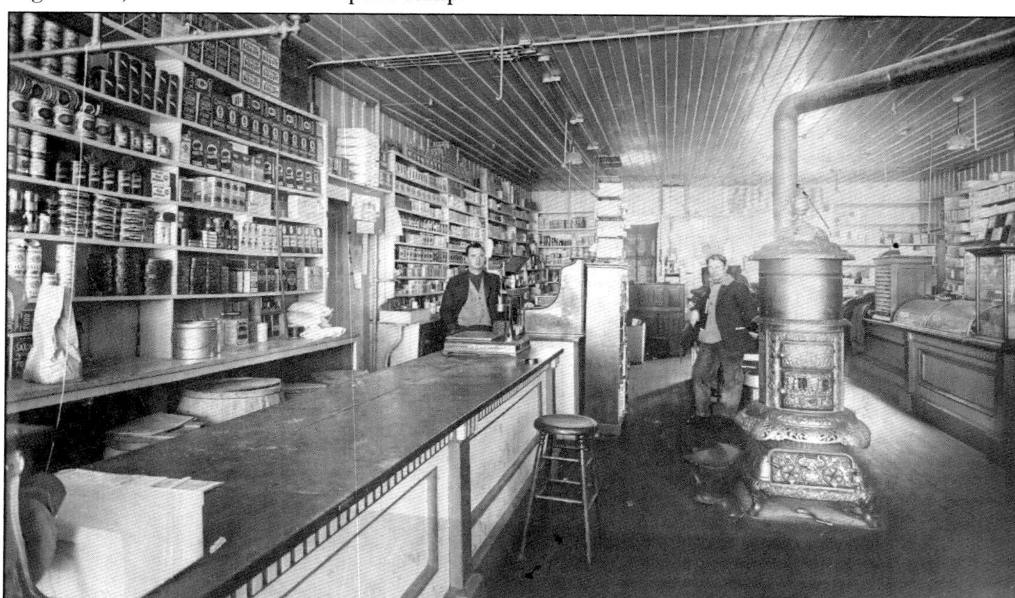

I. D. Hill maintained the store on Main Street in Pine Hill. An 1883 promotional pamphlet for Pine Hill and Summit (later Highmount) advertised ready-made clothing and dry goods, groceries and canned goods, pork and fish, kerosene and oil lamps, boots and shoes, flour and feed, stationery and postage stamps, and fishing and tackle. The store was the embodiment of a true general store.

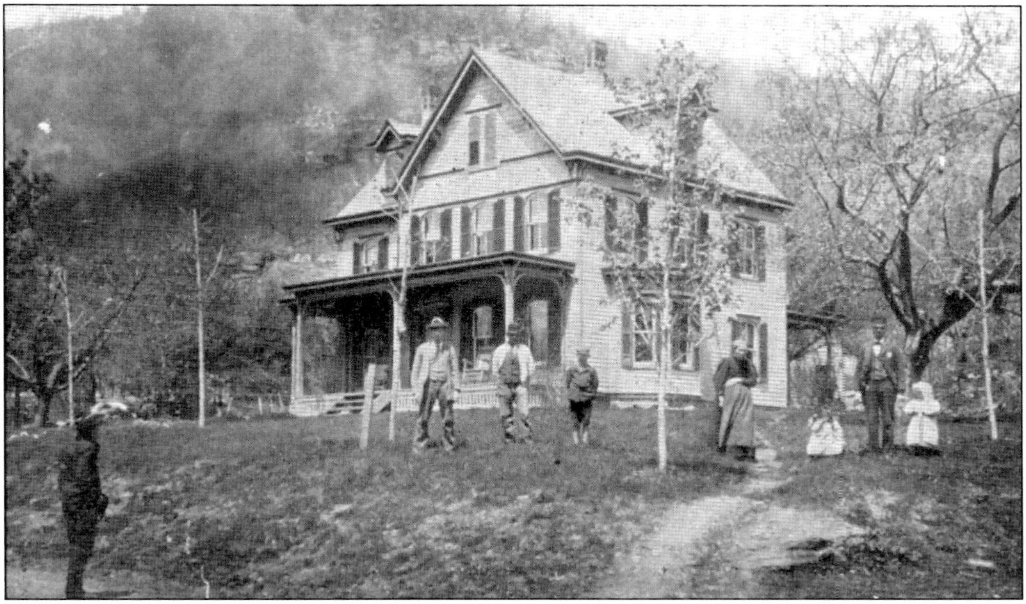

One of many homes that have survived through the decades is the G. B. Riseley residence in Allaben. The hamlet name Riseleys was used for a short time to designate the area between Allaben and Phoenicia, but it faded away after the post office was abolished in 1919. The hamlet was ultimately named after Dr. Allaben. The home still stands across from Shandaken Town Hall on State Route 28.

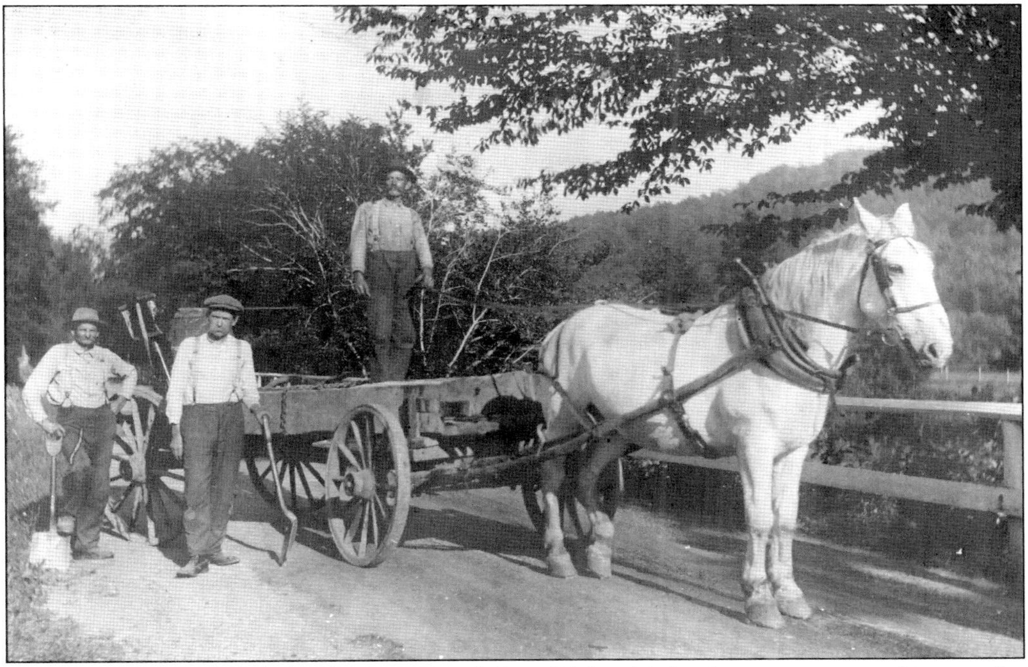

This photograph is labeled "The State Road Gang." Most likely, these men are working on the Ulster and Delaware Turnpike that was paved with planks from the hemlock trees that were stripped for tanning. The plank road was completed in 1850.

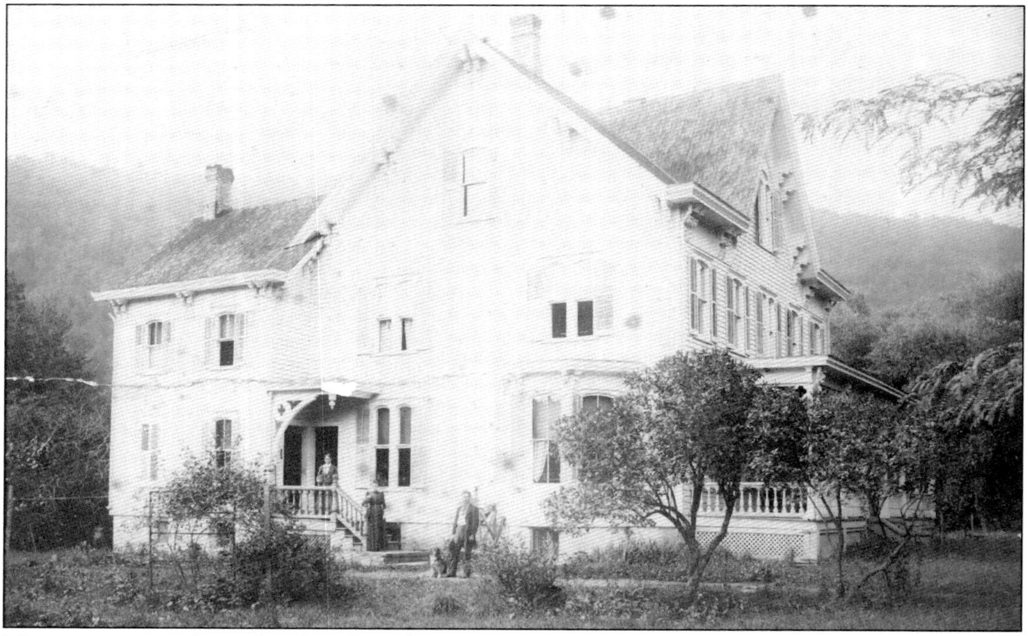

Many enterprises have developed on this acreage in Big Indian that is currently occupied by the Weyside Inn. The name was based on the surname of the property owners—Robert Wey ran the Inn. There was both a tannery and a lumber mill on the site before it was an inn.

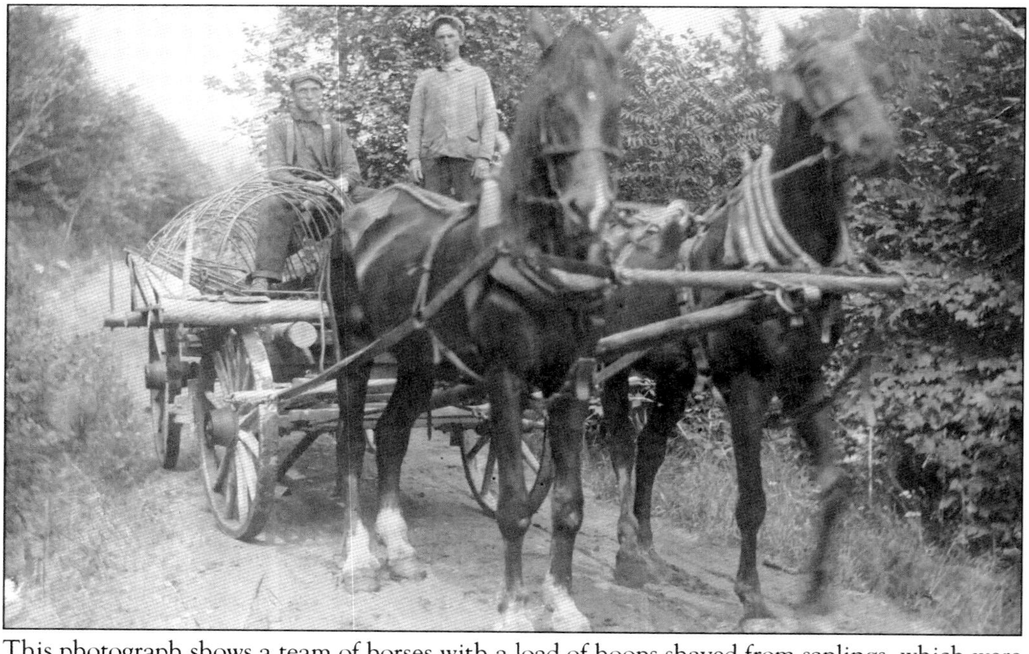

This photograph shows a team of horses with a load of hoops shaved from saplings, which were used to bind barrels and crates. By the 1870s, the hemlock supply, used for tanning leather, was depleted. The resourceful workers turned to hoop shaving as a source of income. In addition to providing income for bark peelers, this was also a way for farmers to supplement their income in the winter months.

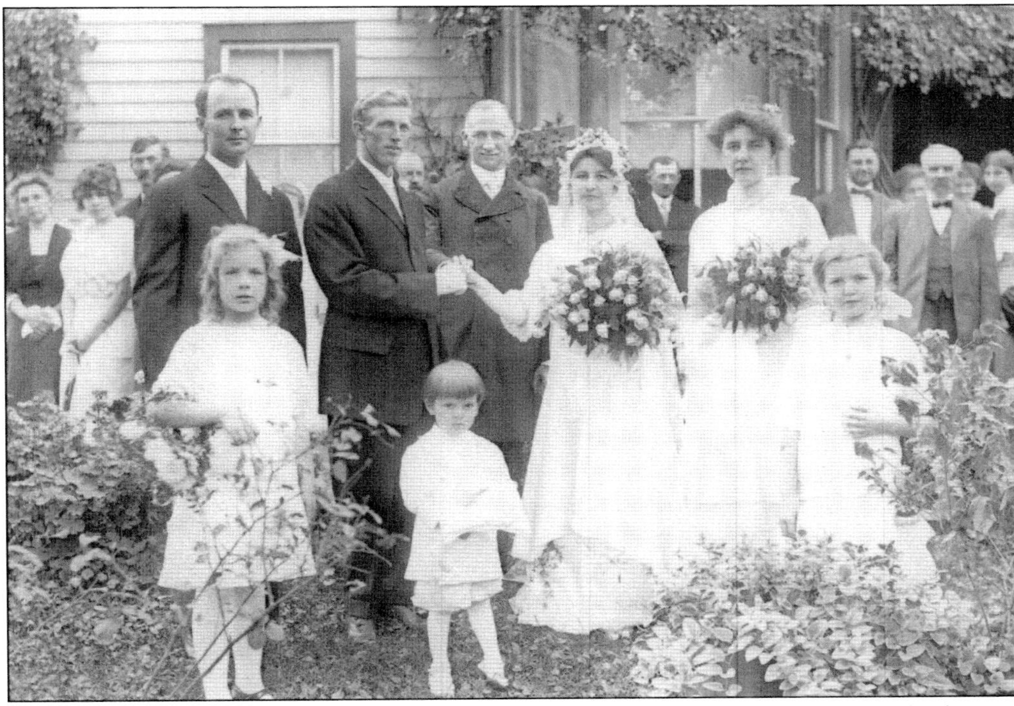

Eva Shultis and E. Short are the happy couple joined at this wedding that took place on September 9, 1914. The ring bearer is Lawerence Buley; to the right of the bride are Mr. Winne, Nell, Egbert, and Grandpa Shultis. The other guests are unidentified.

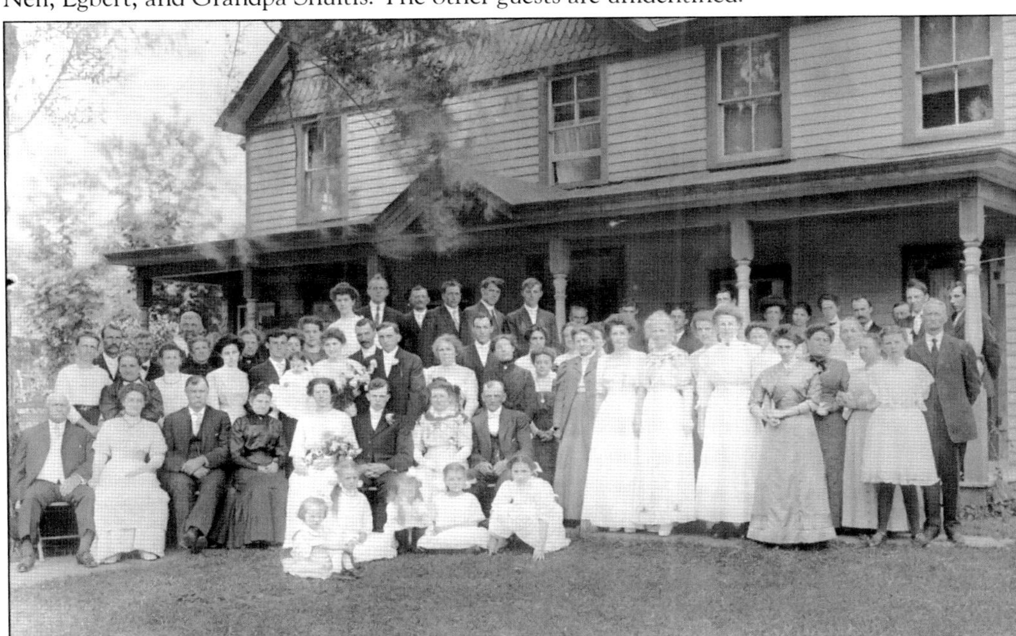

Weddings were simple affairs often held at the homes of family members. Nellie Smith and Grover Hodges were married on June 1, 1911.

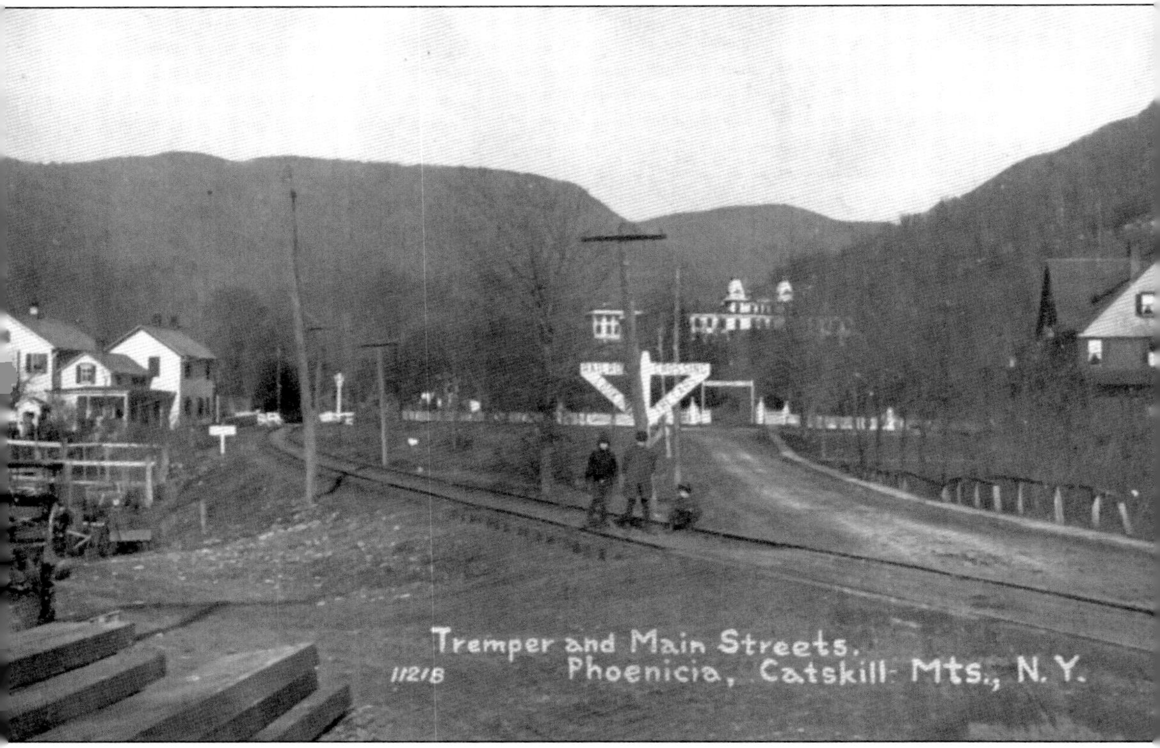

The house on the far right is the 1890 House, which is now restored and is a focal point in the hamlet of Phoenicia, housing several businesses. The drive to the Washington Inn, center, is now Ava Maria Drive. The grounds that once graced the inn are now the setting for an apartment complex. The railroad bed is now used as a drive for businesses on Main Street.

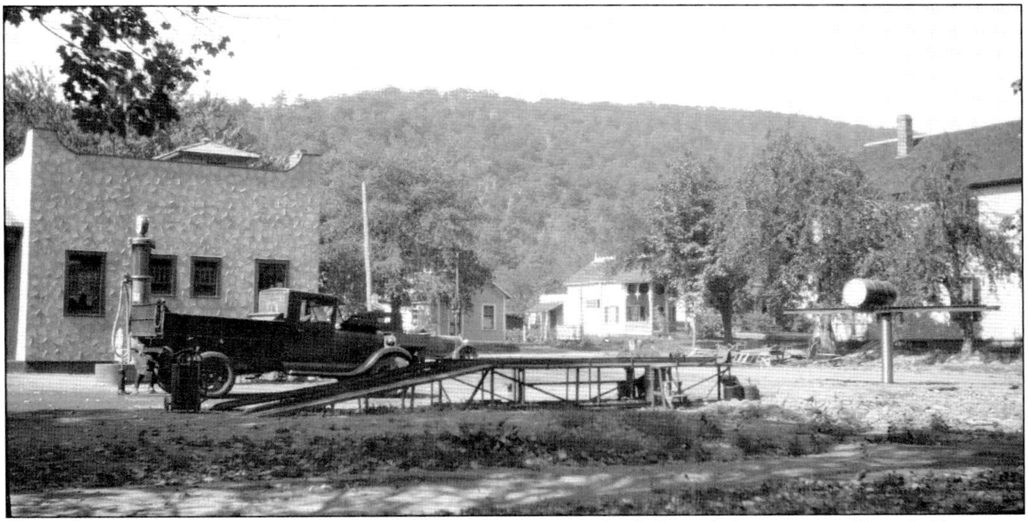

This photograph shows the Alamo Service Station on the left with homes on Church Street in the background. With the exception of the old stucco Alamo building that was replaced in the 1950s; all the buildings in this picture are still standing today.

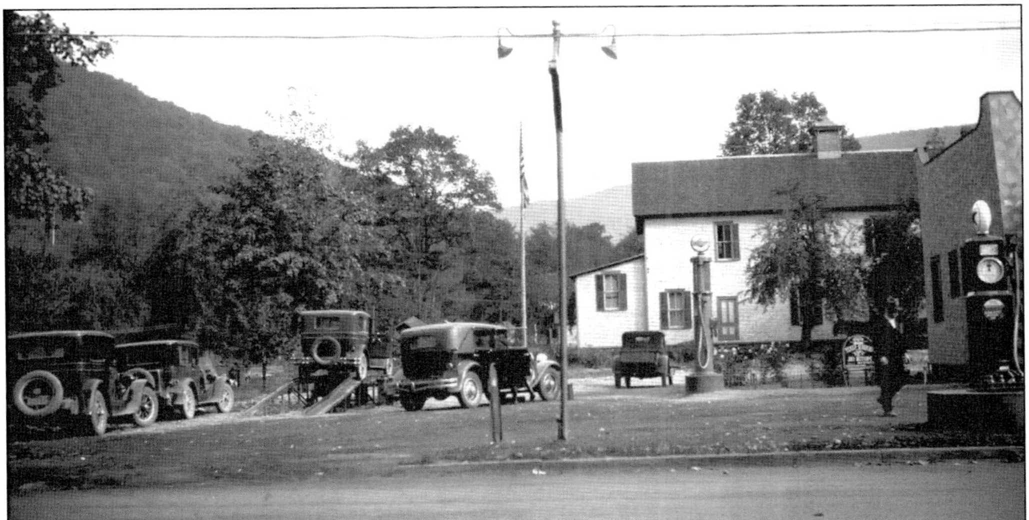

The Alamo Service Station at the corner of Main and Church Streets in Phoenicia was just the place to get an oil change.

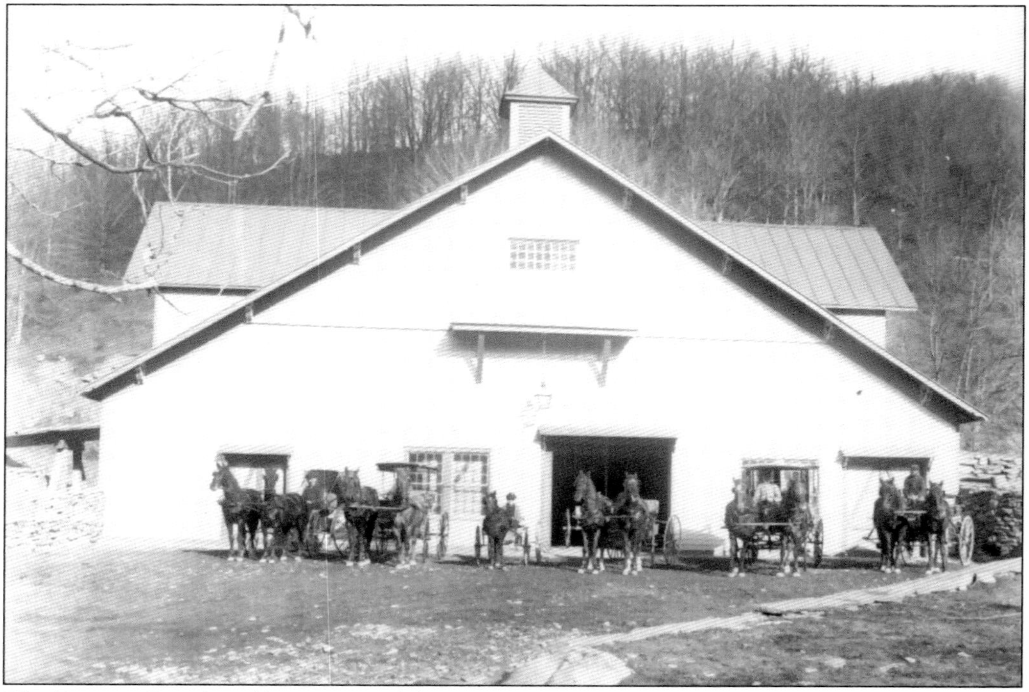

The Barn at Dutch Hill was part of the properties acquired by William O. Schwartzwaelder in Chichester.

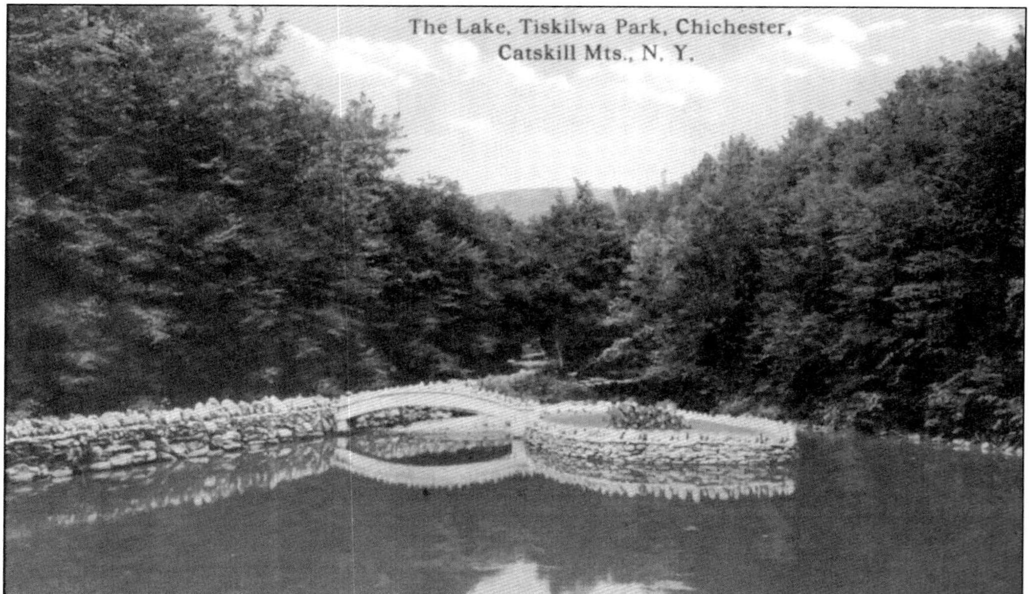

The lake at Tiskilwa Park in Chichester was for the enjoyment of the Schwartzwaelder Factory employees and their families. Built by William O. Schwartzwaelder at a cost of $500,000, the park was named Tiskilwa, "valley of peace and beauty." It is now privately owned.

Two

Schools and Churches

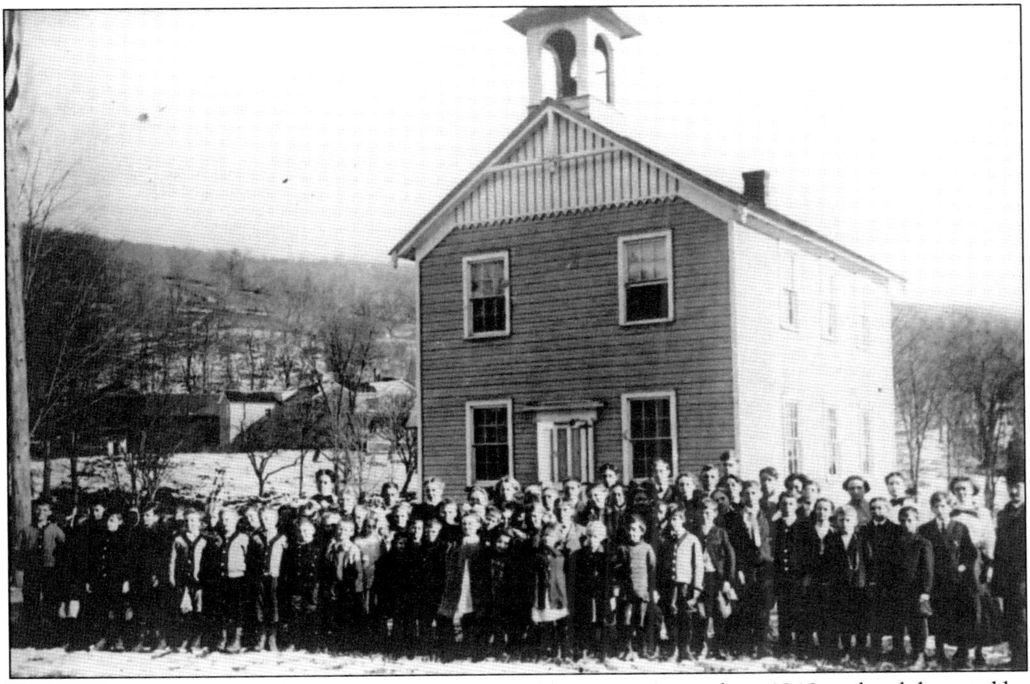

The first schoolhouse in Pine Hill was constructed by James Cornish in 1848 on land donated by R. H. Hill. This building was to the left of the school that was erected in 1925 and now houses the Town of Shandaken Historical Museum. The new building was used until the 1960s when the school district was consolidated.

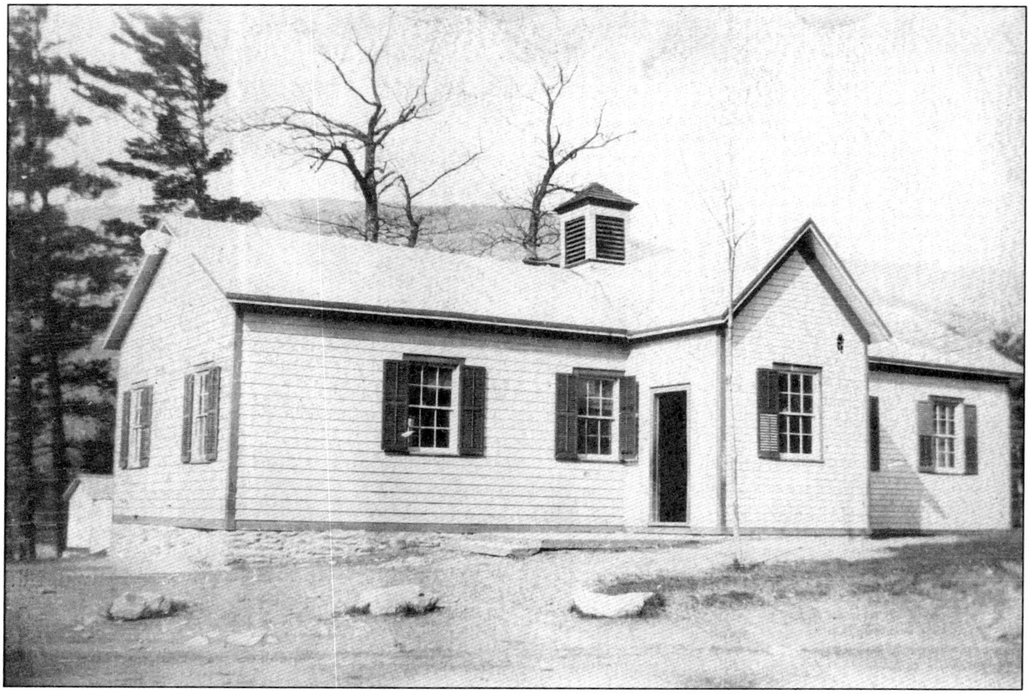

Tremper Schoolhouse was located on current Route 212 on east bank of the Esopus Creek. The school had to be moved to higher ground on the lot after a flood in the 1930s damaged the foundation.

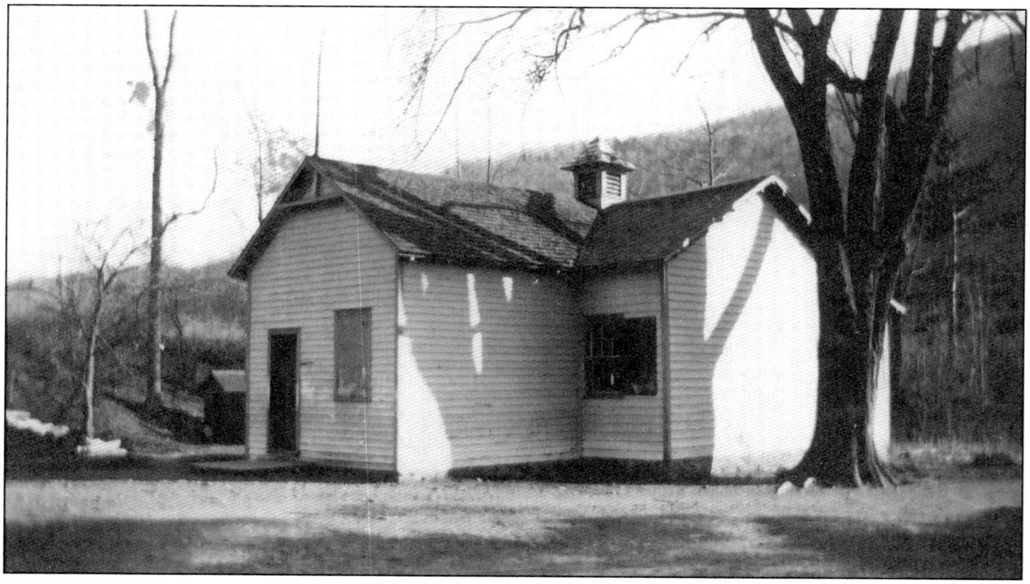

This is an early photograph of the Elm Shade Schoolhouse before the hamlet's name was changed to Allaben.

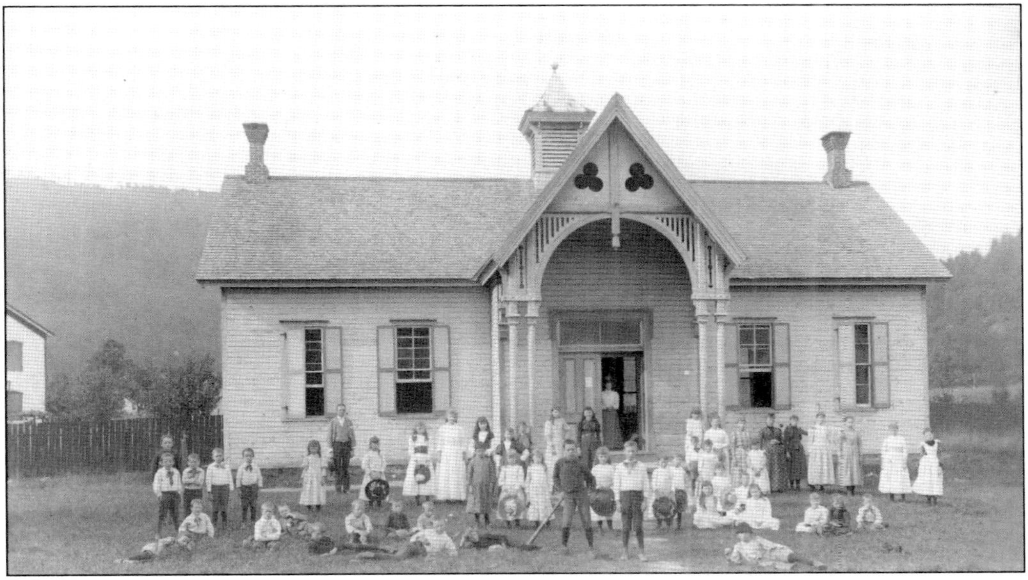

Perhaps to honor the seniors in this photograph of Phoenicia School Senior Department in 1891, only the older students in this photograph were named. From left to right are as follows: Mrs. Harvey Hoyt in the doorway, Dillie Moshier, Prof. J. I. Harkness, Nellie McGrath, Mary McGrath, Claudia Hallenbeck, Nellie Handley, two unidentified, Edith DuMond, Agnes Donohue, Densia Hoyt, Daisy Chase, Carrie Galloway, Miss Marie Longyear, Maggie Eltinge, Nellie Boise, Winifred Winter, and Daisy McGrath.

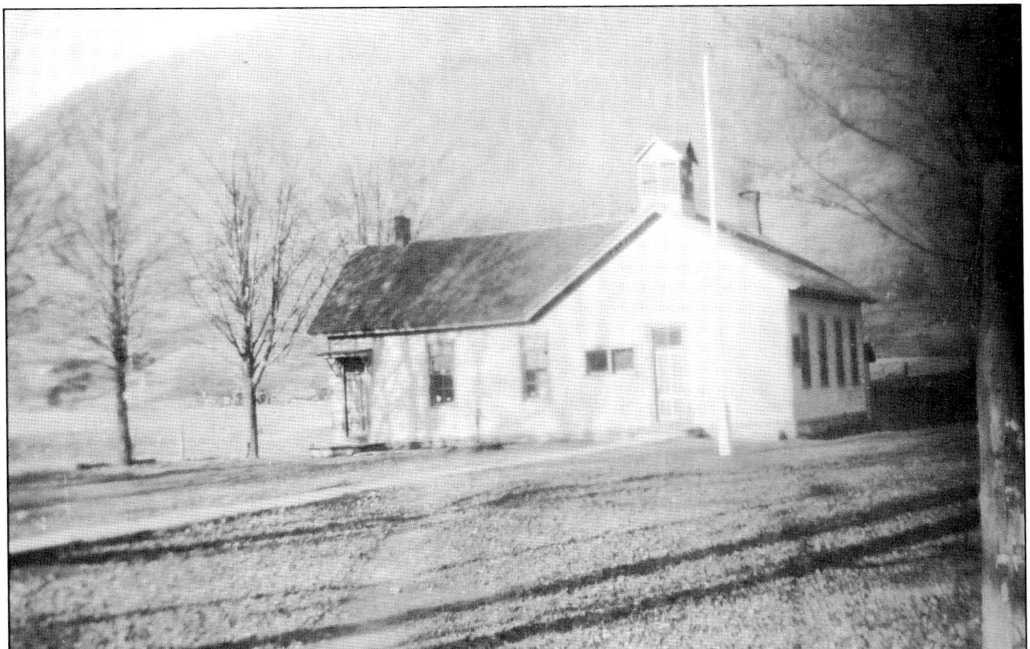

The Shandaken Schoolhouse still stands on State Route 28. After an addition, it became home to the Shandaken Allaben Fire Department.

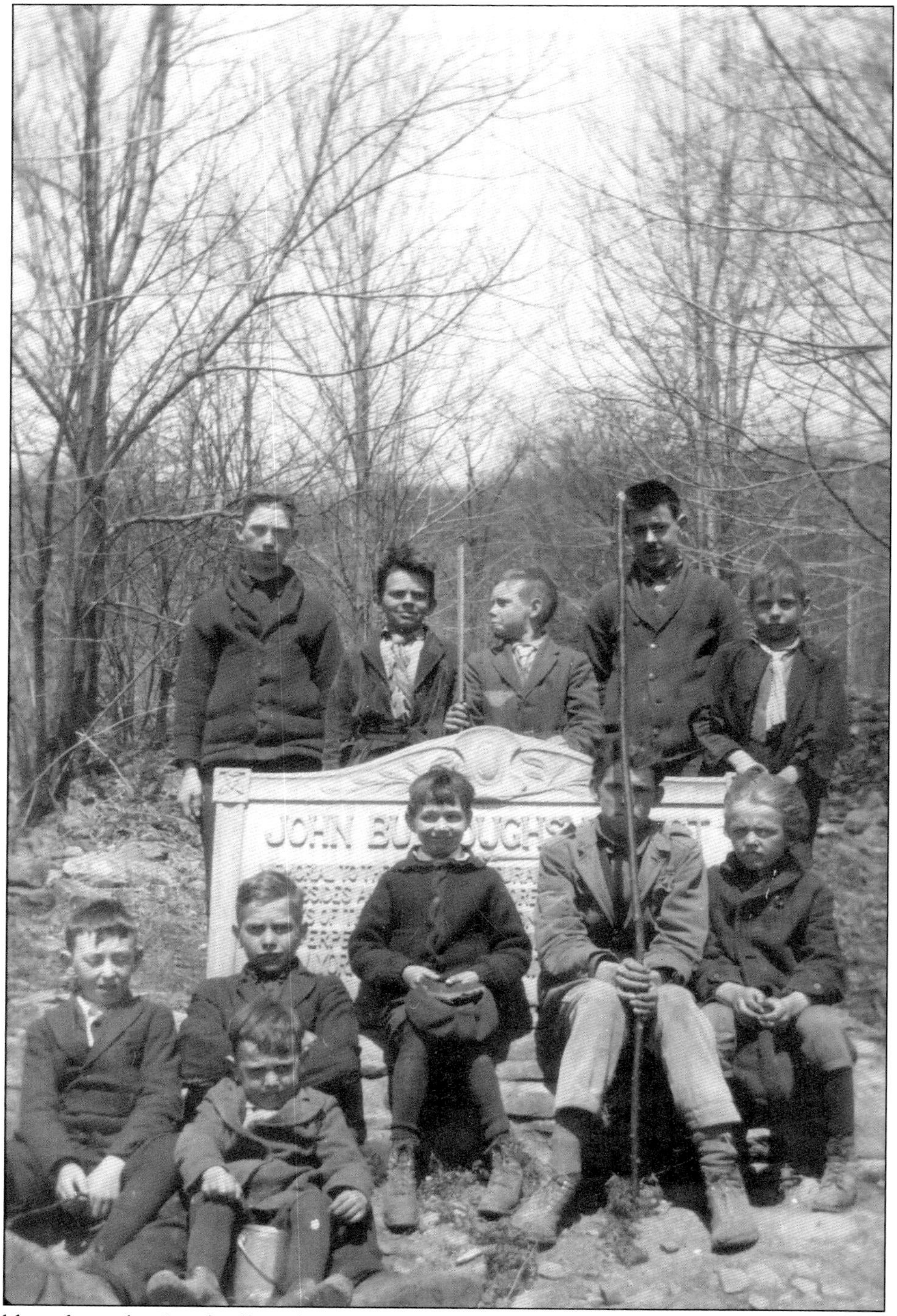

Children from the Smithville School are seen here visiting the John Burroughs Monument in Rochester Hollow in June 1922. From left to right are (first row) Joe Sweeney, two unidentified, Jerome Aley, unidentified, and Roy Hughson; (second row) Joe Hall, Al Eignor Sr., Gordon Maben, Rubin Maben, and Pat Sweeney.

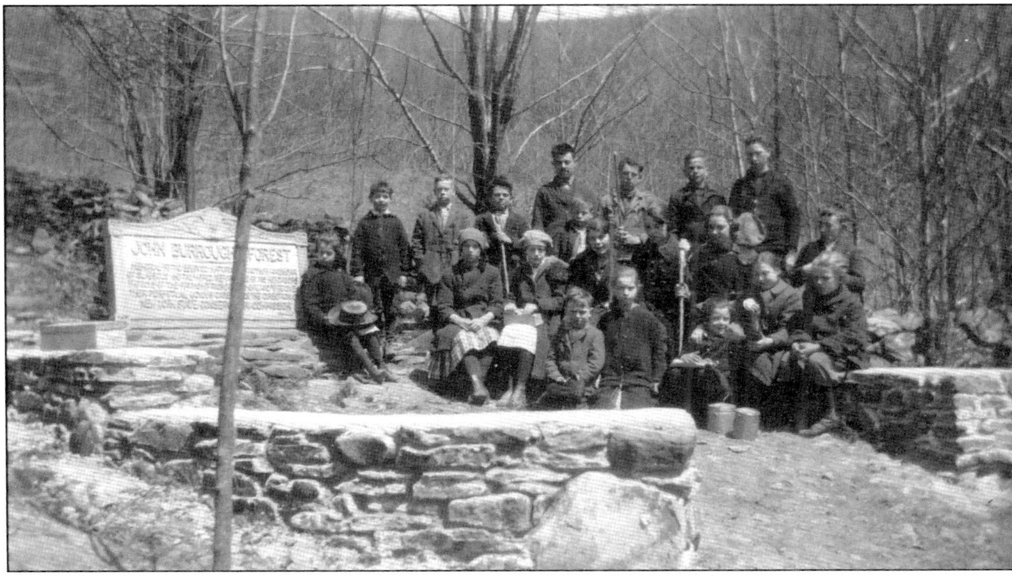

Pictured from left to right are (first row, kneeling) Russul Caldof and Laura Hughson; (seated front) Eleanor Whitney; (on wall) Caroline Hall and Roy Hughson; (seated) two unidentified, Margaret Fennelly, Marjorie Hall, and Joe Sweeney; (back row) Margie Whitney, Jerome Aley, Pat Sweeney, Gordon Maben, Joe Hall, and Viva Maben.

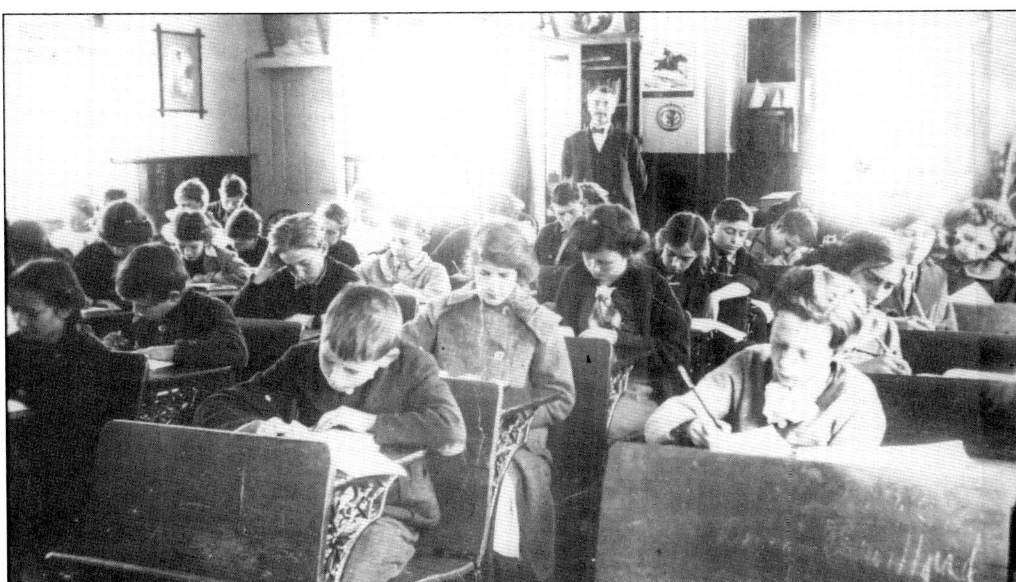

The children in Fred Harrington's classroom are hard at work inside the Smithville School in 1912. The school building is now a private residence, located on State Route 28. Smithville was between Big Indian and Pine Hill.

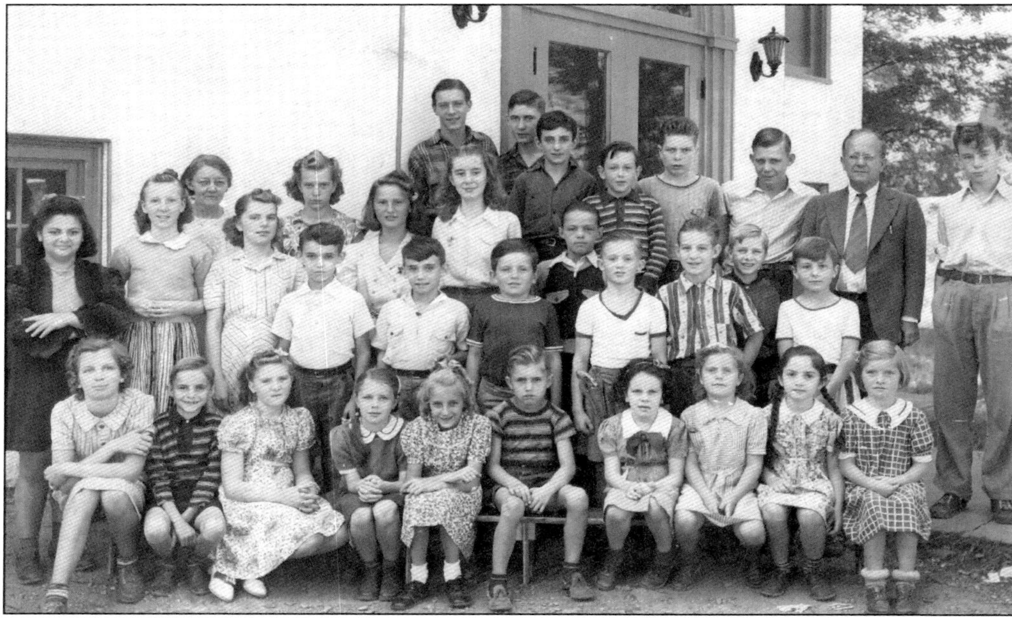

Seen here are students of Pine Hill School in the 1940s. From left to right are (first row) Merrill Hitchcock, sixth; Margaret Merwin, seventh; and Josephine Mancuso, eighth; (second row) James Smith, first; Charles Smith, second; Clifford Benjamin, fourth; and Harold Persons, sixth; (third row) Regina Wallace, second; and Marian Merwin, third; (fourth row) Tony Benjamin, first; Robert Benjamin, fifth; and Harrison W. Gridley, eighth.

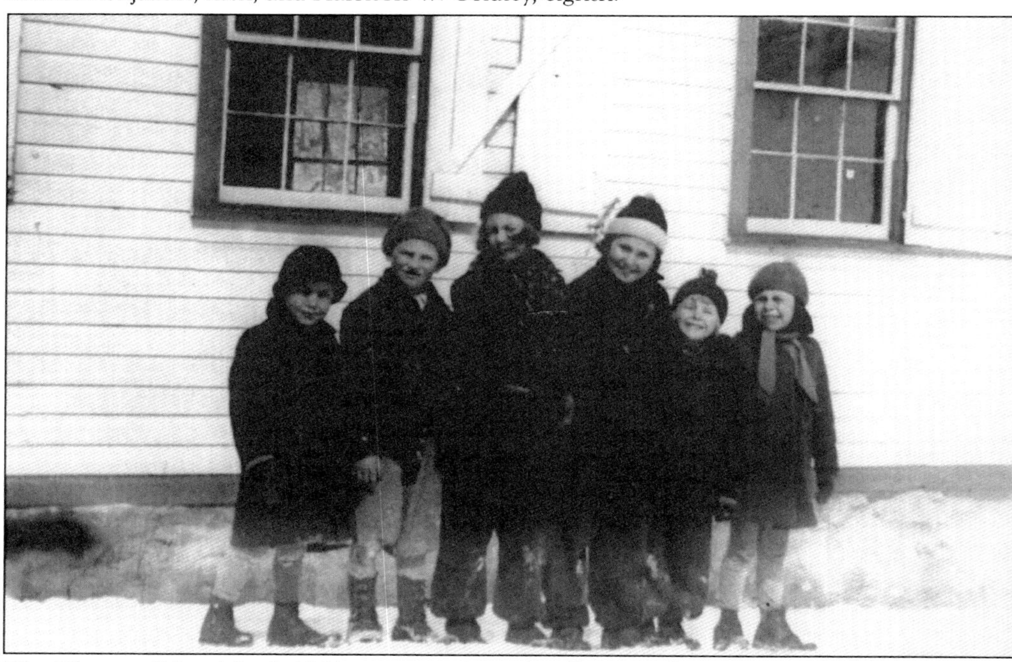

The Oliverea School, built 1886, is yet another schoolhouse still standing and now being used as a private residence. Shown here in their 1937 photograph are Seth Jocelyn, Sigfreid Hermann, Catherine Smith, Barbara Bedell, June Bedell, and Joyce Jocelyn.

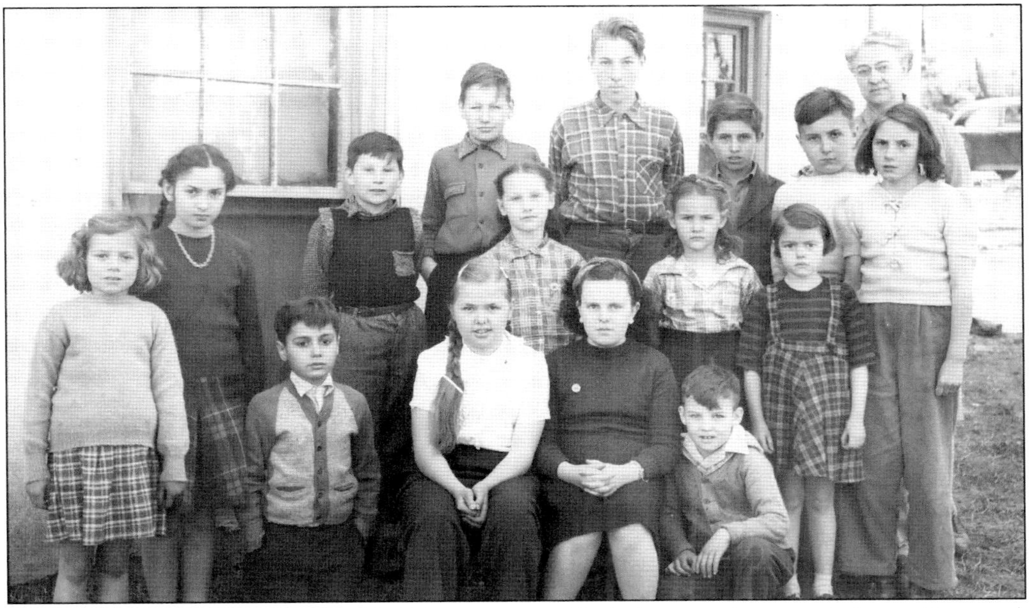

From left to right in this Pine Hill School Spring 1946 photograph are as follows: (first row) Arthur Mosher, Lydia Dammann, Margaret Merwin, and Charles Persons; (second row) Nancy Thompson, Deanna Thompson, Carol Merwin, and Shirley Merwin; (third row) Wilma Simmons, Josephine Mancuso, Raymond Singer, Ronald Singer, David Bennett, Merrill Hitchcock, Douglas Merwin, and Edna Andrews Rover.

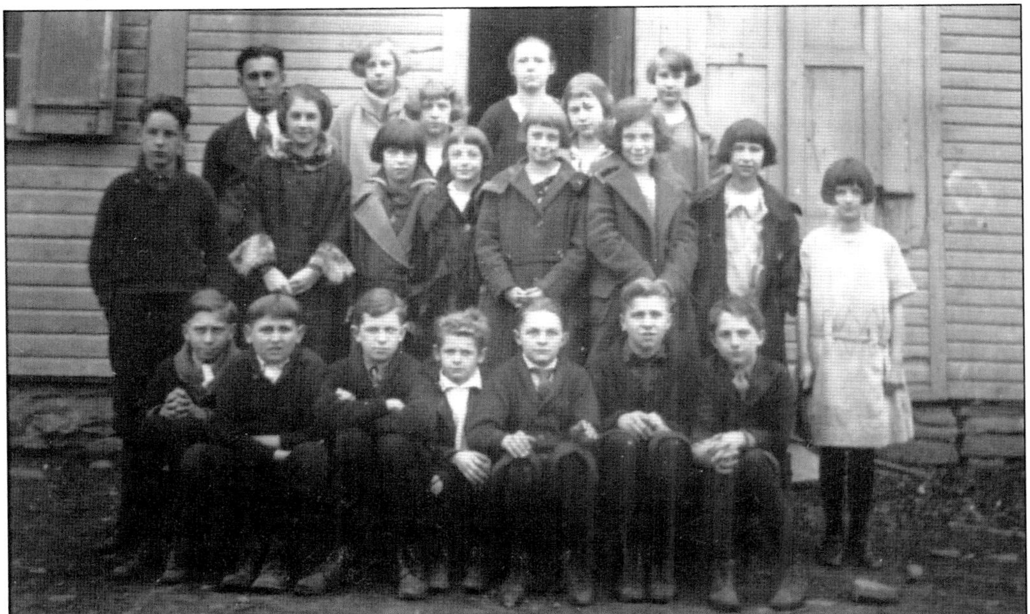

Reginald Bennett, in the back row, was the teacher of this class of the Chichester School, pictured around the 1920s. Others pictured from left to right include the following: (first row) Ronald Sickler, George Oros, Ed Shultis, Homer Smith, William Davis, Volney Smith, and Donald Van Bumble; (second row) Lester Craig, Katherine Knight, Mary Wright, Ray Sickler, and Bessie Shultis.

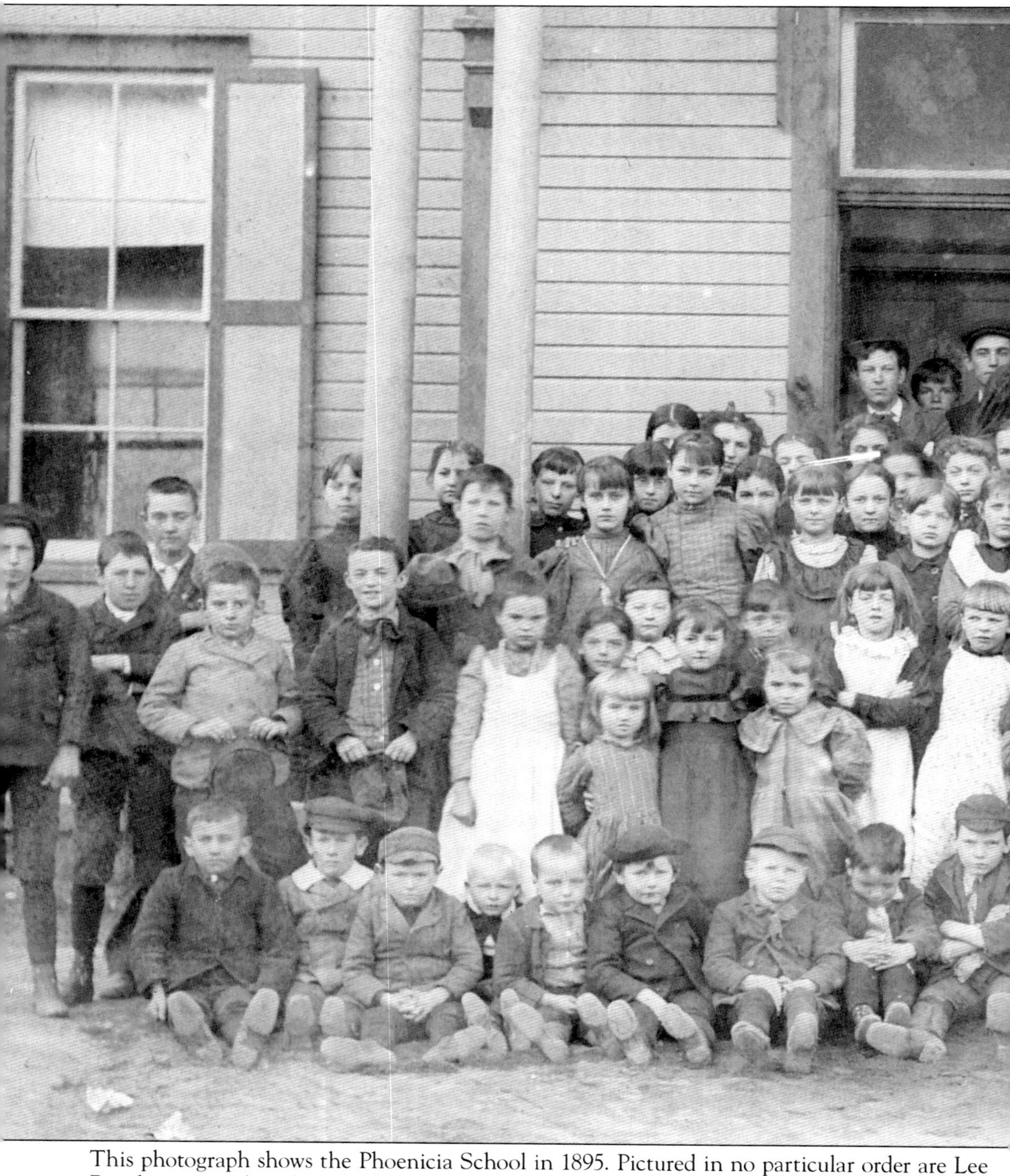

This photograph shows the Phoenicia School in 1895. Pictured in no particular order are Lee Breithaupt, unidentified, George Longyear, Kate Martin, Iretius Van Valkenburgh (teacher), Issac Eltinge, Jennie Reisley (teacher), Daisy McGrath, Denise Hillson, Nellie McGrath, Mary McGrath, Anna Murray, Will Handley, George Martin, Theo Longyear, unidentified, Fred Rosa, unidentified, Will McGrath, unidentified, Mary McSherry, Hilda ?, Belle Murray, Daisy Draffen, Addie Rosa, Belle Handley, Blanche Reynolds, Eva Barbar, Allie Hobertes, Annie Elsworth, Frank Eltinge, Densia Hoyt, Mae Hallenbeck, Marian Mac Dowell, Fanny Wright, ? Wright, Mable

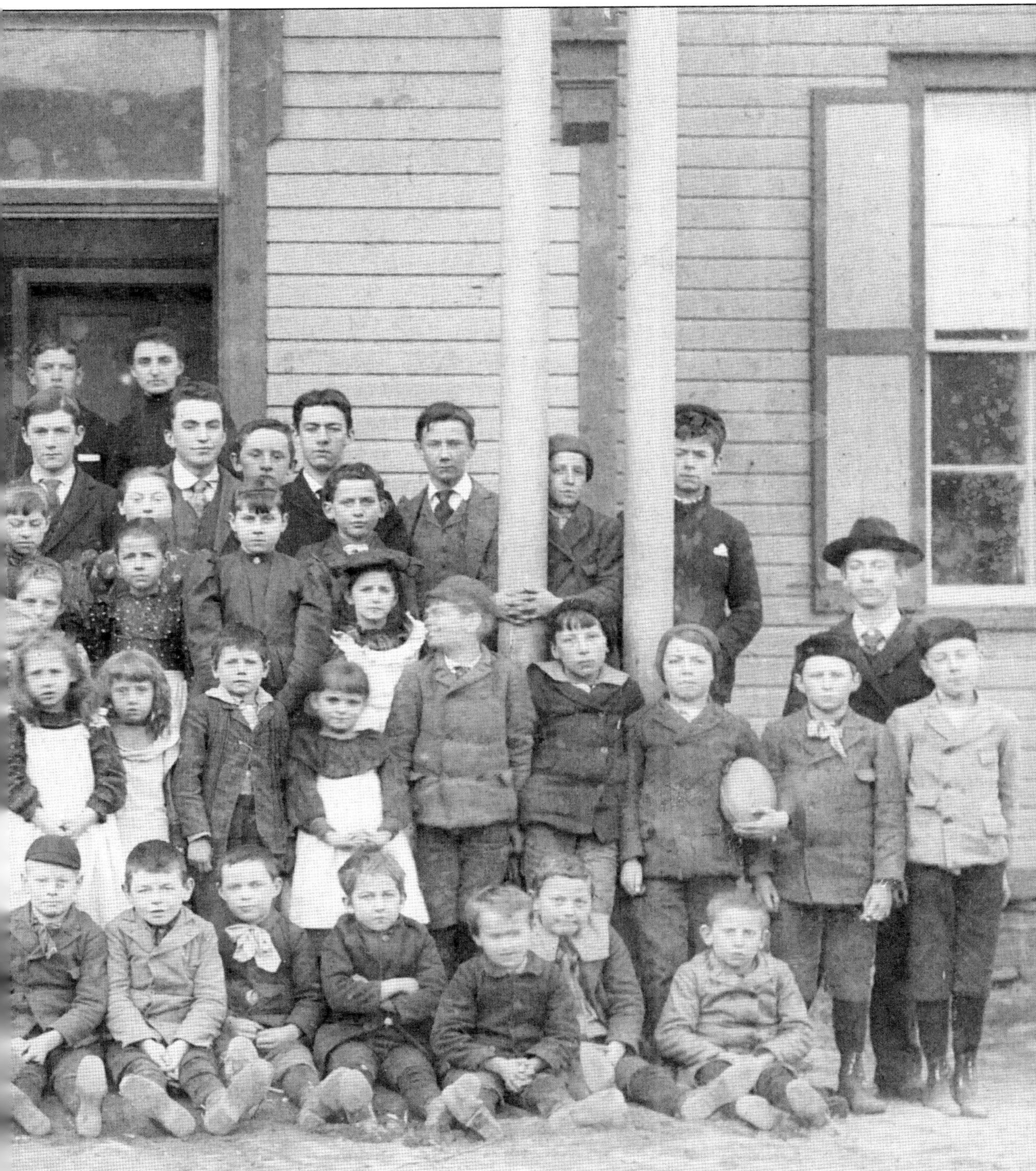

Elsworth, Kate Hallenbeck, Helen Gulnick, Carrie Davis, unidentified, ? Hoberts, Jeff Baldwin, Irving Krom, Merril Temple, ? Murray, Julia Temple, Anna Cornell, Flora Hoyt, ? Cornell, Anna Jamieson, Lizzie Jamieson, Roselie Brown, Jennie Draffen, Belle Longyear, Lizzie Blythe, Mae Blythe, Florence Draffen, Lillah Draffen, Effis Ellsworth, Frank Brown, Harry Breithaupt, Grant Burgher, Wilber Van Steenburgh, George ?, Ralph Longyear, George Hillson, two unidentified, Ed Elsworth, unidentified, Clarence Voss, three unidentified, Fred Voss, ? Brown, Willie Cornell, unidentified, ? Jamieson, Lewis Barbar, and Cornell Longyear.

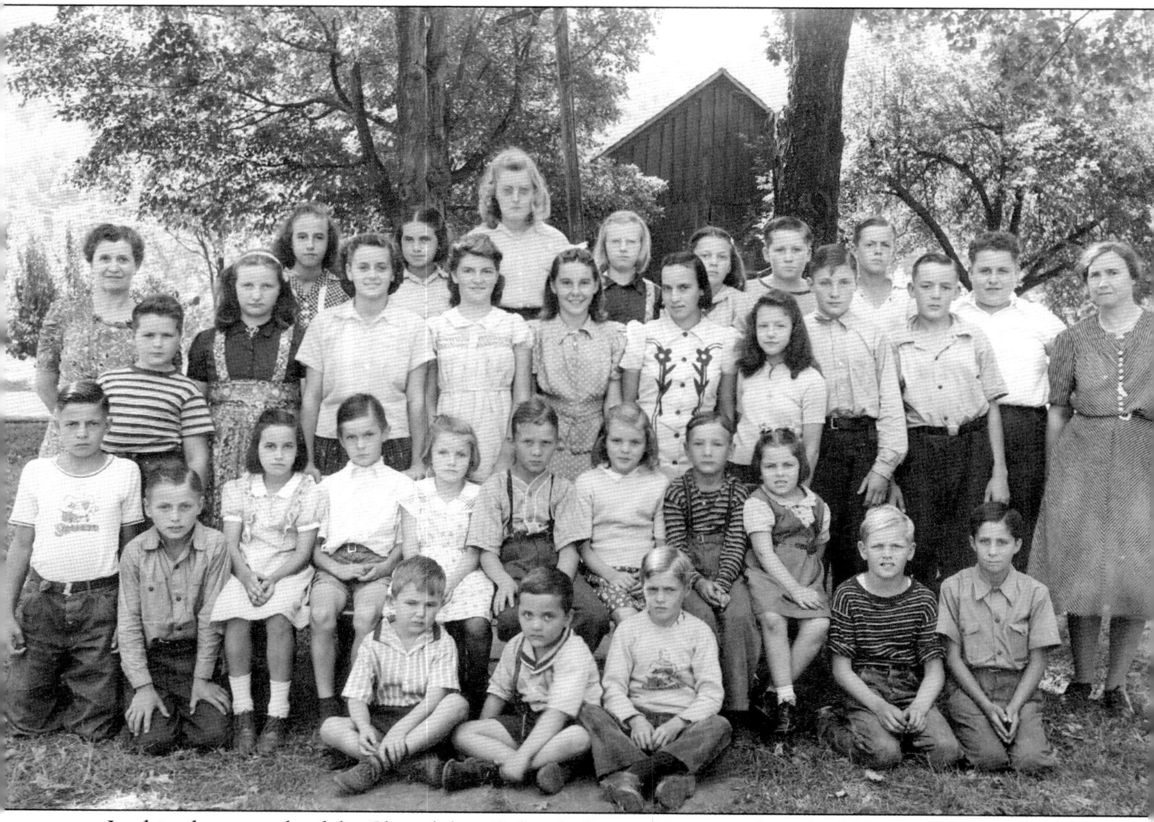

In this photograph of the Shandaken School, the students are identified from left to right as follows: (first row) Donald Ocker, Fred Kurtz, Claude Gossoo, Fred Gossoo, and Alfred Yerry; (second row) Carlton Buley, Gerald Herdman, Anna Lockwood, Robert Hummell, Julia Herdman, John Ford, Nancy Rosa, Kenneth Kurtz, and Jeanette Butlerrea; (third row) Edward Townsend, Beatrice German, Charlotte Redmond, Eleanor Gossoo, Lillian Decker, Marjorie Lockwood, Grace Hoffman, Paul Herdman, and Clarence Kurtz; (fourth row) Beatrice Lockwood, Gertrude Lockwood, Helen German, Kathryn Kurtz, Jerome Gulneck, Findley Gossoo, and Barnett Balkeslee.

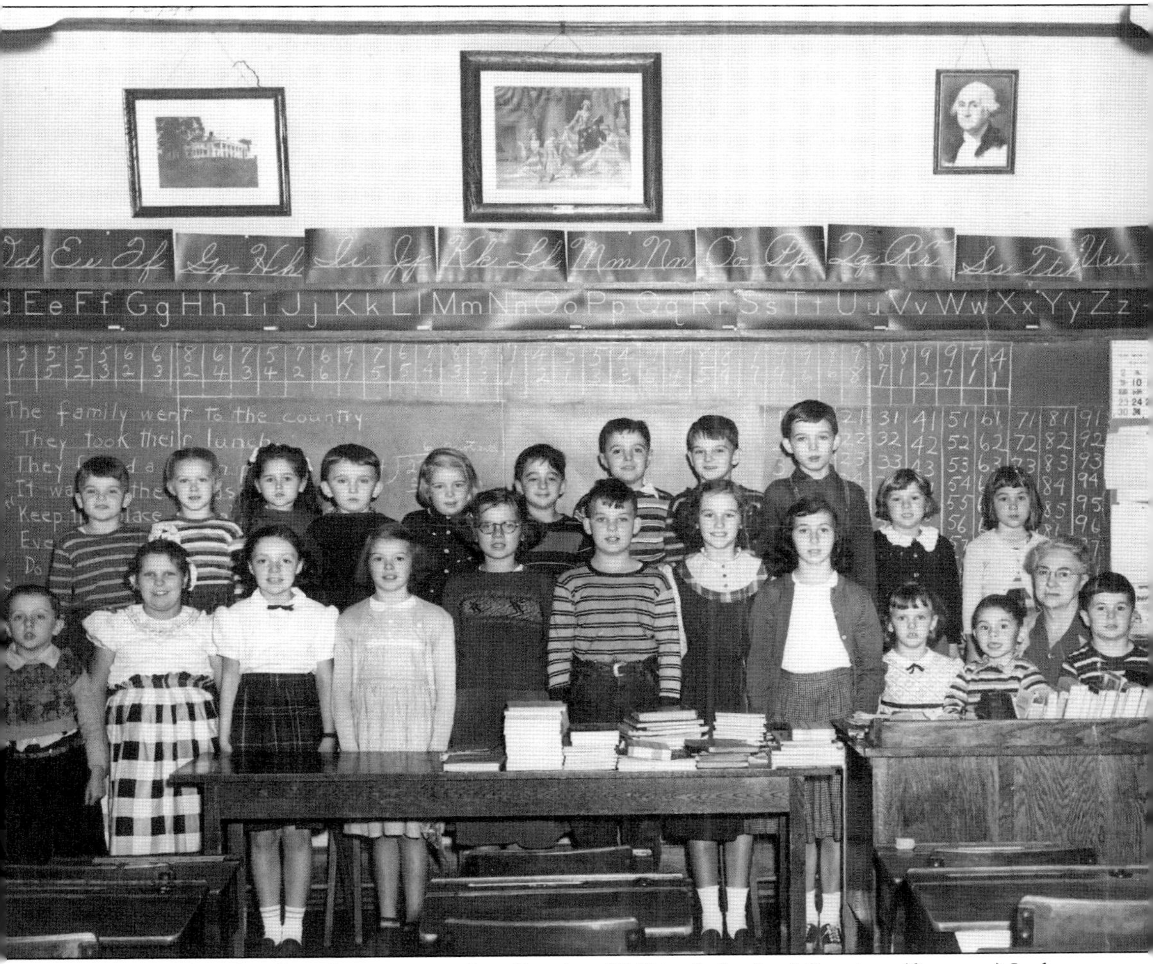

These Pine Hill School students pictured in October 1949 include the following: (first row) Jack Leiching, Beverly Merwin, Grace Gogarty, Carol Merwin, Wilma Simmens, Charles Persons, Deanna Thompson, Brenda Griffen, Louise Thompson, Frank Sanchis, Edna Andrews, and Wayne Griffin; (second row) Bill Ennist, Joan Smith, Dorothy Morck, Warren Smith, Pat Cure, John Dugan, Harry Roberts, Bob Ennist, Lowell Smith, Rosie Simmons, and Nancy Claudy.

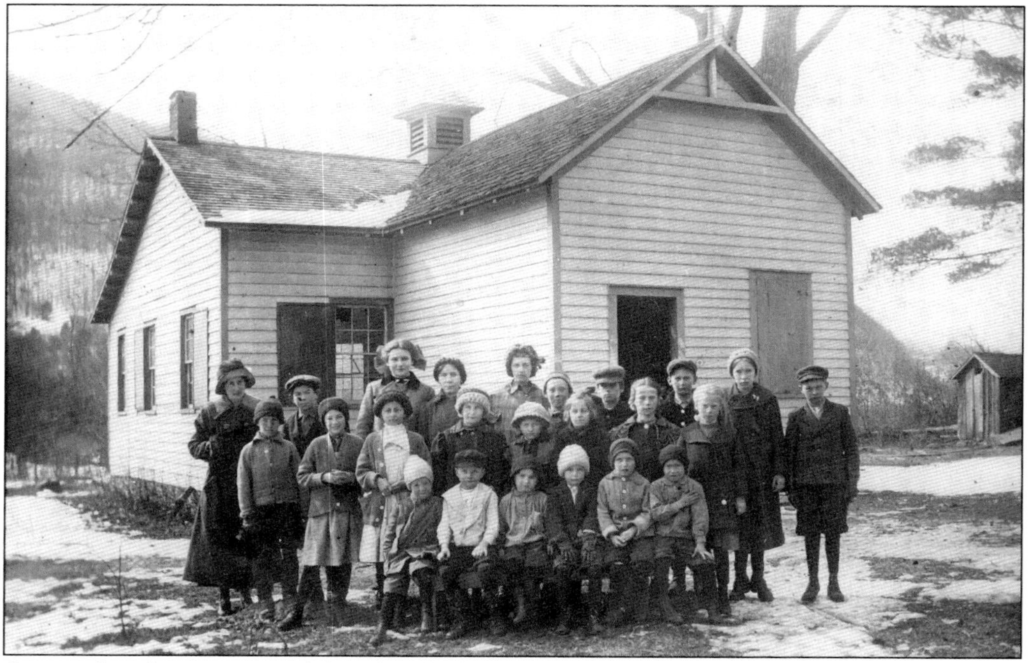

Quite a few class pictures of the Elm Shade School, shown here in the early 1900s, still exist. Unfortunately, the names of the students are lost to time.

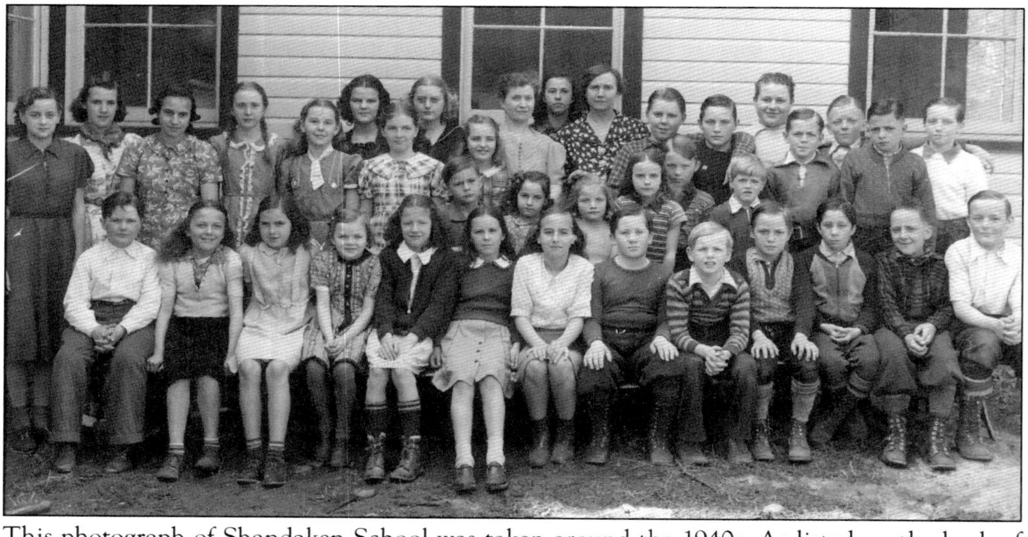

This photograph of Shandaken School was taken around the 1940s. As listed on the back of the photograph are (first row) Edward Townsend, Kathryn Kurtz, Gertrude Lockwood, Nancy Rosa, Grace Hoffman, Nellie VanEtten, Beatrice Lockwood, Jerome Gulneck, Fred Rosa, Gerald Herdman, Nash Dunham, and Clarence Kurtz; (second row) Beatrice German, Anna Lockwood, Julia Herdman, Joan VanEtten, John Ford, and Claude Gossoo; (third row) Charlotte Redmond, Doris Townsend, Marjorie Lockwood, Laura Harbig, Lillian Decker, Hilda VanEtten, Elanor Gosoo, Beatrice Redmond, Mary Rosa, Inez Satterlee, Bertha Lockwood, Anna Riseley, Norman Carpenter, Paul Herdman, Barnett Balkeslee, Findley Gossoo, Sidney Ford, Carlton Buley, and James Gulneck.

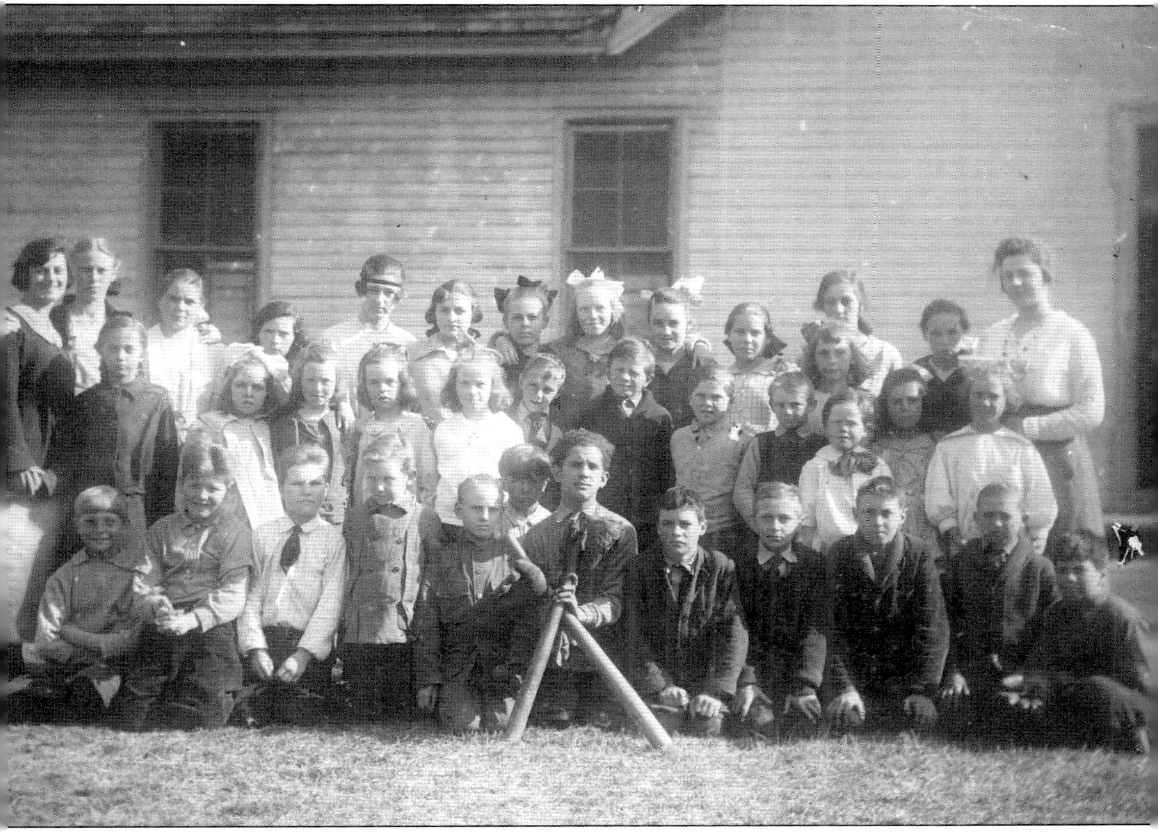

Pictured here is Shandaken School in the spring of 1919. From left to right are (first row) Forrest Dutcher, Clement Dyer, Charlie Dyer, Harold Garrity, Chester Krom, Russell Dutcher, Charlie Menzies, Charlie Ford, Ray Yerry, Ivan Ford, Marshall Yerry, and Lela Winchell; (second row) Florence Van Dusen, Florence Fouhy, Beulah Coons, Margaret Searle, Helen Knight, Arnold Yerry, Andrew Hinkley, Harold Peck, Carl Yerry, Norbert Fouhy, Esther Olmstead, and Phyllis Ousterhoudt; (third row) Florence Knight, Gertrude Yerry, Ruth Fouhy, Dema Misner, Neta Hinkley, Josephine Knight, Luella Garrity, Ella Humphrey, Olive Yerry, Margery Gulneck, and Laura Platt.

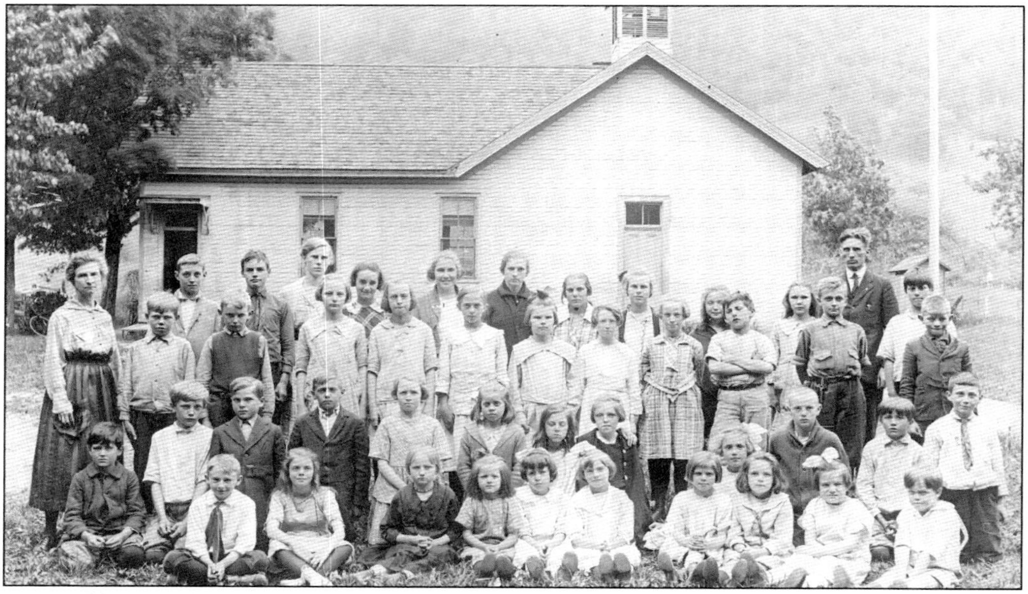

Pictured here is Shandaken School in the spring of 1920. Pictured are (first row) Harold Peck, Betty Clarck, Hazel Brandow, Helen Hanson, Phoebe Rowe, Elnora Van Dusen, Madeline Clarck, Vivian Fouhy, Lelah Winchell, and Norbert Fouhy; (second row) Robert Huntington, Forrest Dutcher, Carl Yerry, Arnold Yerry, Dorothy Coons, ? Yerry, Esther Olmstead, Florence Fouhy, Phyliss Osterhoudt, Floyd Brandow, Russell Dutcher, and Billy Gonzales; (third row) Harold Garrity, Ometa Brandow, Freda Irwin, Florence Van Dusen, Evelyn Dyer, Beulah Coons, Helen Knight, Harry Kelleher, Ray Yerry, Marshall Yerry, and Andrew Hinkley; (fourth row) Ivan Ford, Charles Ford, Florence Knight, Ella Humphrey, Linda Griffin, Olive Yerry, Josephine Knight, Josephine Gonzales, Stella Cornell, and John Clarck.

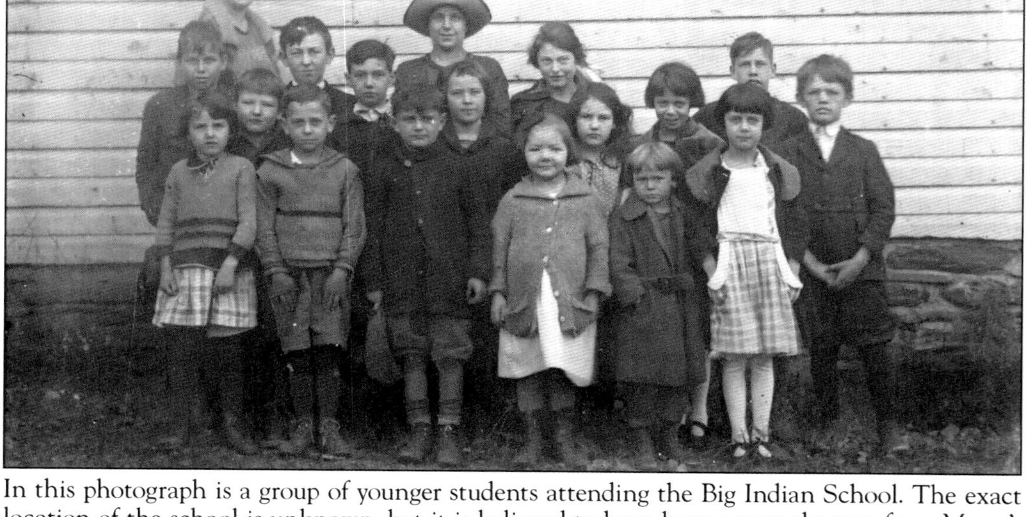

In this photograph is a group of younger students attending the Big Indian School. The exact location of the school is unknown, but it is believed to have been across the way from Morra's Market on Oliverea Road.

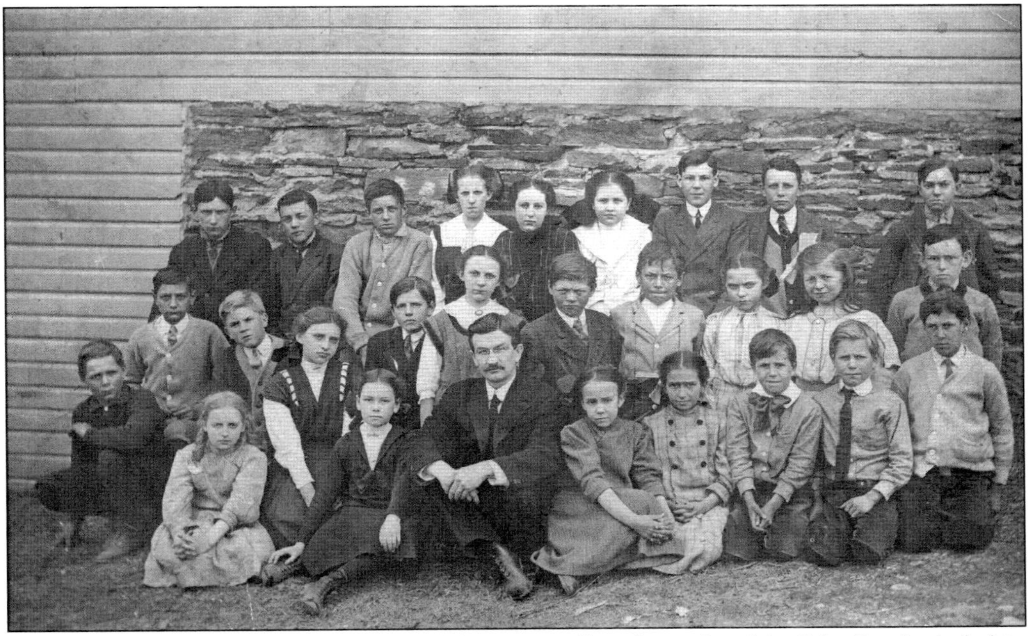

Pictured here is the "Upstairs Class" of the Pine Hill with teacher Mr. Schaffer. Included in this photograph are (first row, second from left) Beatrice Murray, Dorothy Cole (third from left), Mr. Schaffer, and Inez ?; (center row, third from right) Marguerite ?, and Andrew Cole (far right).

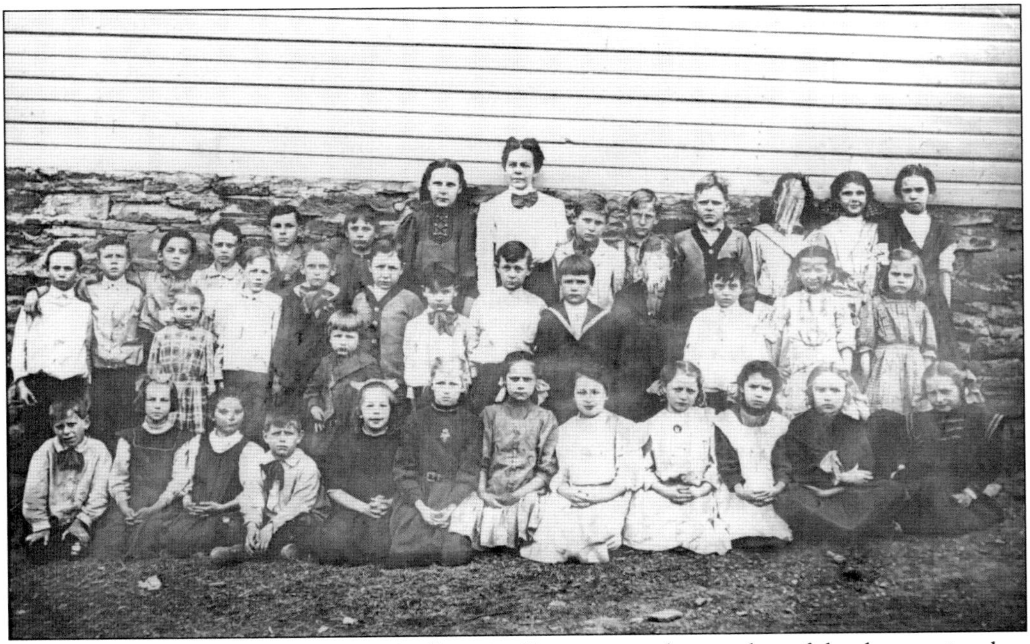

Possibly a fellow instructor to Mr. Schaffer, Miss Kerr is named as teacher of the downstairs class in the Pine Hill School in this class photograph.

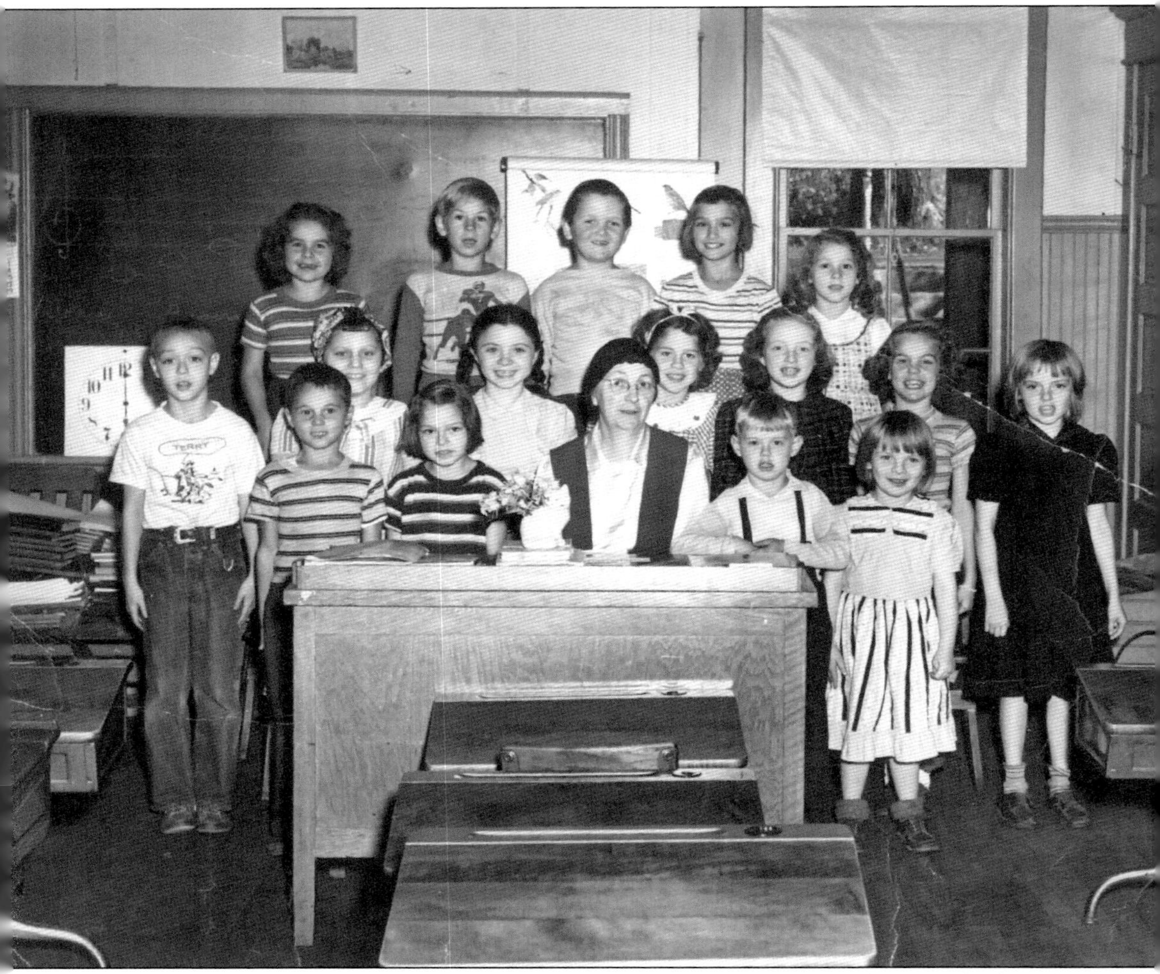

This 1948 class photograph of the Allaben School includes students from grades first through fourth. Pictured are (first row) Bruce Storey, Arlene Quick, Miss Maine, Walter Rider, and Ernestine Rider; (second row) Terry Grant, Patricia Knight, Delphine Torntegy, unidentified, Babette Decker, Arlene Dutcher, and Maryann Rider; (third row) unidentified, Robert Jones, Larry Dutcher, Elaine Quick, and Blanche Miller.

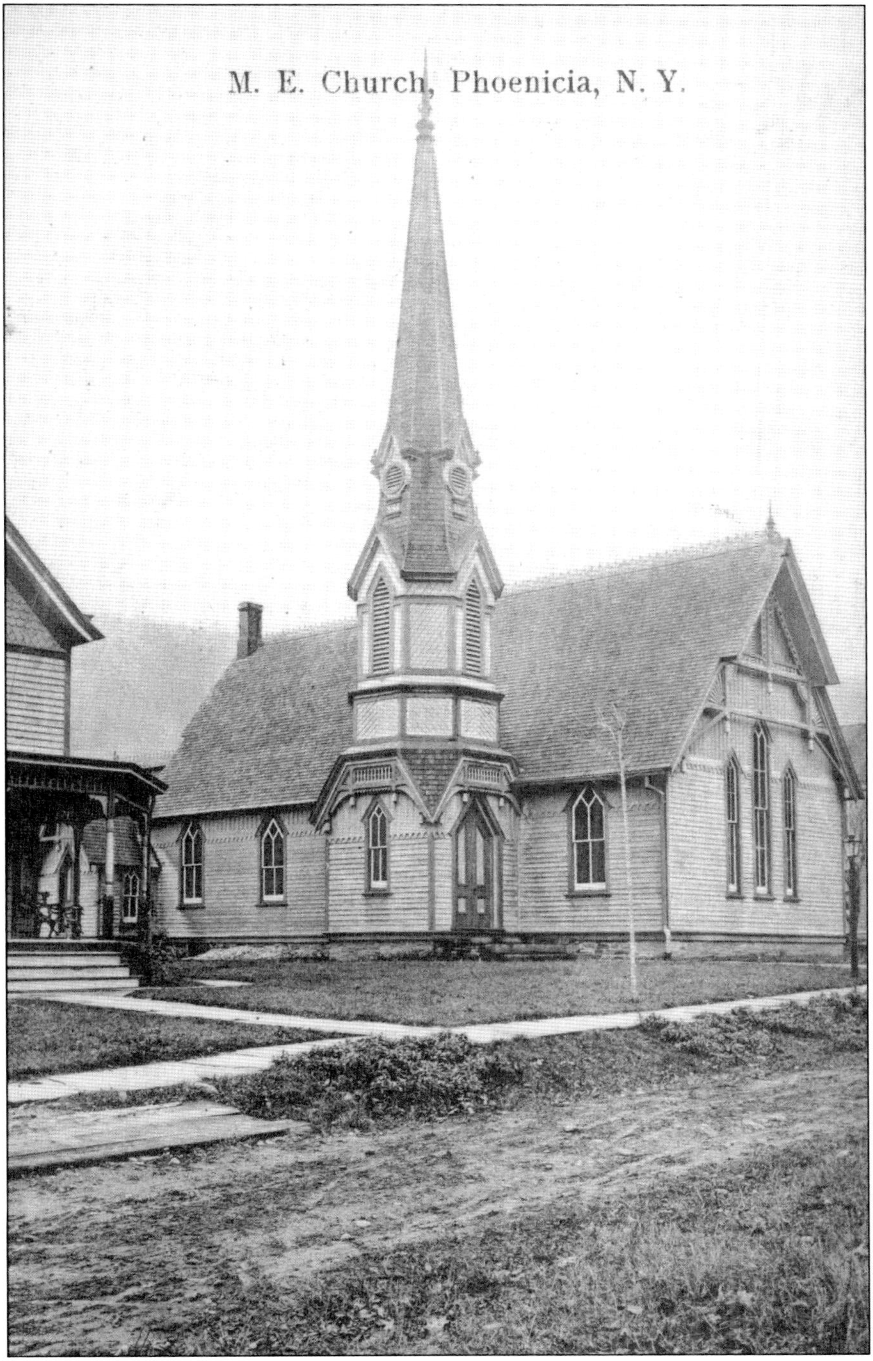

The Methodist Episcopal Church on Church Street in Phoenicia owes its beginnings to a community meeting held at the home of Mrs. Winters, the wife of a prominent Phoenicia doctor. That night, the Ladies' Aid Society was formed with a mission to build a church for the community. The charter members were Mrs. Winters, Sarah M. Bouse, Alice VanDemark, Mrs. P. Johnson, and Mrs. J. J. DuBois.

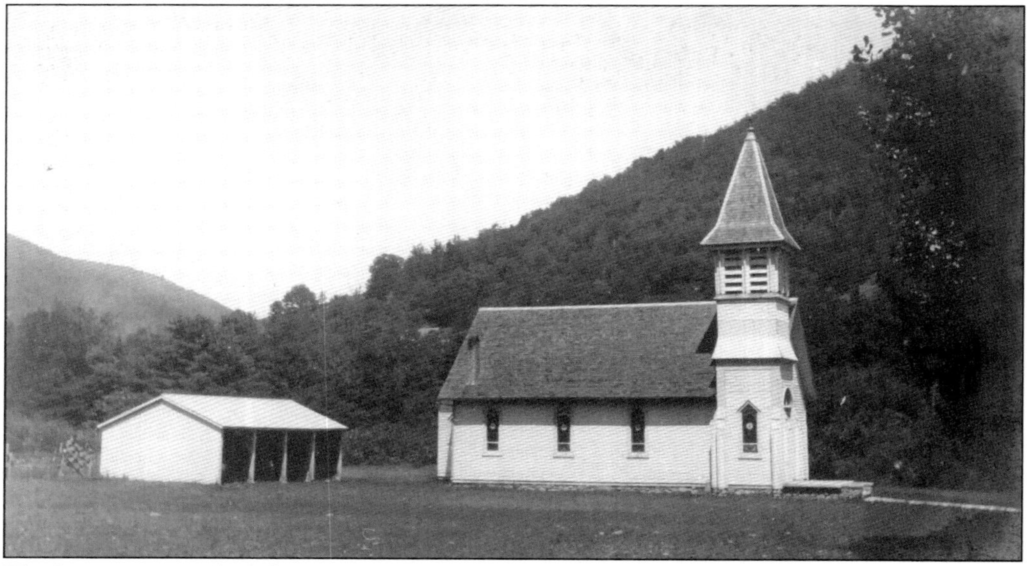

The late 1960s marked the end of services for the Methodist church on Church Street in Big Indian. In May of 1967, the Shandaken and Big Indian Methodist churches and the Pine Hill Community Church merged and became known as the Methodist Memorial Church. The new congregation spread from Highmount, almost to Phoenicia, and included several valleys.

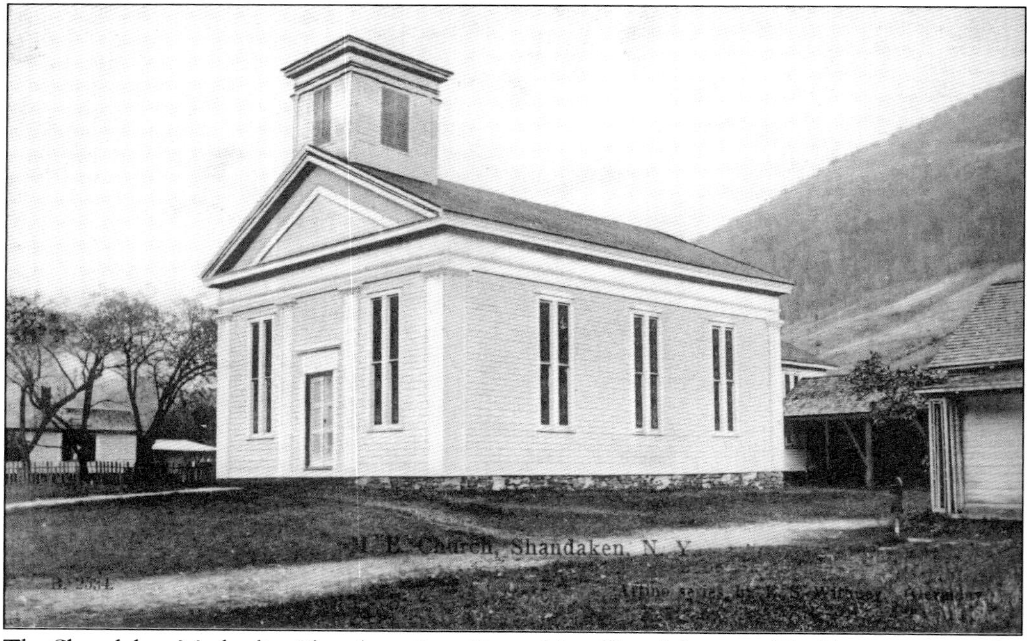

The Shandaken Methodist Church on State Route 28 in Shandaken is still holding services today and is an important hub of the community.

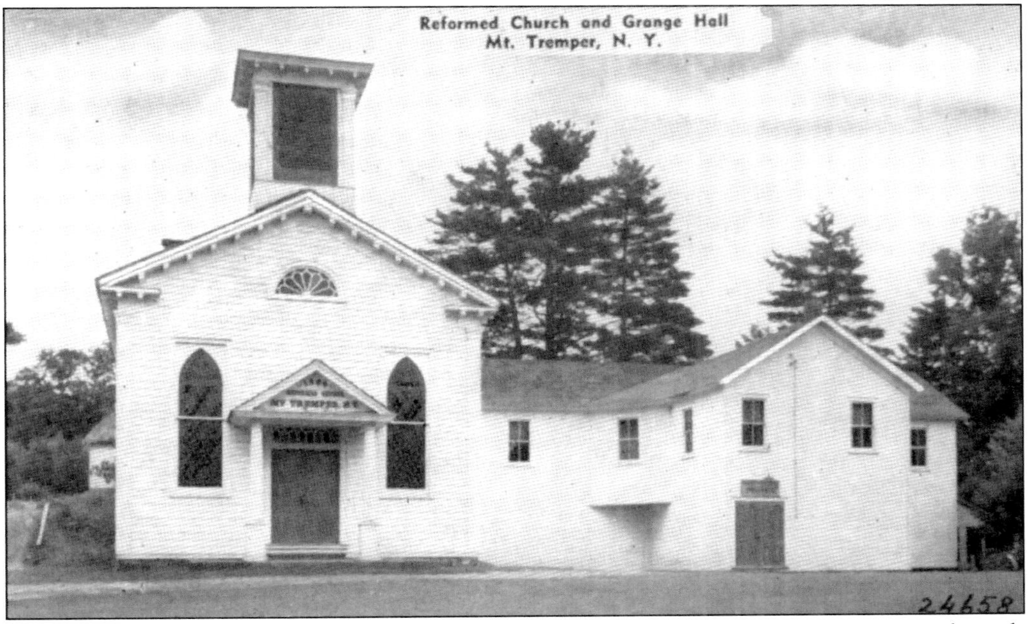

Mount Tremper Reformed Church is located on State Route 214 in Mount Tremper. It is a branch of the Dutch Reformed Church of Kingston that dates back to the 1600s. The addition was home to the local chapter of the National Grange.

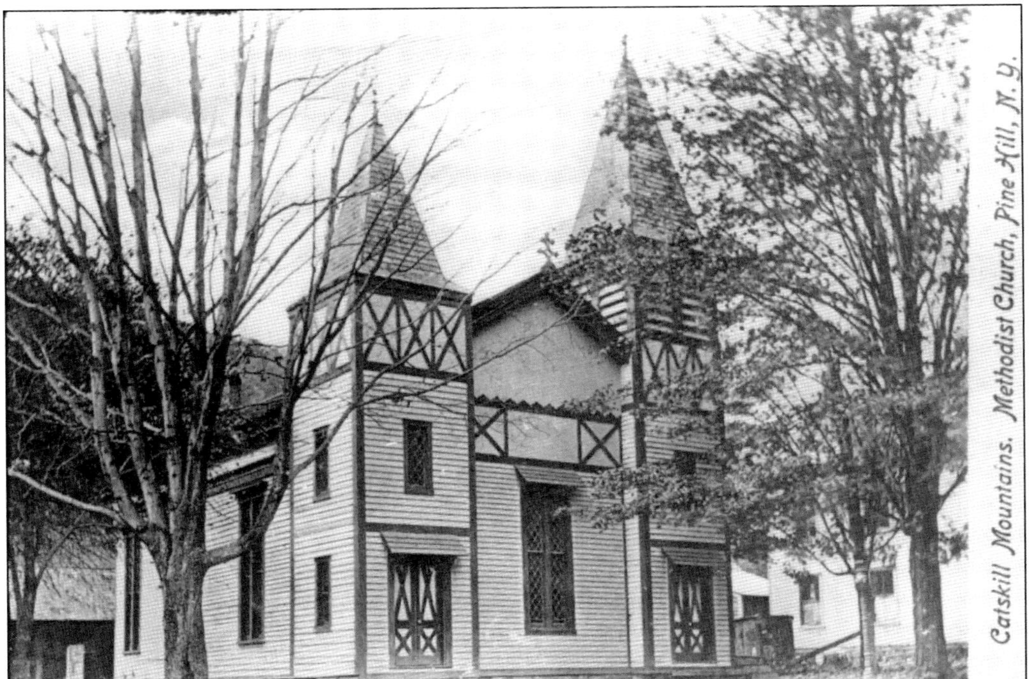

The Pine Hill Community Church discontinued services after consolidation with the Methodist churches. Like many quasi-public buildings in the community it has been adapted for use as a private home.

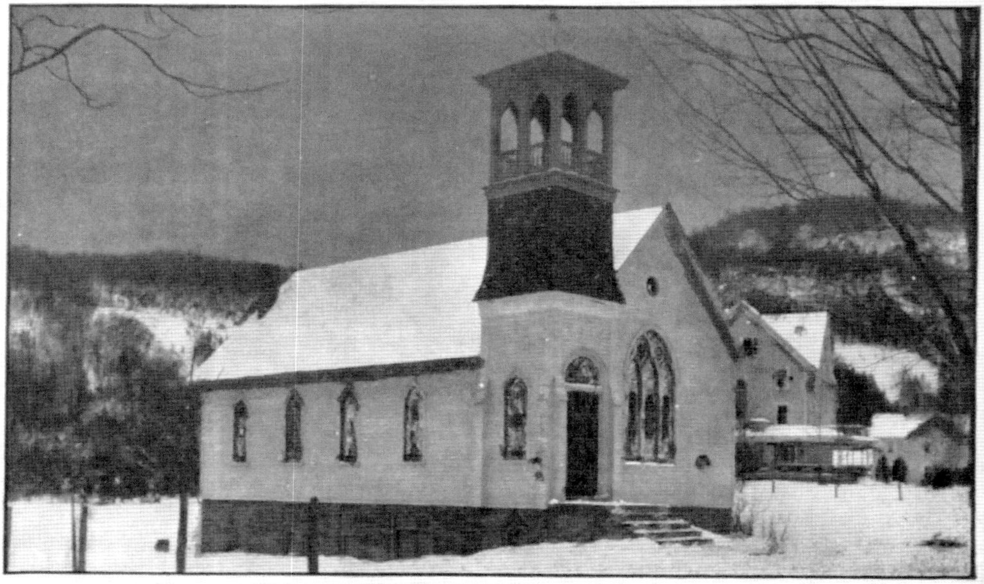

BAPTIST CHURCH, PHOENICIA, N. Y.

Like most of the congregations, Baptists built their church in the heart of the growing hamlet. This church is located on Main Street in Phoenicia.

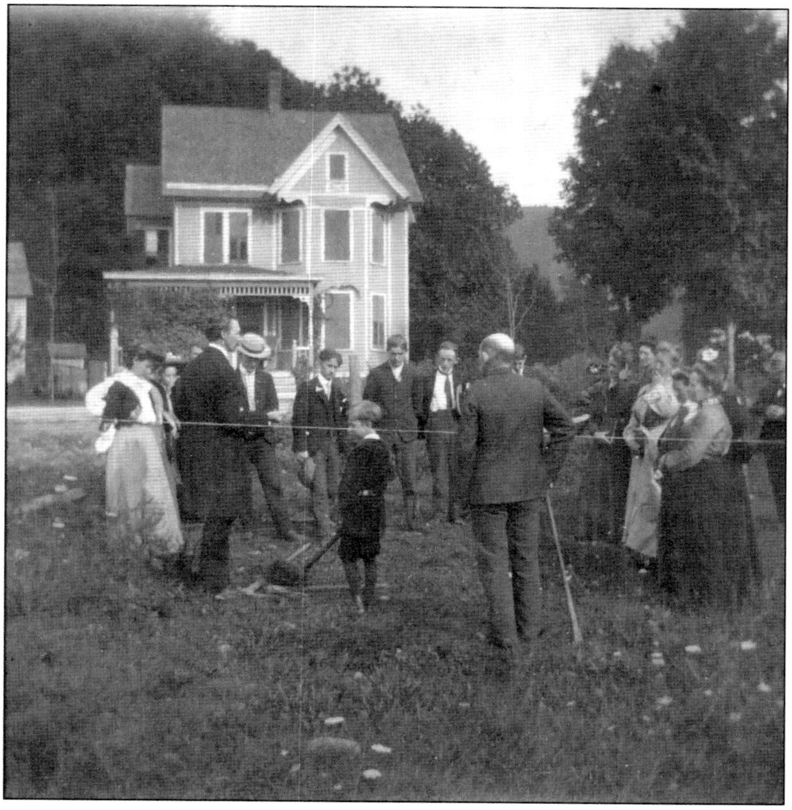

This 1904 photograph shows community members breaking ground for the Baptist church on Main Street in Phoenicia.

Built entirely of native bluestone in 1904, the St. Francis DeSales Church on Main Street is a surviving Catholic place of worship in the area today.

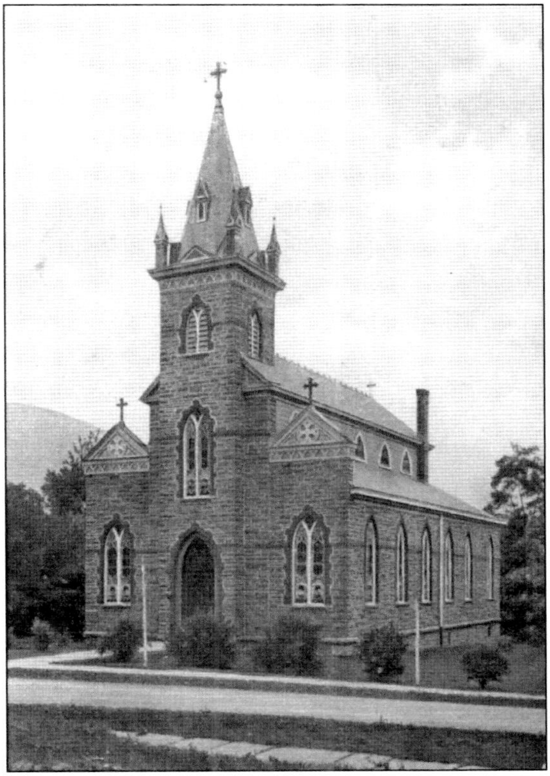

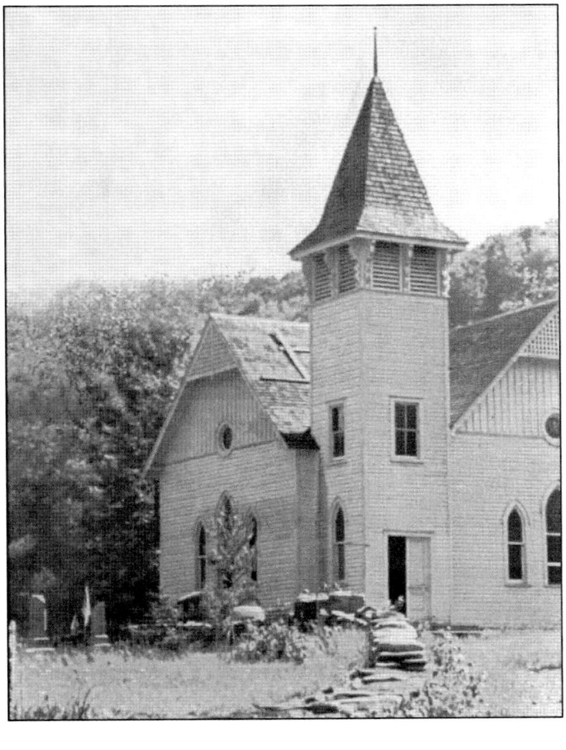

The Oliverea Church was on McKinley Hollow Road, adjacent to the Oliverea Cemetery.

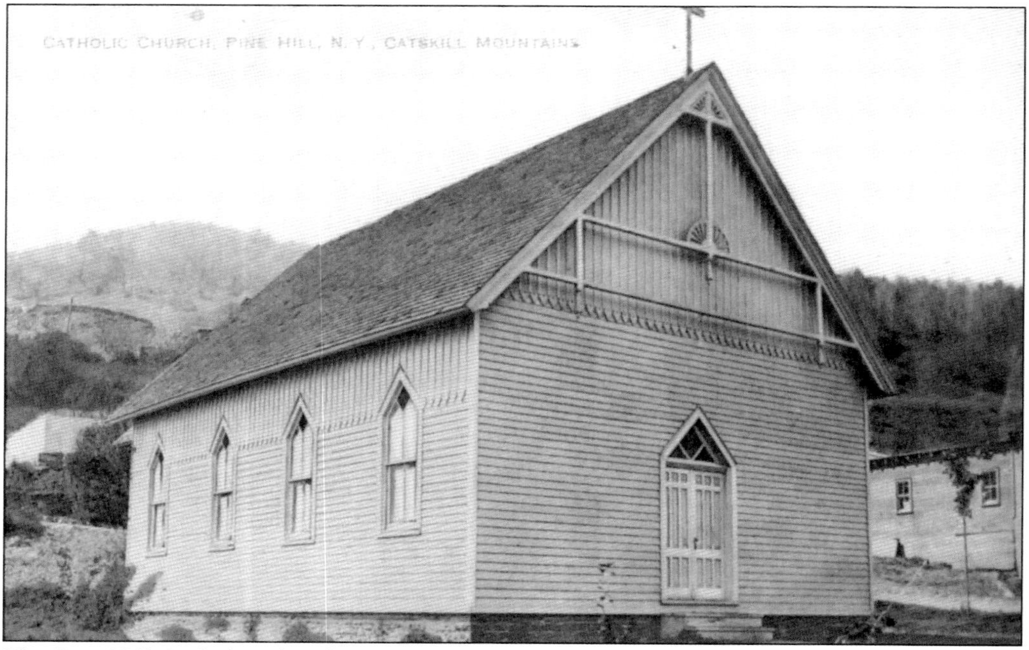

The Pine Hill Catholic Church is believed to have been built for the Irish Catholic indentured servants who would come to work in the hotels during the summer season.

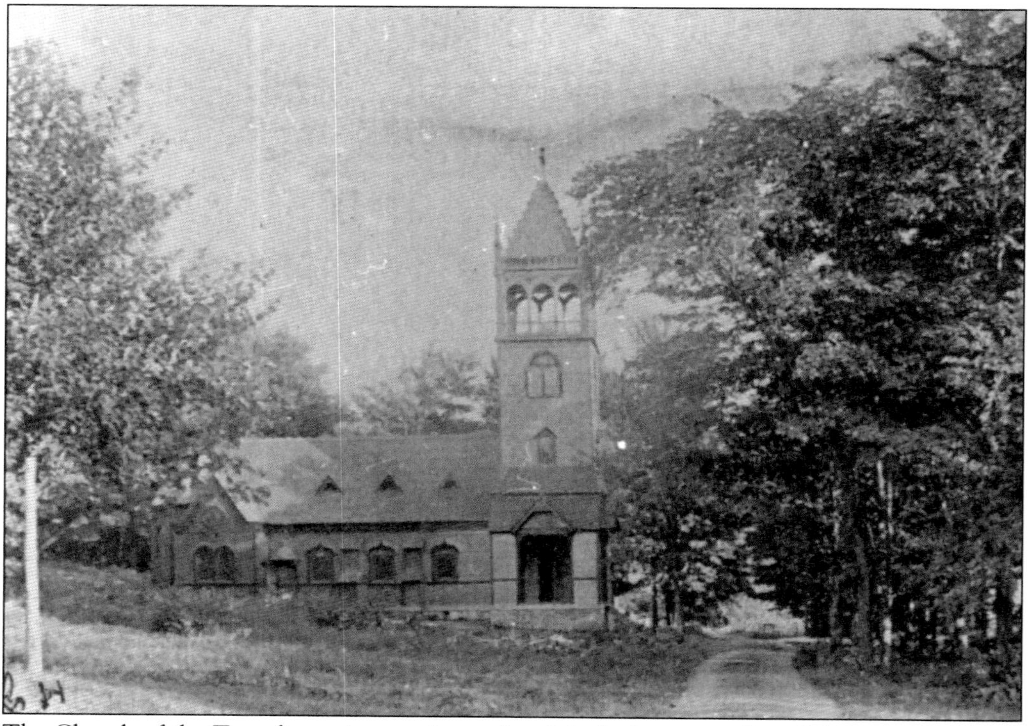

The Church of the Transfiguration was located on Maple Avenue in Pine Hill.

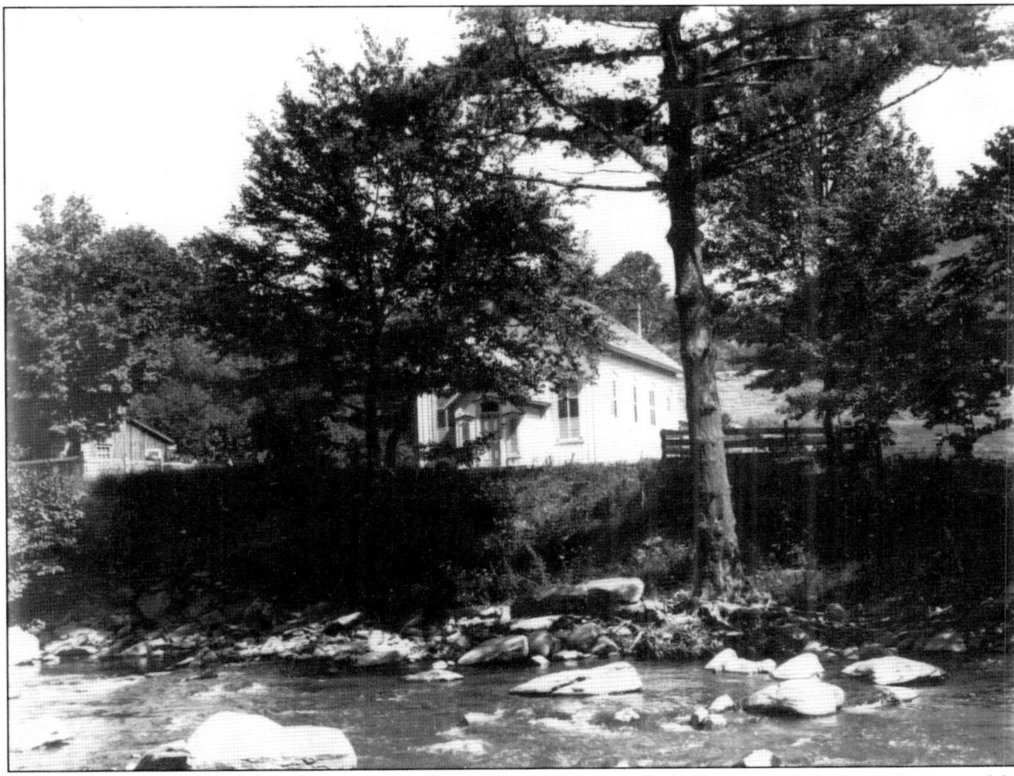

After purchasing the properties that encompassed the town of Chichester, William O. Swartzaelder called the Chichester Church St. Paul's, after their home church in Flatbush, New York.

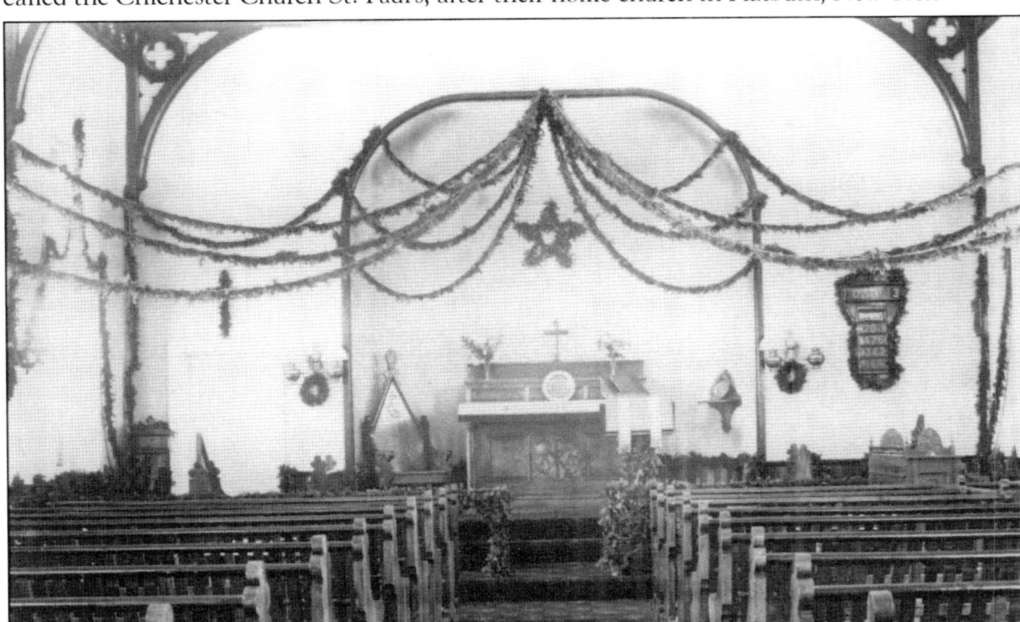

The interior of the Chichester Church is decked out for Christmas in 1899.

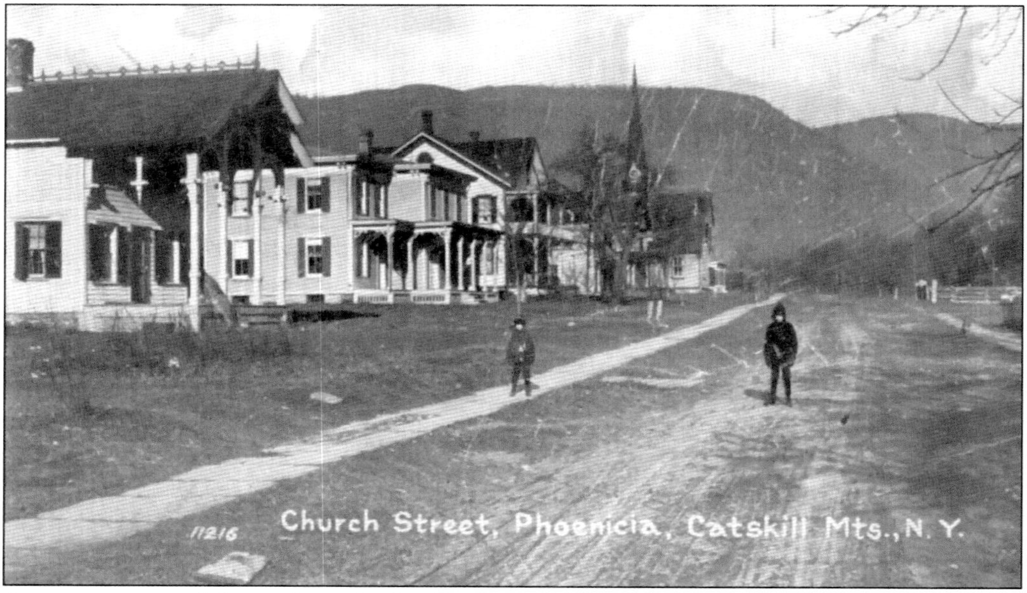

A picture postcard shows the early development of Church Street in Phoenicia. Although the street's formal name is Newton Avenue, it is commonly known as Church Street.

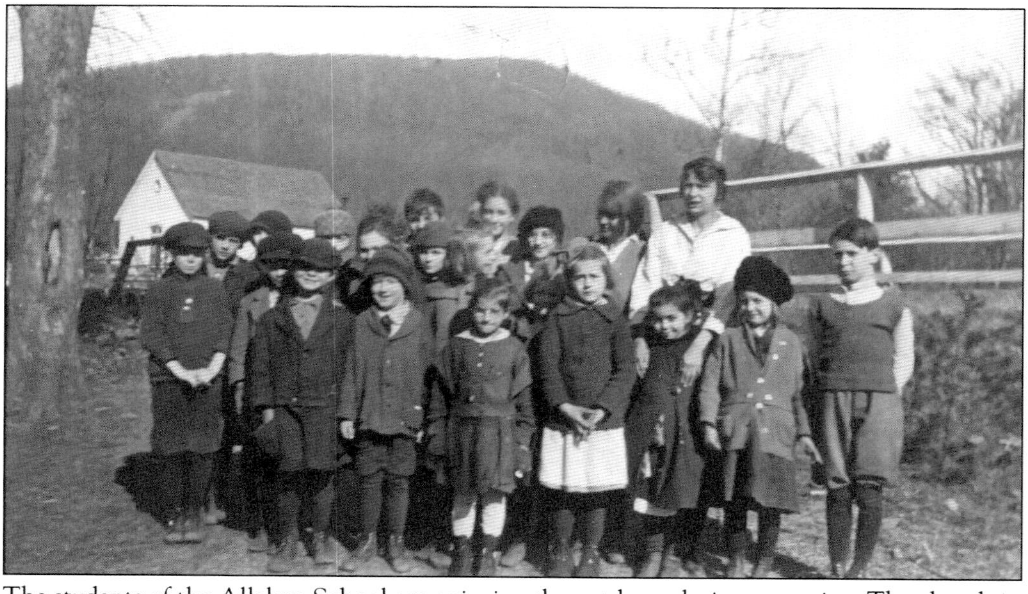

The students of the Allaben School are enjoying the outdoors during an outing. The church in the background is the Free Methodist.

Three

Business and Industry

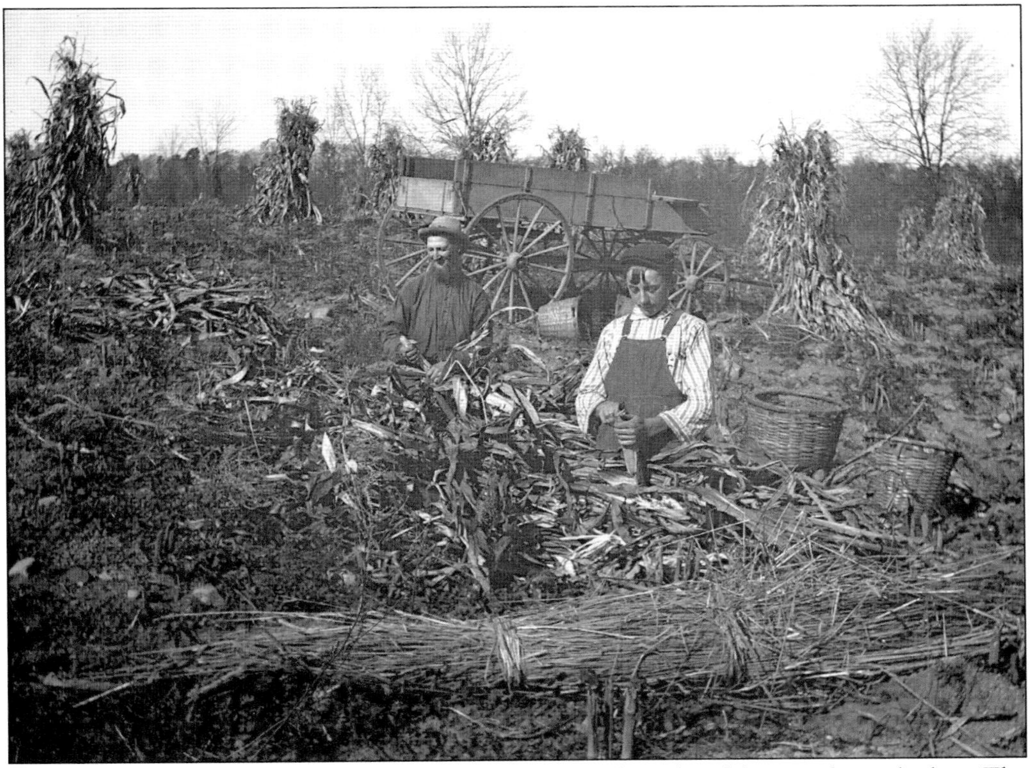

Cornhuskers are working hard in the field. Many farmed in Shandaken in the early days. The census of 1890 showed that most residents worked the land as farmers, but most farms were gone by the mid-1900s.

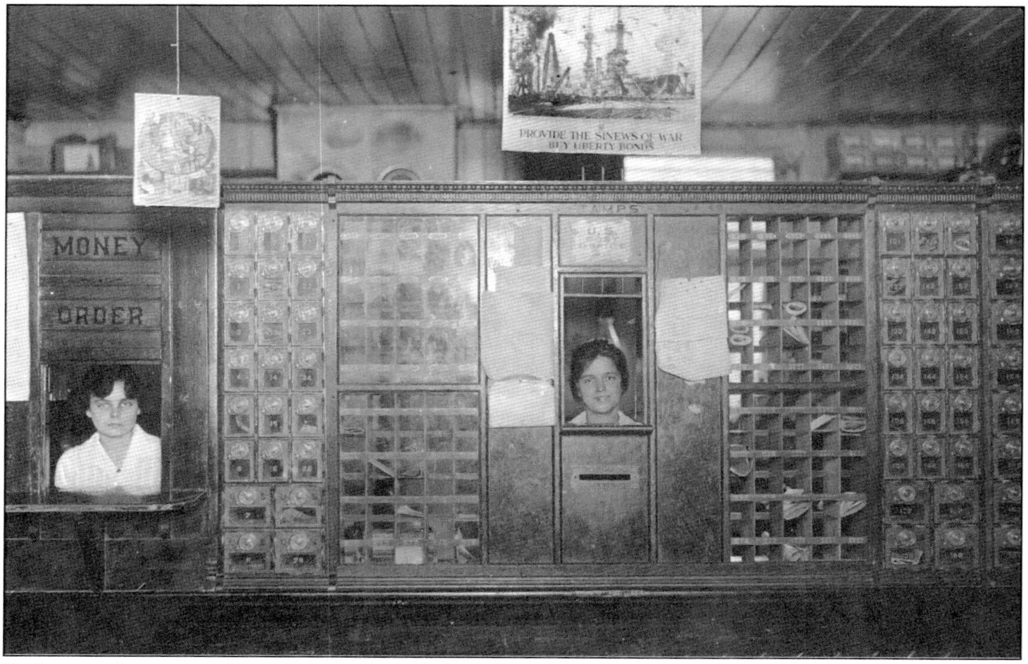

Before modern post offices became standalone businesses, Phoenicia's post office was once nestled in McGrath's store, now the Nest Egg on Main Street. Pictured here around 1917 are postal clerks Orpha Wright Nollner and Francis Hill.

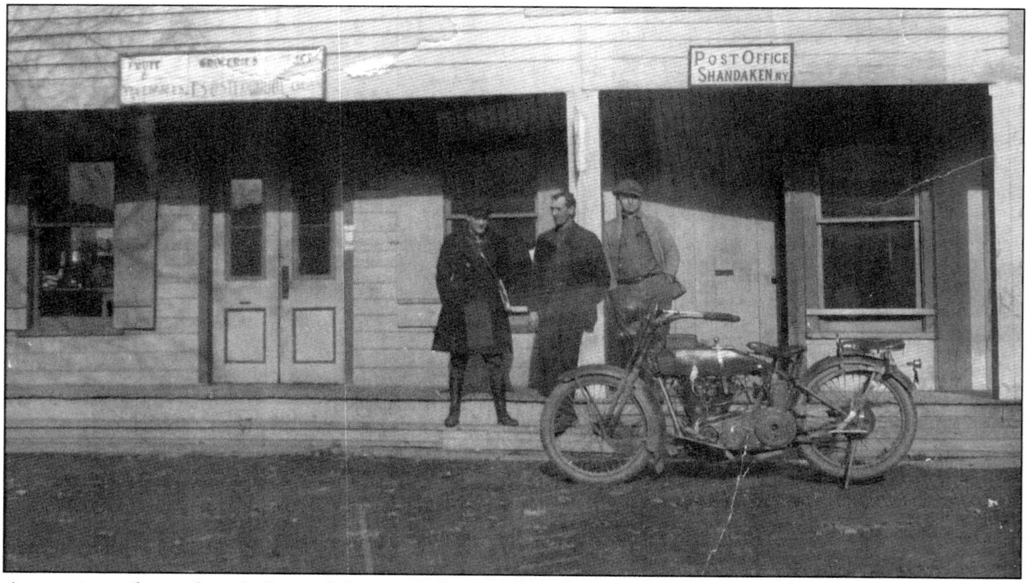

A courier takes a break from delivering the mail with residents in front of the Shandaken Post Office around 1918.

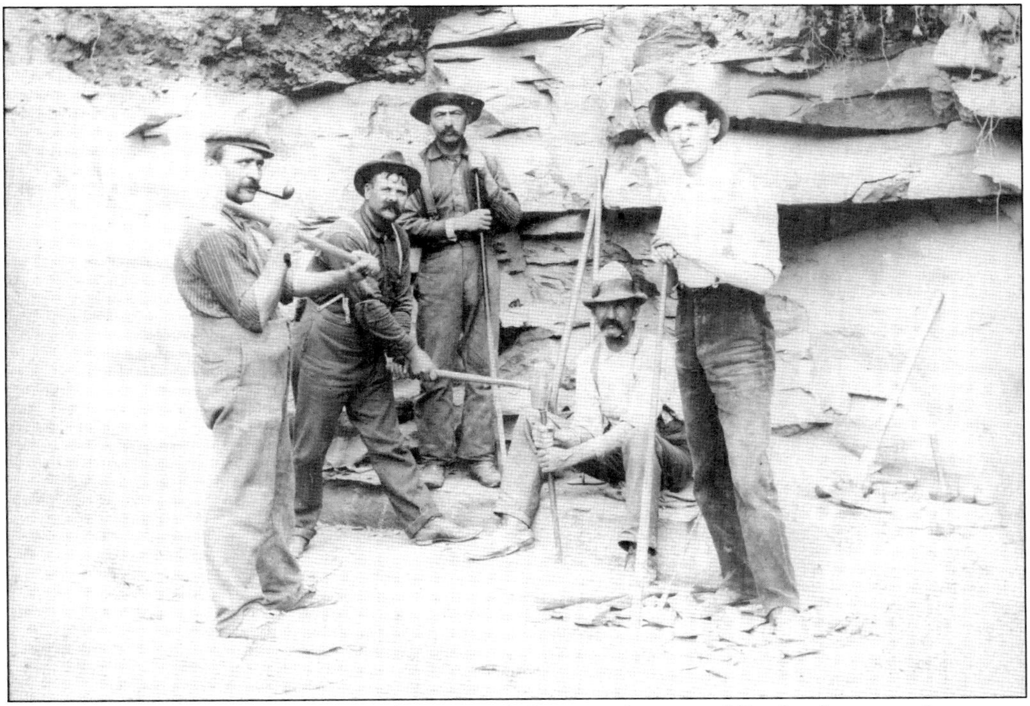

Quarrying was briefly a popular industry until the introduction of Portland cement became a cheaper alternative. The quarry workers in this picture are, from left to right, Orville Smith, Ros Merwin, Albert Benjamin, unidentified, and Rob Thompson.

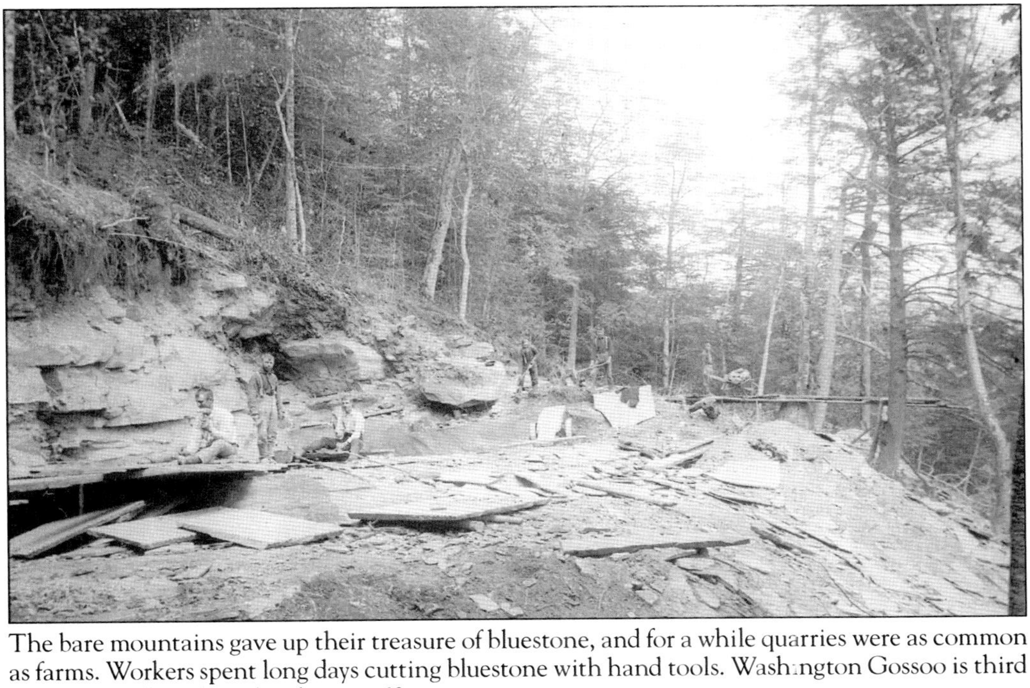

The bare mountains gave up their treasure of bluestone, and for a while quarries were as common as farms. Workers spent long days cutting bluestone with hand tools. Washington Gossoo is third from left, still working hard at age 63.

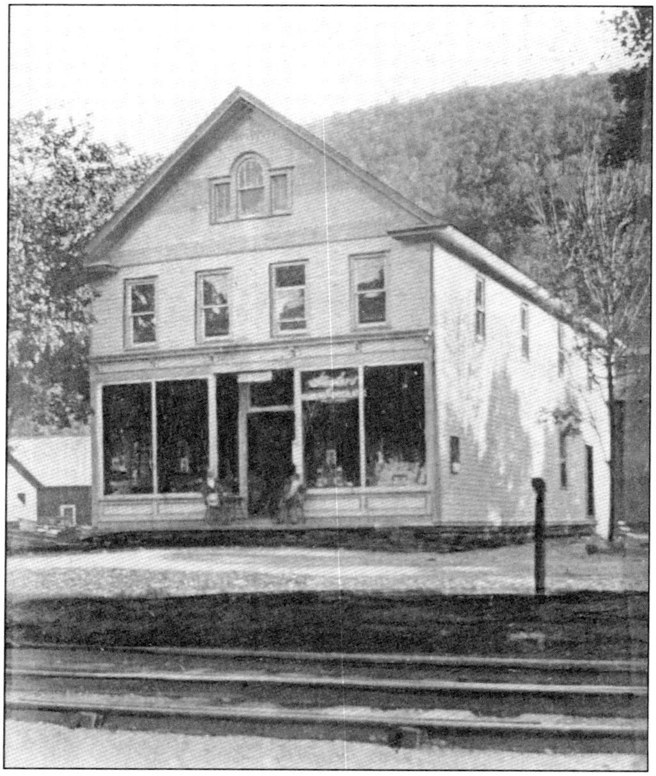

Bryants Store was located in Big Indian. The tracks in the foreground are part of the line that ran from Kingston to Oneonta. An extra engine was often added at this point to assist the train in climbing the summit at Highmount.

Much is known of the Chichester Chair Factory, yet Shandaken's Whitney Chair Factory was no less important as a major employer. It opened in 1869 and was located on the same site as the Sherrill Tannery. The Whitney family also ran a general store and a hotel in Shandaken.

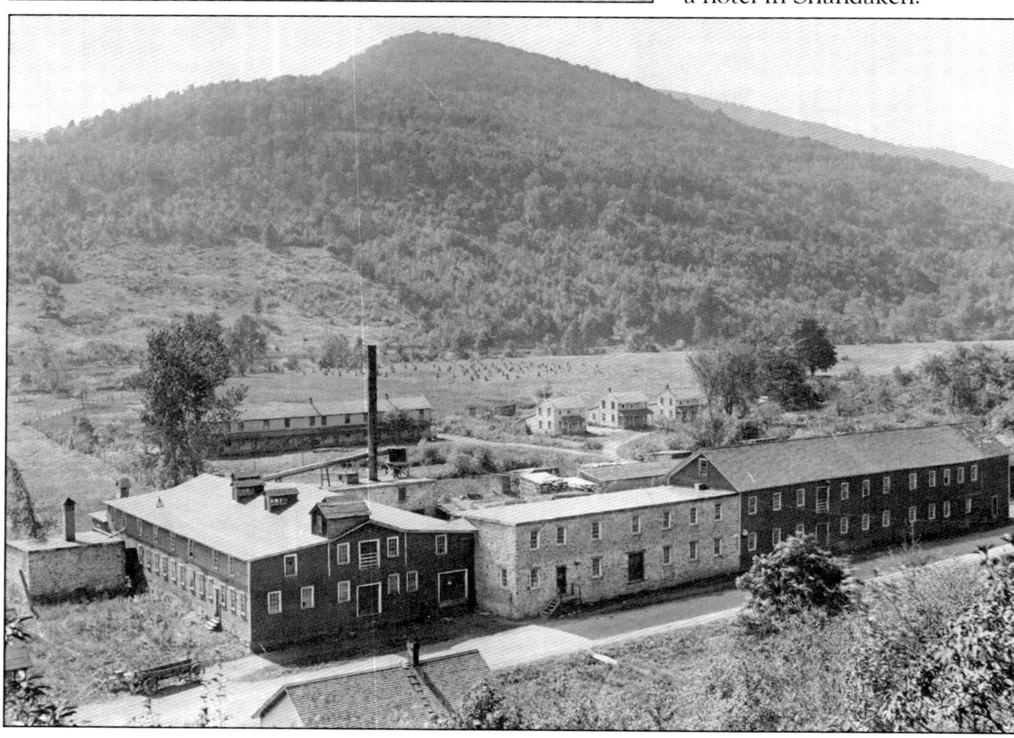

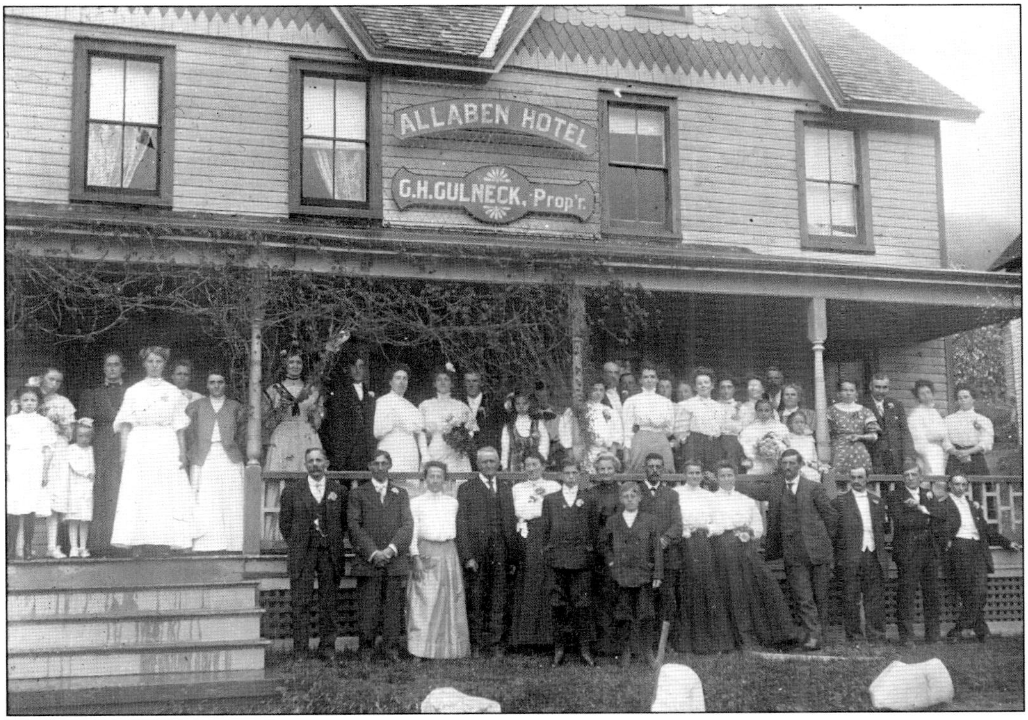

The Allaben Hotel, of which G. H. Gulneck was proprietor, on State Route 28 is the setting for this wedding picture. The photograph is of the wedding of Laura Marian Gulneck and Elwyn Taylor Hoar. The building is now a private residence. This section of State Route 28 was renamed Evergreen Road after the straightening of the original road.

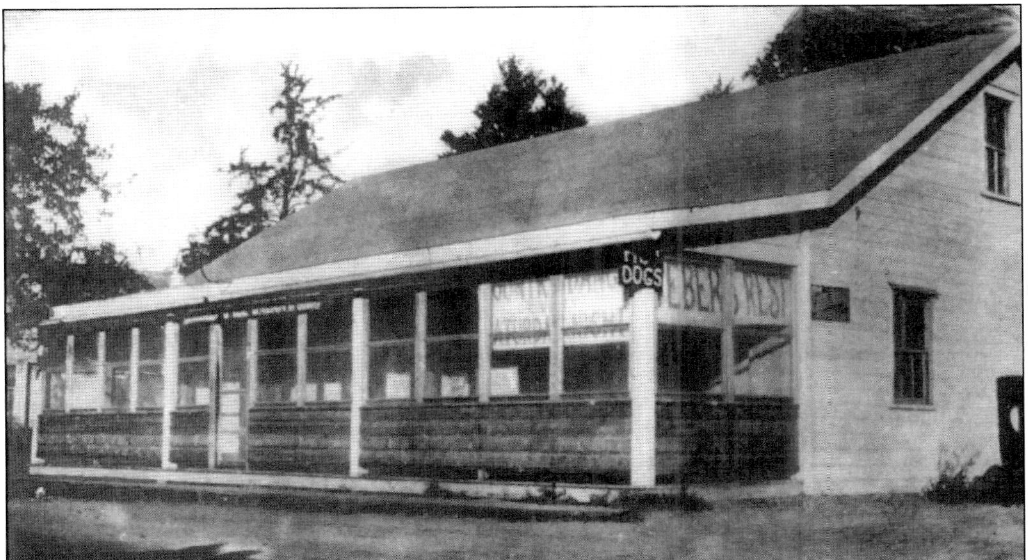

Weber's Rest in Mount Tremper was a delicatessen and lunchroom in the 1930s through the 1950s. The building located on State Route 214 has been several businesses over the years and is still in use today.

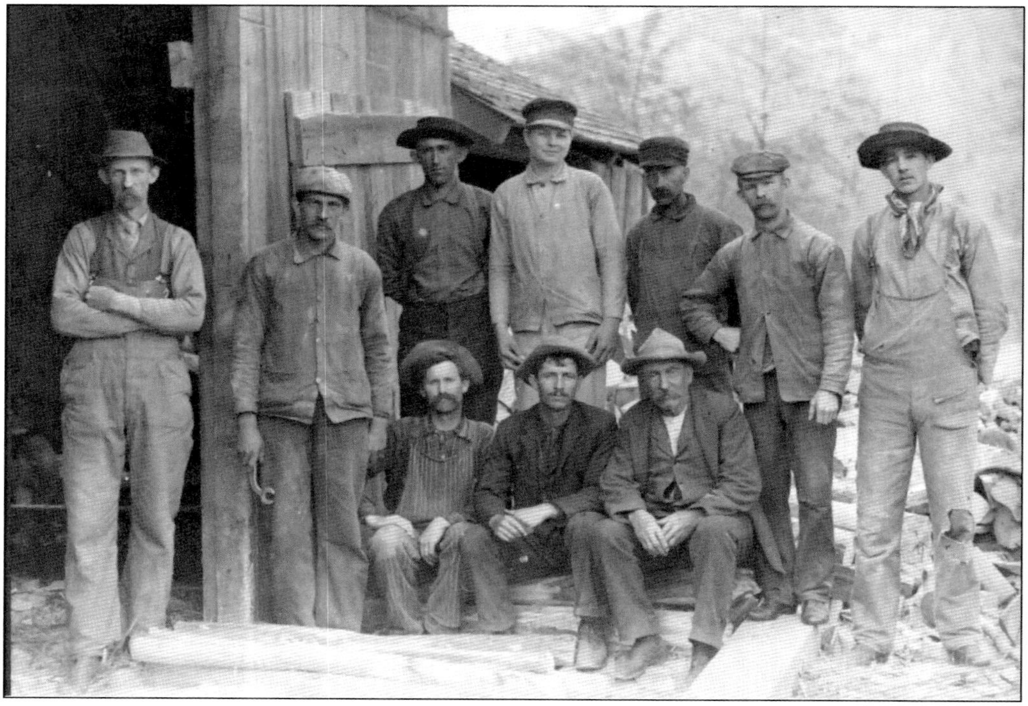

The Excelsior Mill workers pause for a more formal portrait during a workday. The workers in this picture are, from left to right, (seated) Mel Finch, Gene Gormley and Mr. Burgher; (standing) Sol Burgher, Joseph Rider, William Ennist, Howard Johnson, David Jamison, Varnum Rider, and Will Mack.

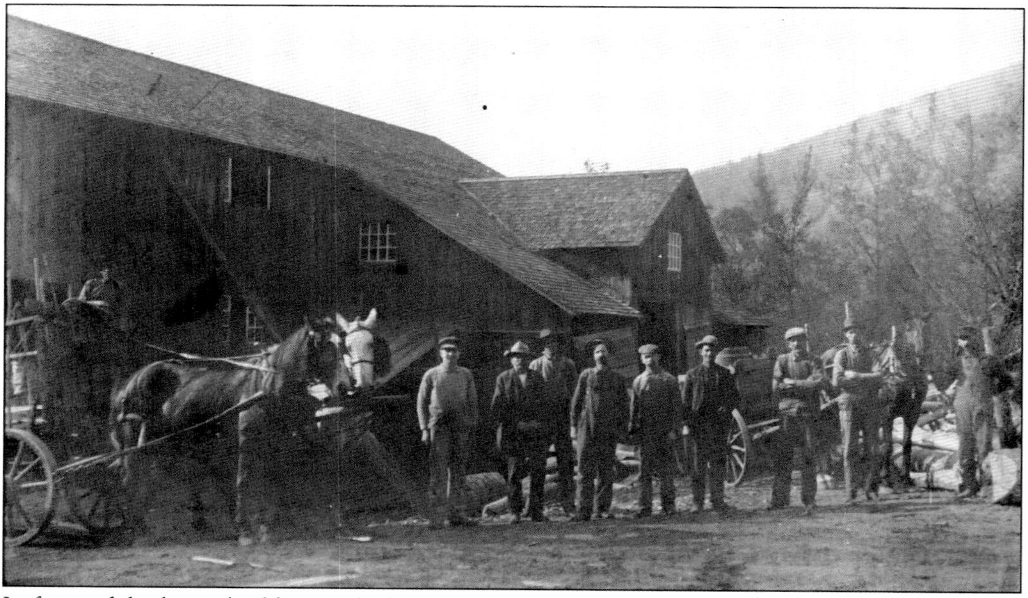

In front of the larger building with the horse teams, workers from the Excelsior Mill are (seated) Mel Finch, Gene Gormley, and Mr. Burgher; Sol Burgher, Joe Rider, Will Ennist, Howard Johnson, Dave Johnson, Varmun Rider, and Will Mack.

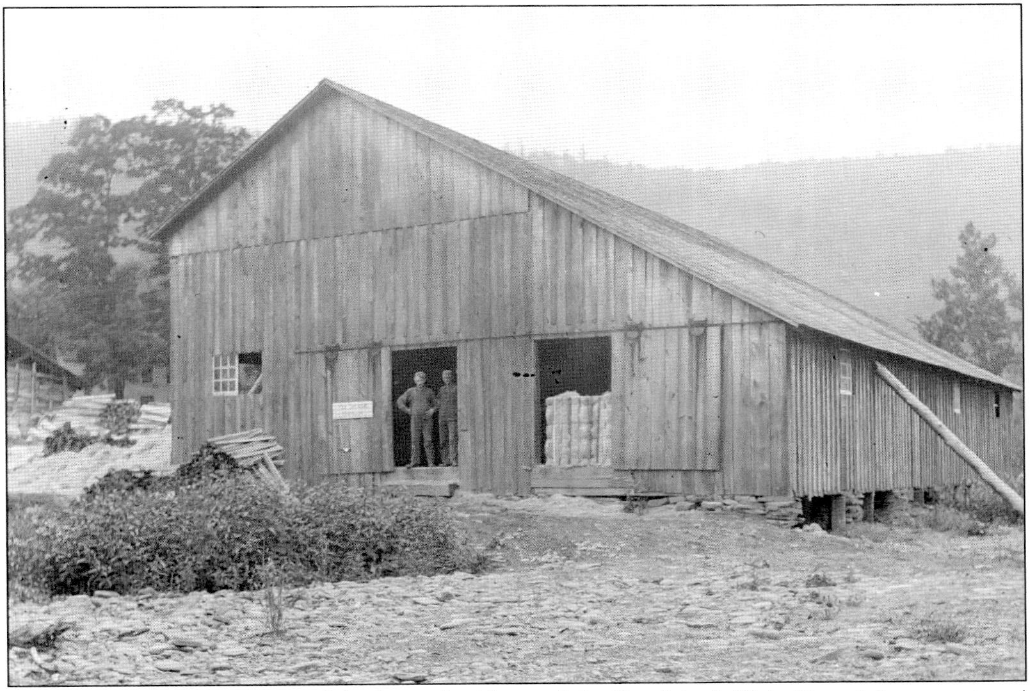

This photograph shows one of the larger buildings of the Excelsior Mill in Shandaken, reprinted from a glass negative. (Courtesy of Richard Schaedle.)

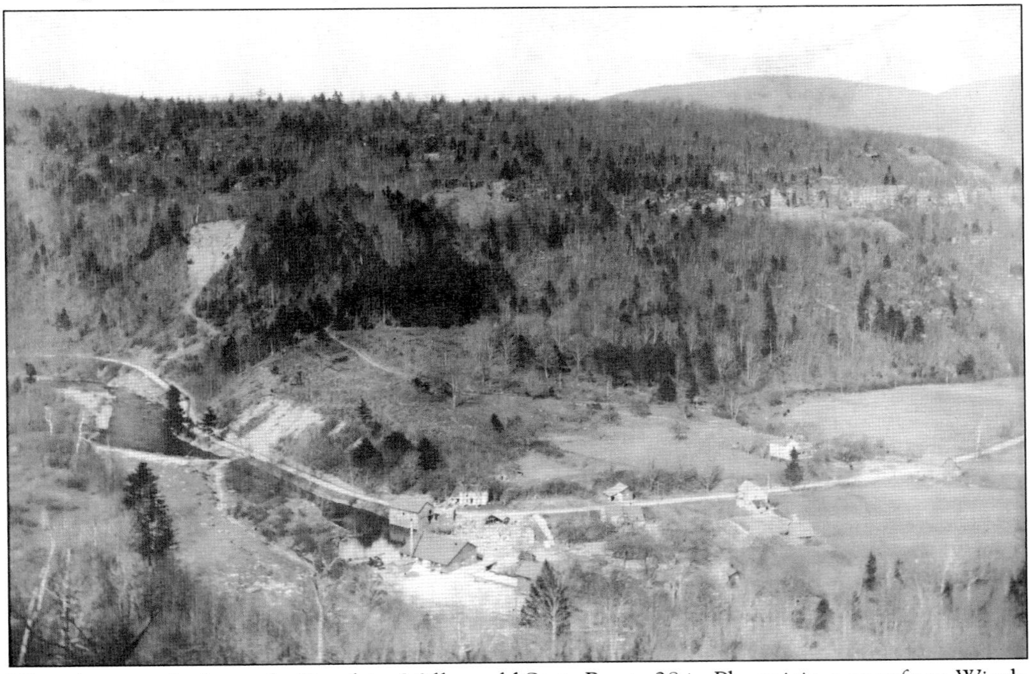

This photograph shows the Excelsior Mill on old State Route 28 in Phoenicia, across from Windy Ridge. To the right is the Jameson Farm. Also pictured are the Lounsbury and Burgher homes. The mill is long gone but the foreman's house is now a private residence.

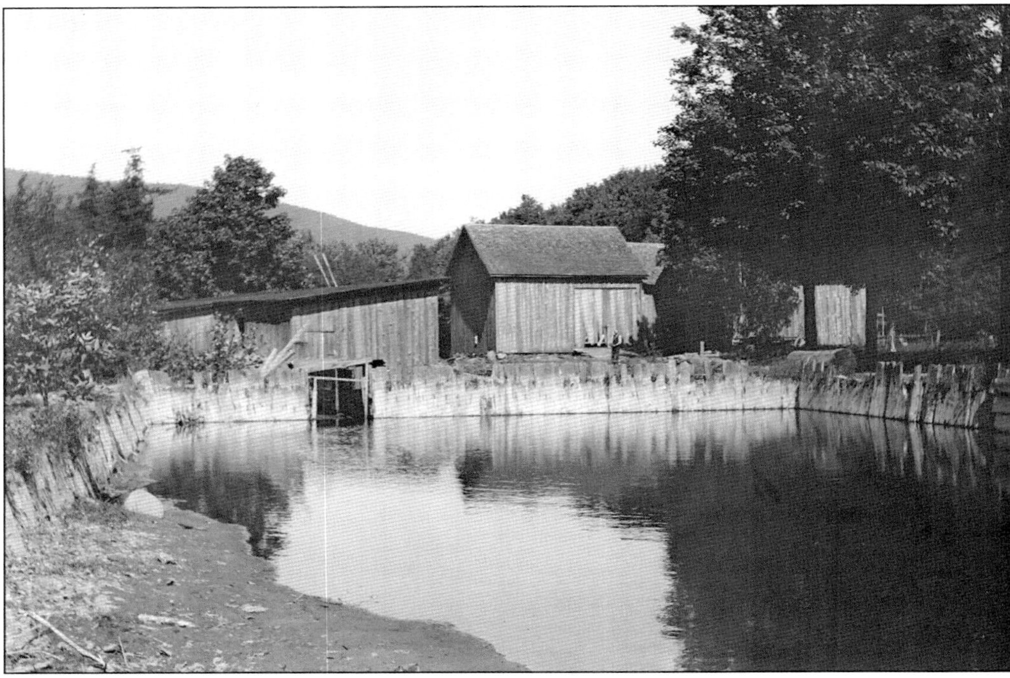

The dock at the Excelsior Mill was built up on the bank of the creek to hold the logs waiting to be sawn. (Courtesy of Richard Schaedle.)

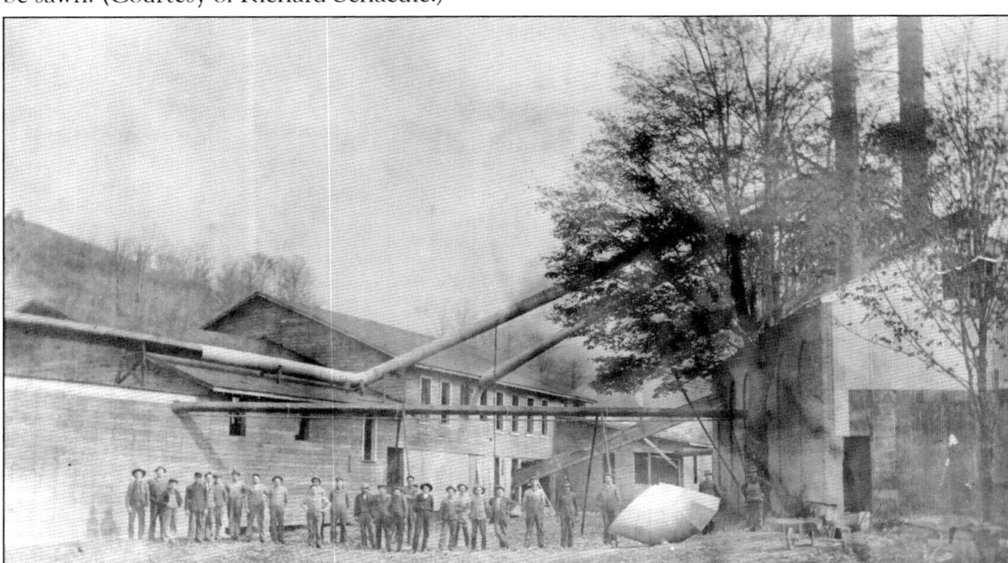

In a letter to his cousin Byron Dutcher, Richard Bennett wrote the following regarding the Riseley's Lumber Mill in Oliverea: "Our grandfather, Andrew C. Bennett, was the foreman and George's father, Clarence Bennett, was the caretaker even after the mill shut down. The building on the [right] used waste lumber to make steam as the whole mill ran on steam. Behind the center building was a pond where they dumped the logs. A ramp took the logs up to a 6-foot saw that cut the slabs, planks and boards."

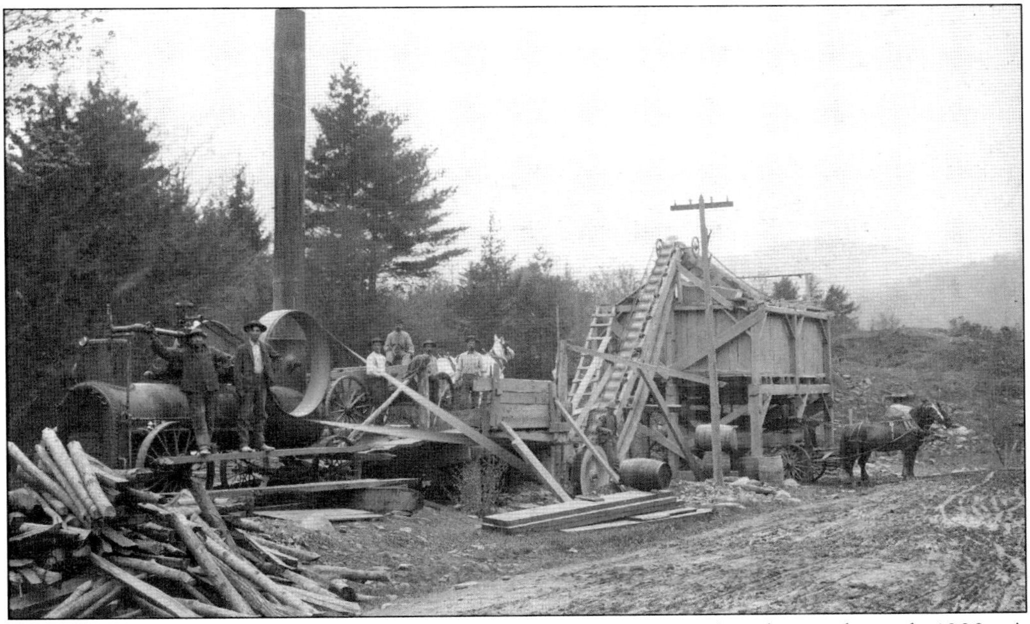

The Cruickshank Mill was one of the many local mills that popped up during the early 1900s. A 1924 issue of the *Catskill Mountain Reflector* advertises the Big Indian Wood Products Co., Ltd, established in 1911. They produced crates, cooperage stock, veneer for crates, lumber, shooks, and boxes. J. H. Cruickshank was the president and W. H. Cruickshank was the secretary and treasurer.

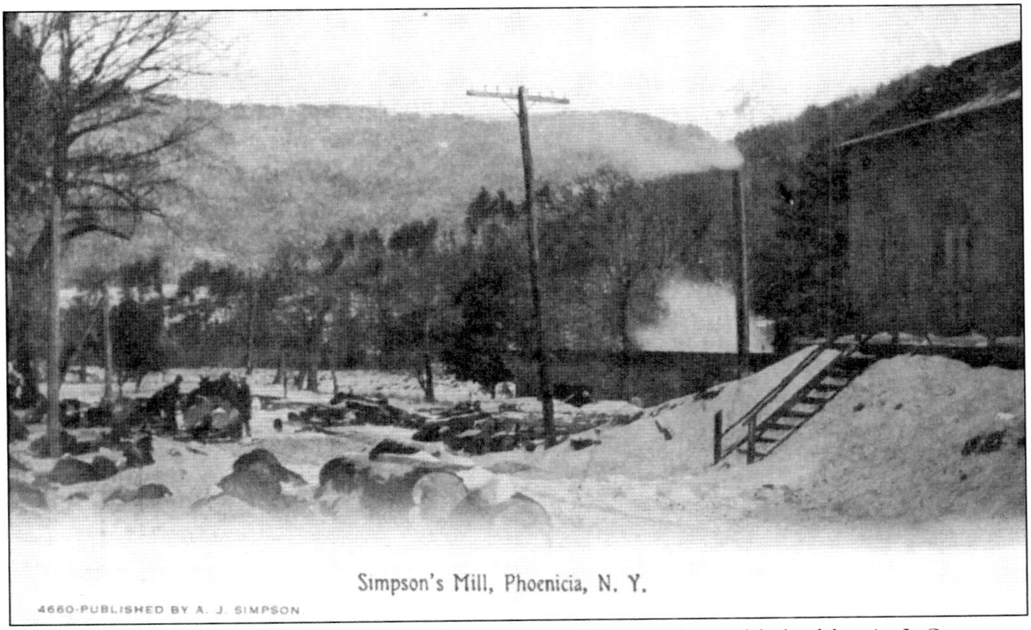

This postcard titled "Simpsons Mill, Phoenicia, N.Y." was also published by A. J. Simpson. Although the exact location is unknown, it was most likely located just south of Phoenicia where the Simpsons Ski Slope was at a later date. A. J. Simpson was a very pioneering individual, and it is not implausible he would run a mill.

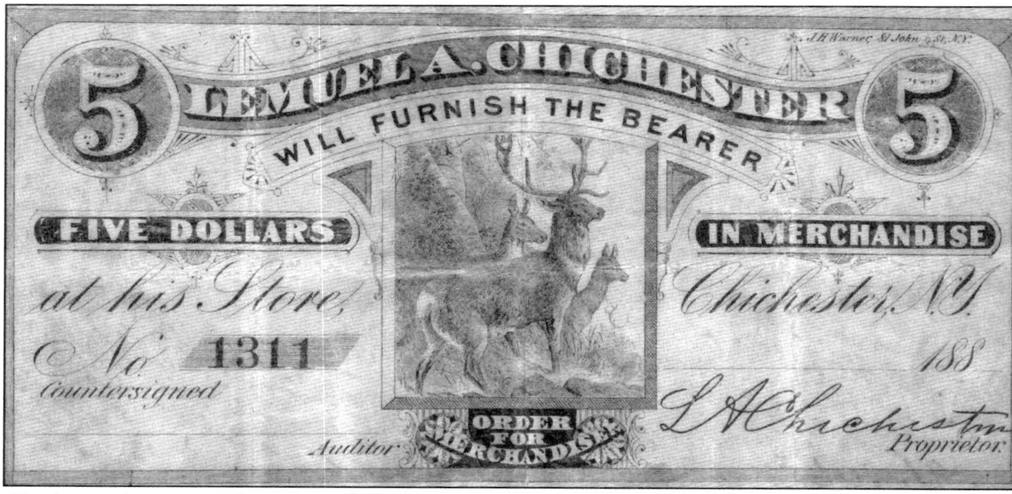

Chichester factory workers not only lived in company houses, but were also paid with company scrip to be spent at the Chichester General Store. Mr. Lemuel L. Chichester died on March 31, 1903. His obituary stated, "In our memory he will never die, and any little acts of kindness done by this noble man in helping the poor will never be forgotten and often spoke of with tearful eyes."

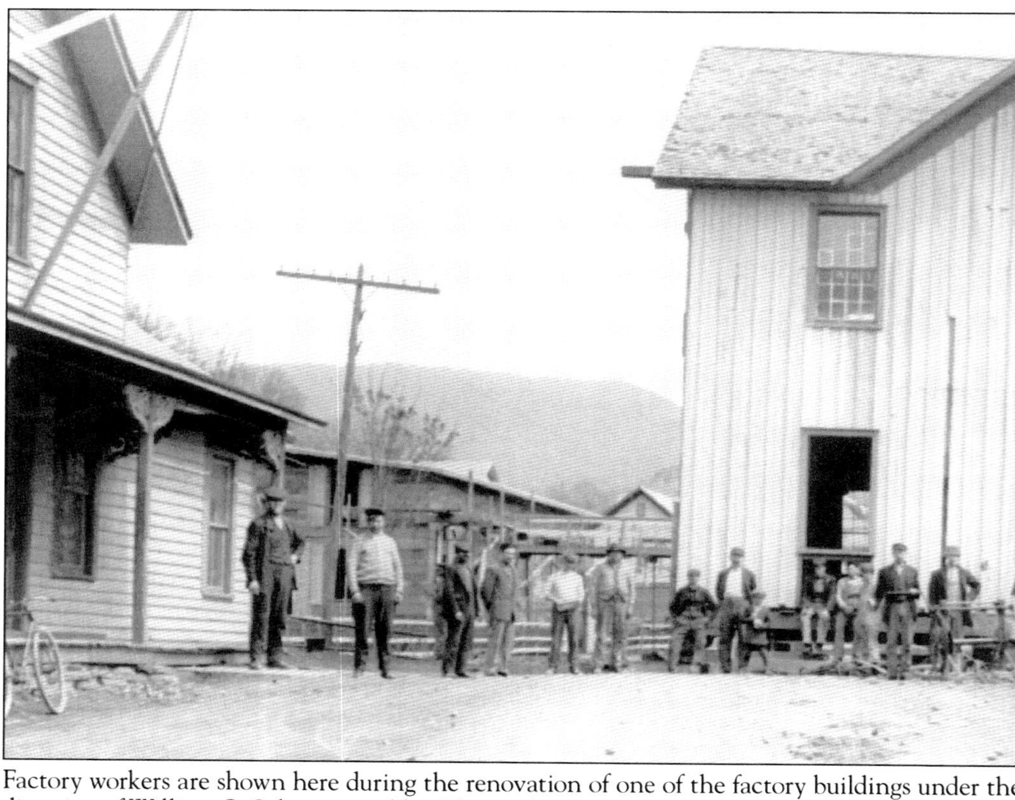

Factory workers are shown here during the renovation of one of the factory buildings under the direction of William O. Schwartzwaelder. The newly named and reinvigorated complex was viable for many years until the days of the Great Depression took its toll.

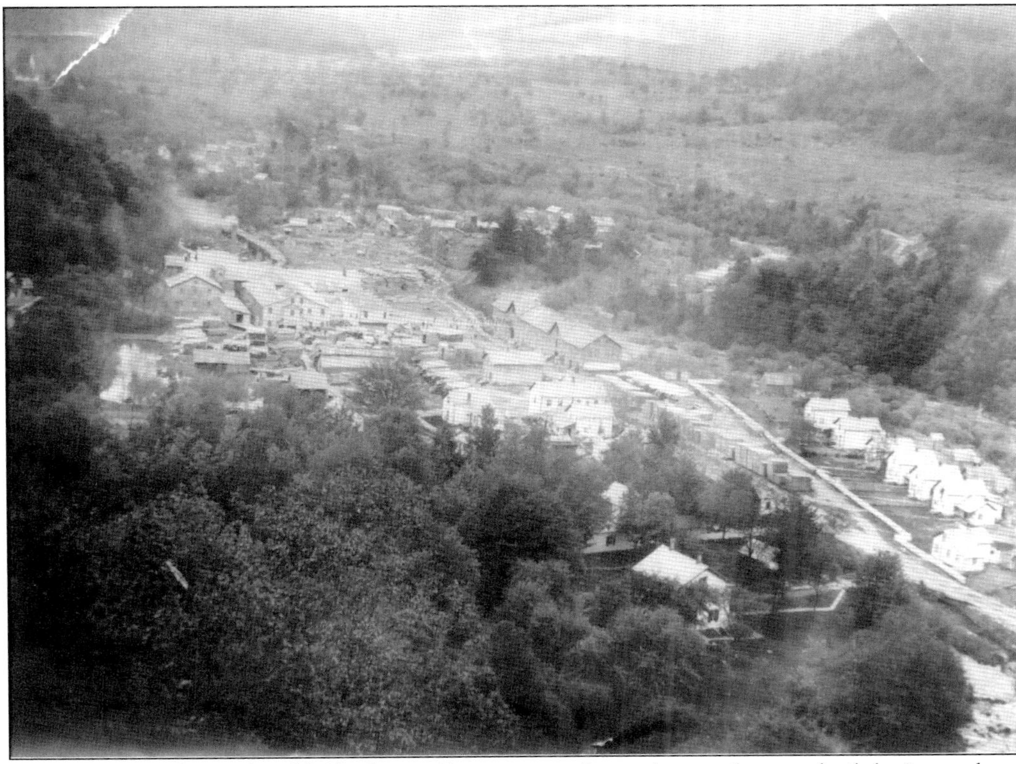

Down in the valley is the old Chichester Factory complex and town that was built by Lemuel and Frank Chichester and their partner Josiah Partridge. In 1866, Mr. Partridge sold out his share to be followed by Frank Chichester, leaving Chichester as the sole owner. Frank Chichester maintained the business through 1884, when Schwarzwaelder bought him out.

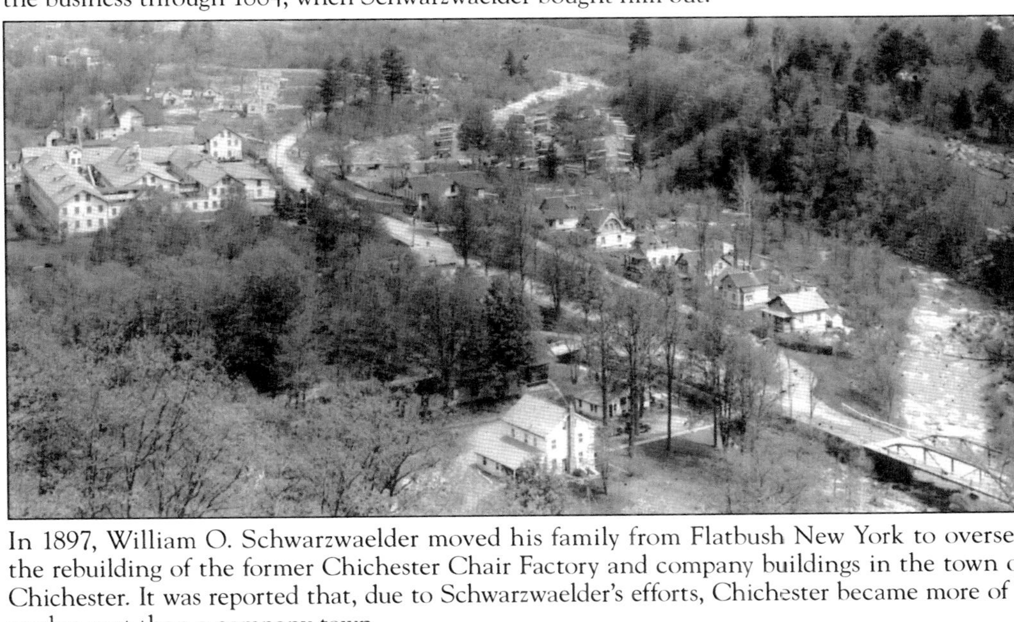

In 1897, William O. Schwarzwaelder moved his family from Flatbush New York to oversee the rebuilding of the former Chichester Chair Factory and company buildings in the town of Chichester. It was reported that, due to Schwarzwaelder's efforts, Chichester became more of a garden spot than a company town.

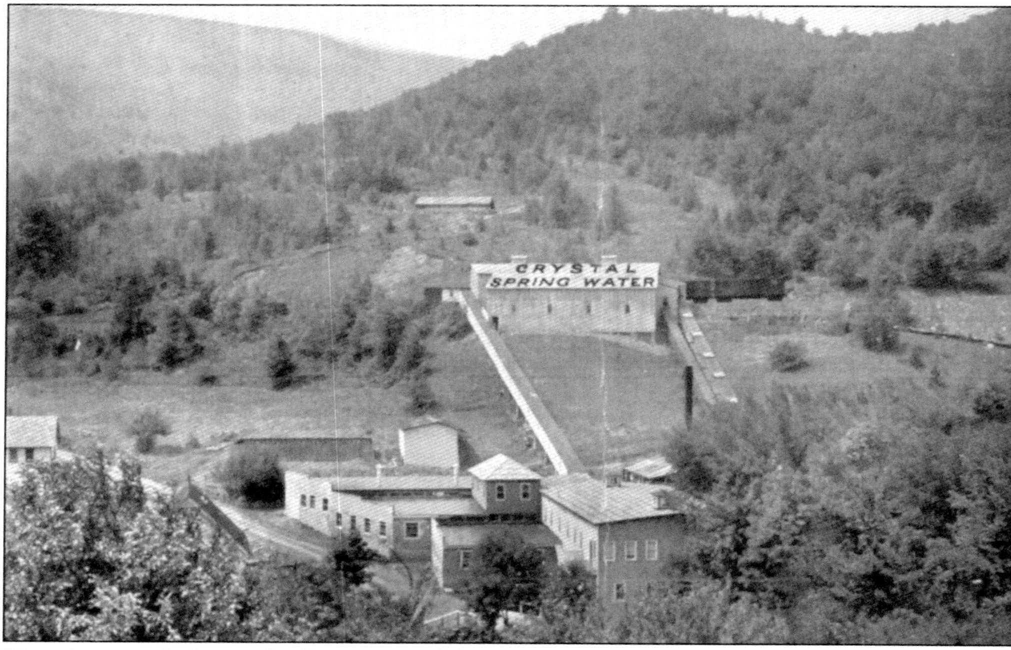

This photograph shows a bird's-eye view of the Crystal Spring Water bottling plant on Bonnieview Avenue in Pine Hill. Established in 1901, the company promised that the whole bottling operation was done by machinery and from the time the water left the spring until it was delivered to the consumer, it touched nothing but glass.

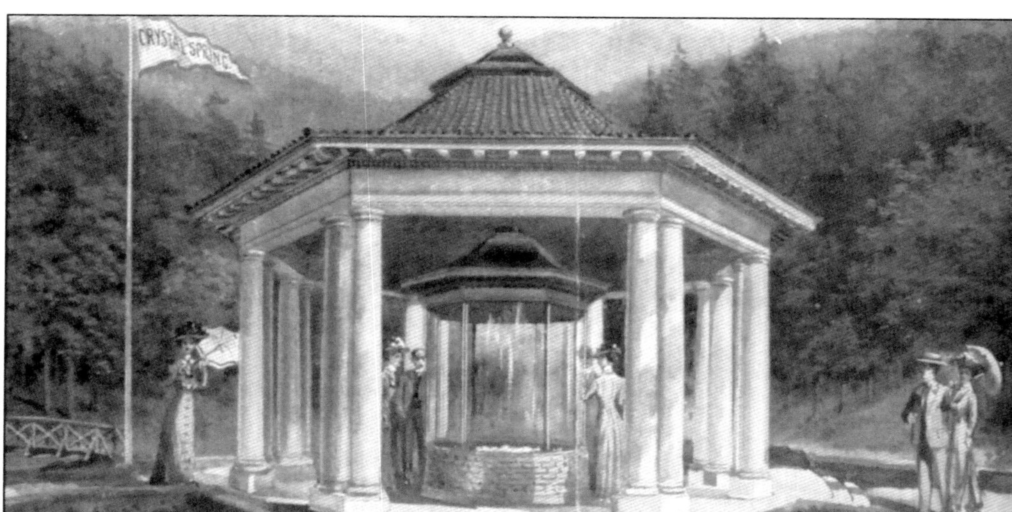

This illustration from a Crystal Spring Water advertising brochure is captioned "The Spring Pavilion and arcade on Belle Ayr Mountain 2,200 feet above tidewater." The spring still produces water today, although the village now draws water from adjacent wells.

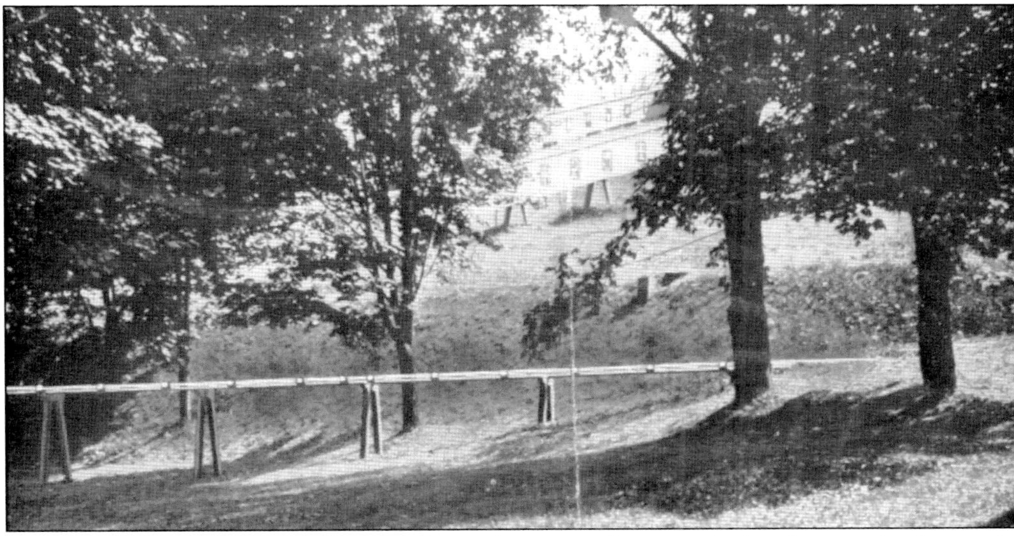

The glass pipeline delivered the water from the spring down to the bottling works, by gravity alone. After bottling, the three conveyors would carry the cases up the mountain to be loaded into railroad cars. A fire in September 1923, thought to have been caused by an electrical storm, destroyed the shipping station and most of the largest elevator.

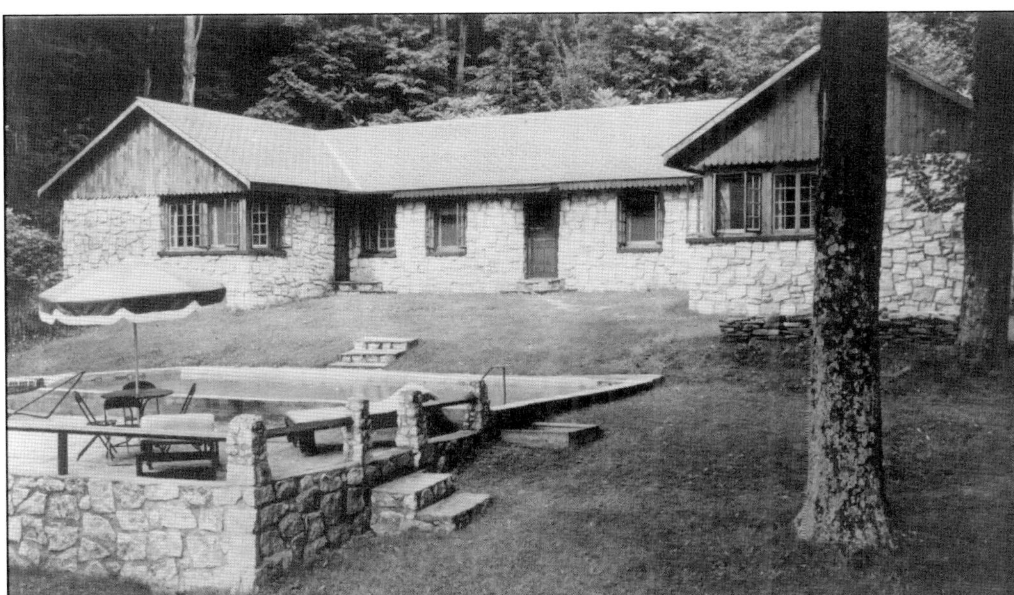

The Little Castle in the Woods, built of fieldstone and Norway spruce, was owned and operated by Herr Max von Stoltzenberg and his wife, Frau Emmy. Situated on a hillside in Oliverea, they served organic food with charming Bavarian-style hospitality.

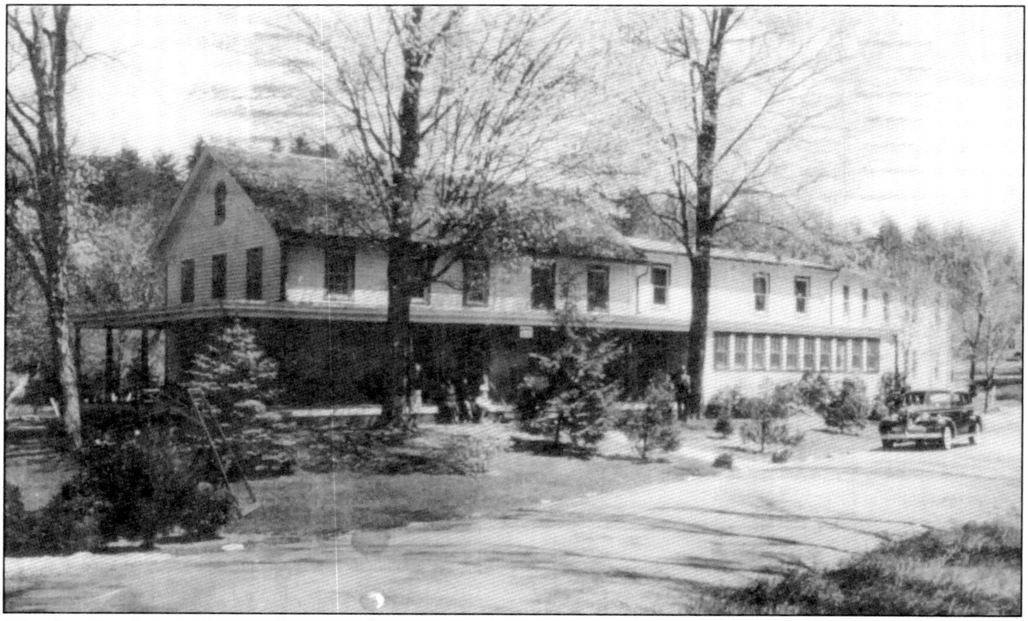

The La Duchesse Anne, formerly known as the Brookside House, was lost to an early morning fire in January of 1996.

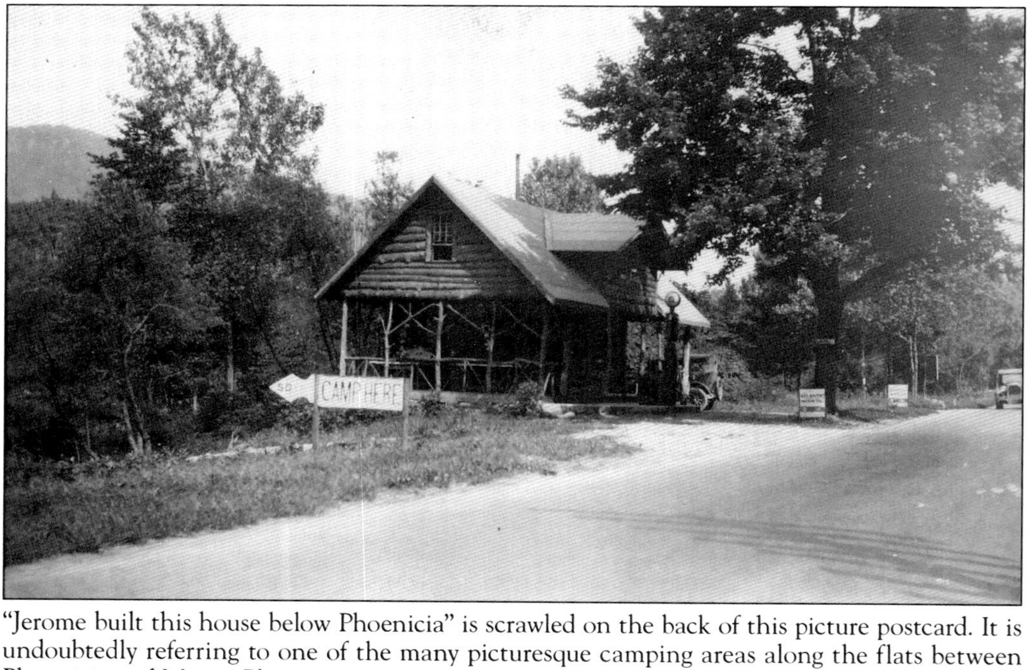

"Jerome built this house below Phoenicia" is scrawled on the back of this picture postcard. It is undoubtedly referring to one of the many picturesque camping areas along the flats between Phoenicia and Mount Pleasant.

Four

Civic and Social Organizations

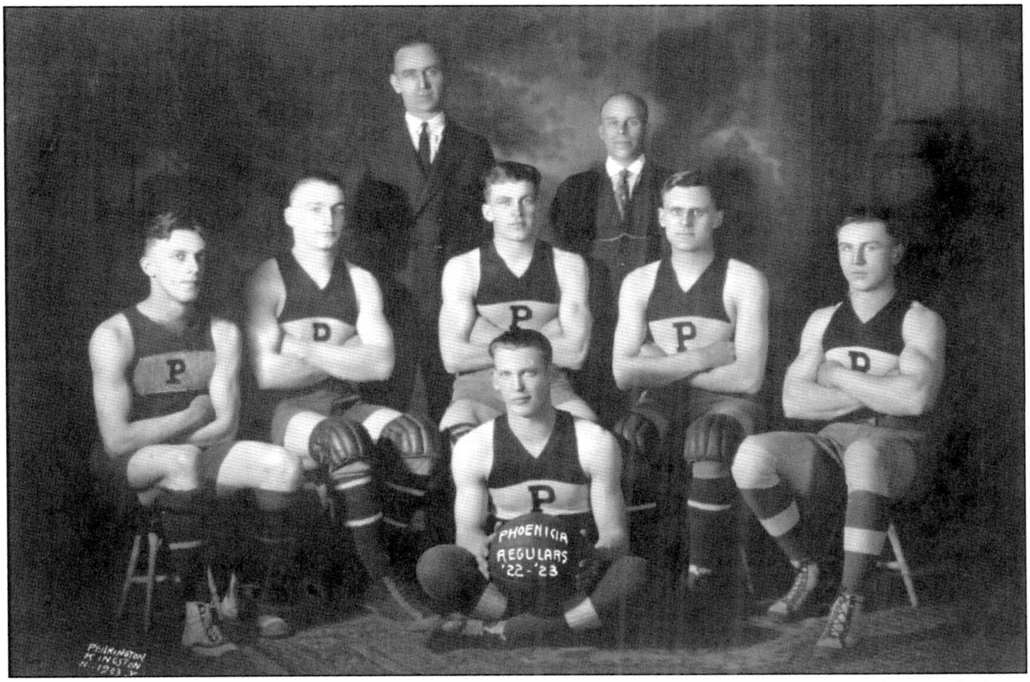

This photograph shows the Phoenicia Regulars: Kenneth Ennist; Levan Merrihew; Herbert Townsend; Carroll Simpson; Conrad Gross; Earl Somerville; William Malloy, manager; and Walter Smith, assistant.

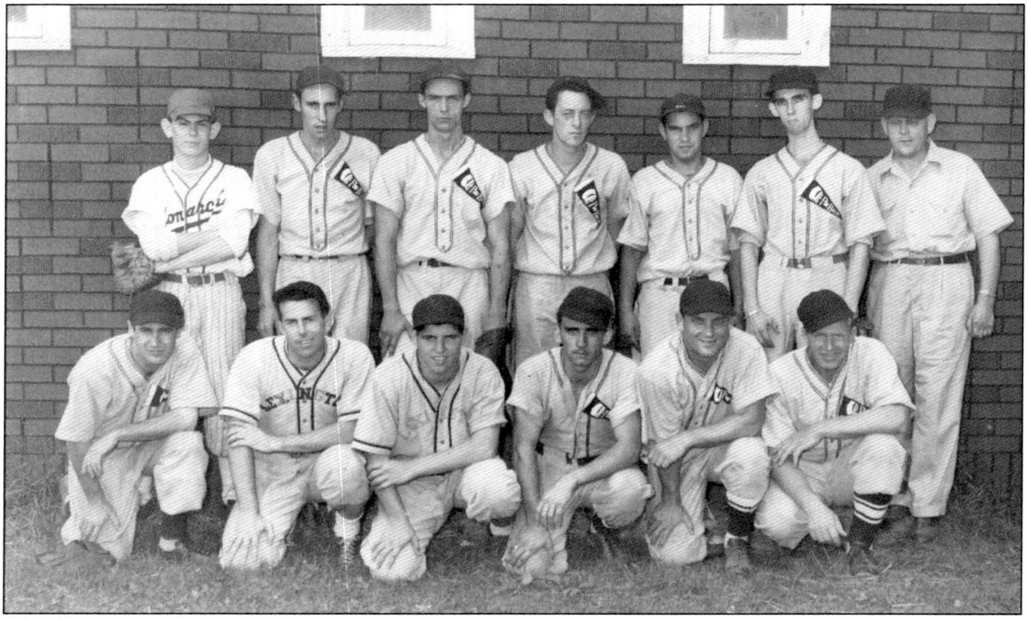

This photograph of the Pine Hill baseball team was taken in August 1951. From left to right are (first row) Fred Bogdan, Jack Wallace, Gilbert Turner, Charles Smith, Hokey Thompson, and Stanley Benjamin; (second row) ? Zimmerman, Douglas Ousterhoudt, Clifford Benjamin, George Seward, Charles Myers, James Smith, and William Knigge.

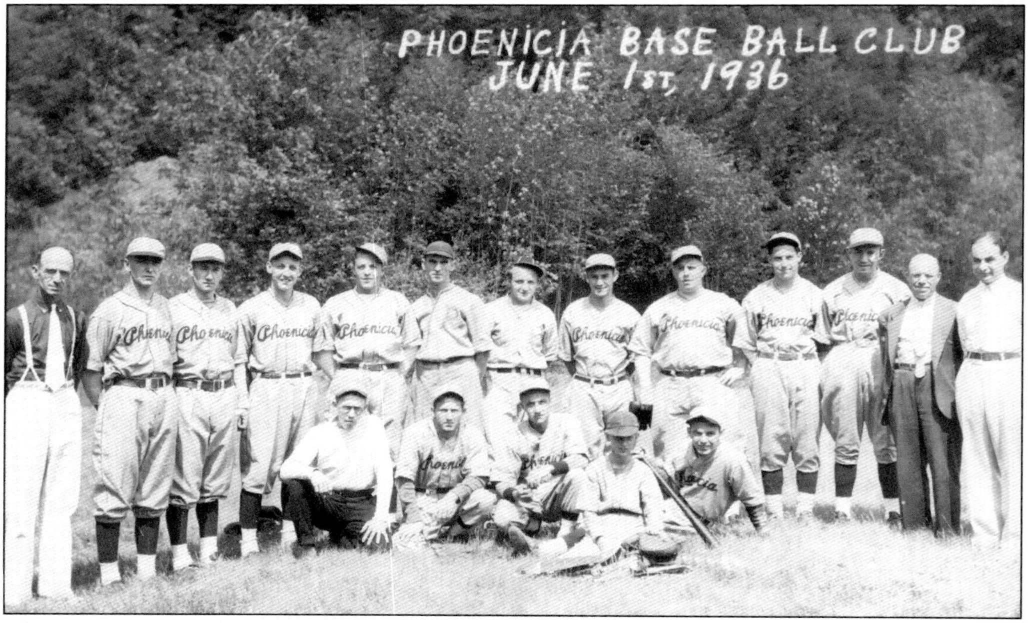

This June 1, 1936, photograph shows the Phoenicia baseball team. The players are, from left to right, as follows: (seated) Dan Ennist, unidentified, Joseph Gordon, unidentified batboy, and Arnold Bell; (standing) William Malloy Sr., William Malloy Jr., ? Egan, Ward Dunham, Barnard Todd, Percy Rosa, Charlie Buck, Earl Benjamin, and Walter Smith. The unidentified players were from Kingston. Each player received $10 per day to play.

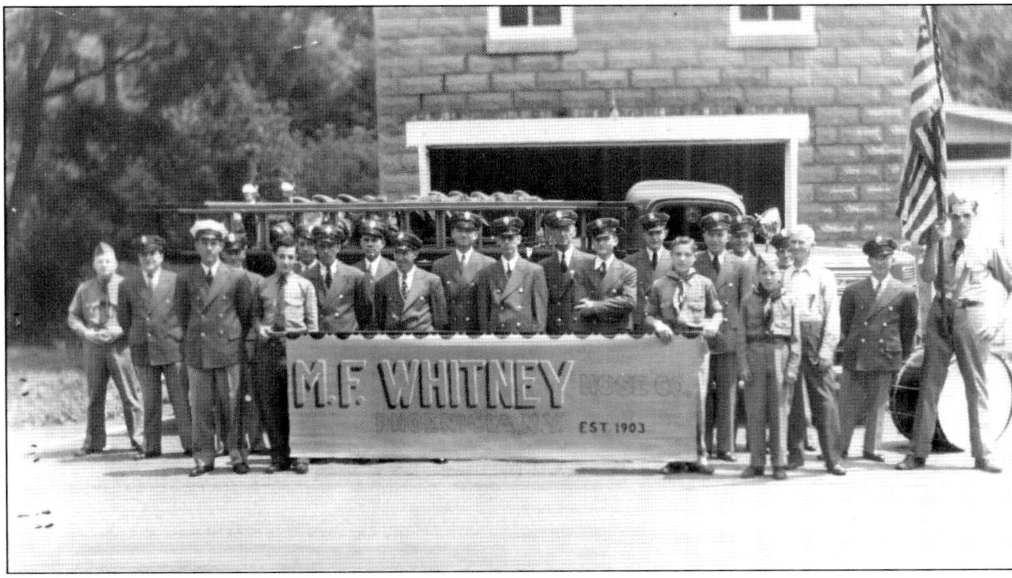

Volunteers from the M. F. Whitney Hose Company were photographed at their original headquarters on Church Street in Phoenicia. They eventually moved into the old schoolhouse on State Route 214, and this building has since been converted to a private residence.

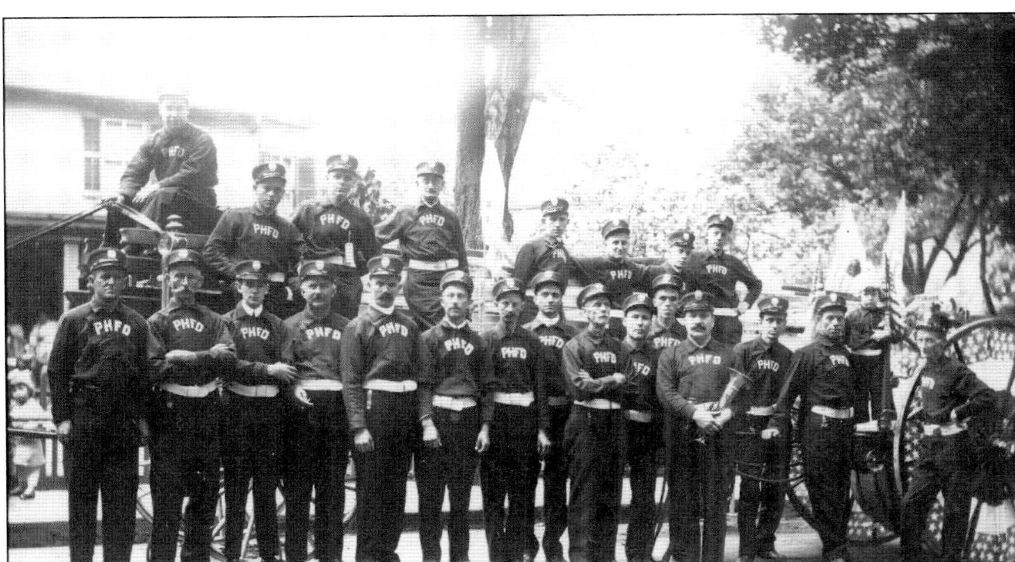

Parades were an important part of rural life and the local fire companies were always in attendance. Here the Pine Hill firemen are dressed for a parade in 1906.

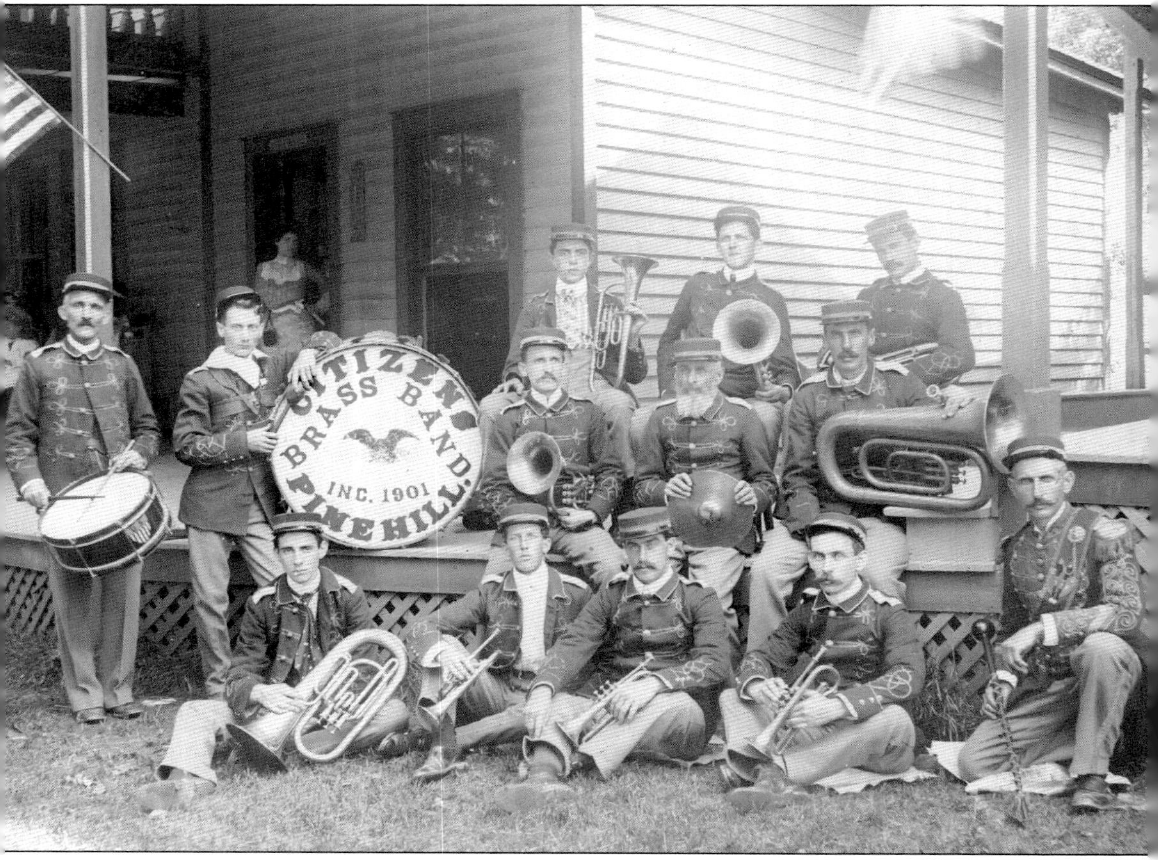

This photograph of Pine Hill Citizens Brass Band was taken in front of the Colonial Inn on Main Street. The band members are as follows: (first row) Charles Smith, Orville Smith, Robert Eignor, Chester Hoffman, and Casper Smith; (second row) Elmer Cure, Willis France, Joe Mason, Lory Peet, and Charles Rose; (third row) unidentified, unidentified, and Grant Morgan. Coronet and brass bands were a very popular form of entertainment at hotels, parades, and social functions.

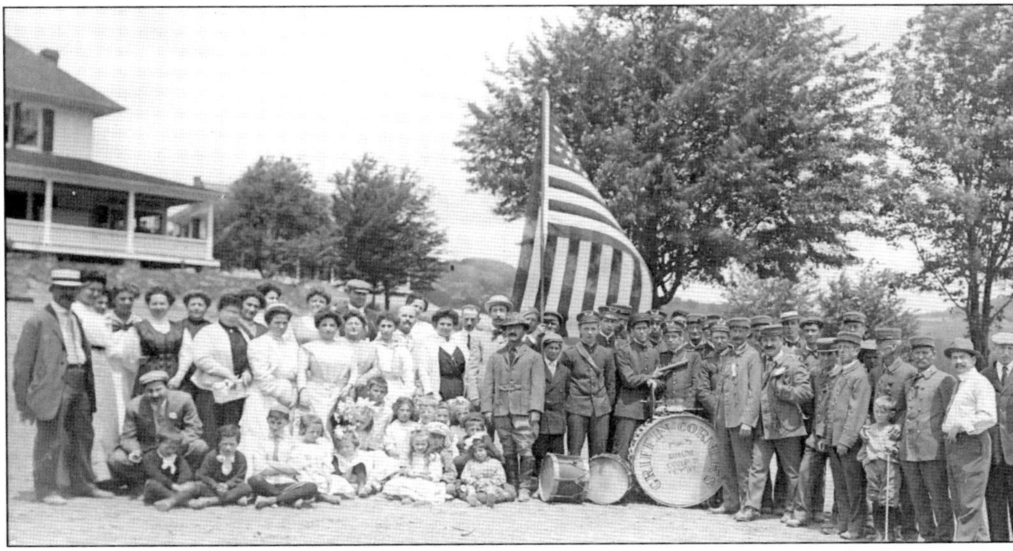

A group of citizens gather for Fourth of July in Chelsea Park, a development nestled between Pine Hill and Highmount. Griffen's Corners was the first town over the county line into Delaware County, renamed Flieschmanns. It was not uncommon for different towns to assemble together for holiday celebrations as such events were important social gatherings of the day. Note that on the back of this photograph is the following: "Grandpa Smith is holding the flag."

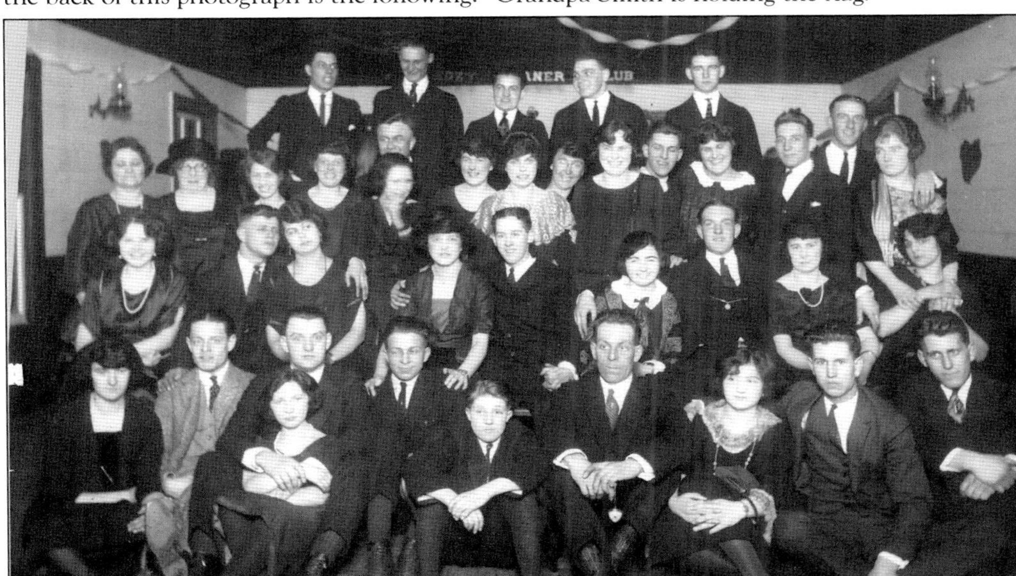

This group photograph shows the Cozy Corner Club. The members are as follows: (first row) Marian Winchell Aley, Emily Smith Gaughan, Russel Merrihew, Ezra Hearn, Jerry George, Veen Townsend, unidentified, and Cecil Satterle; (second row) Katherine Hornbeck, Andrew Satterle, Goldie Peet Murray, Gladys Morgan, Steve O'Conner, Margaret Forbes, Marshall Winchell, Margaret " Babe" Goldman, and unidentified; (third row) Blanche Smith, Mrs. A. D. Hill, Addie Hill, Ruth Cure, Fred Cure, Elsie Smith, Anna Eignor Moran, Maugerite Smith, Ora Townsend, Lil Merrihew, Edith France, ? Johnson, unidentified, Eddie Hitchcock, Earl Gosso, and unidentified; (fourth row) Ernie Hinkley, Tait Persons, Izzy, unidentified, and Charlie Smith.

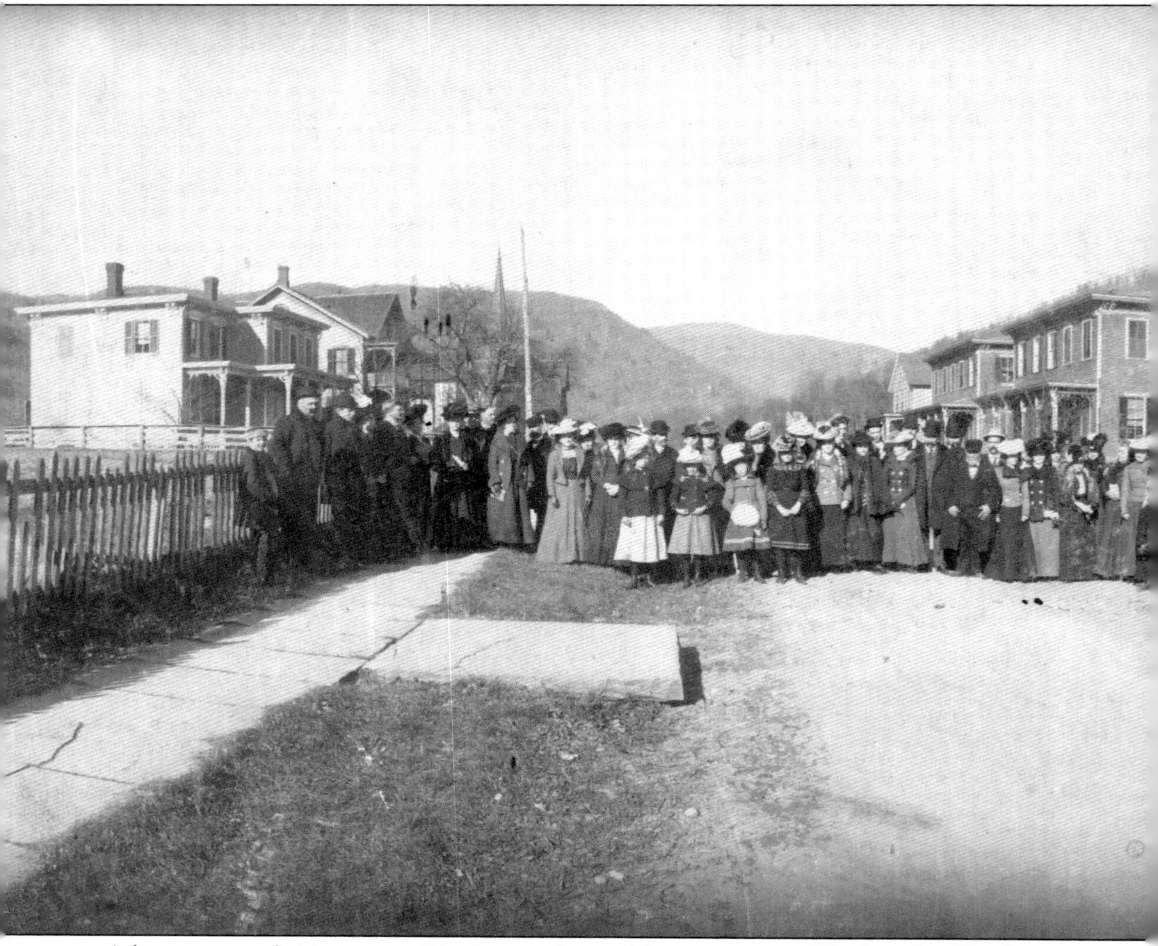

A large group of citizens, possibly the members of the International Order of Odd Fellows, poses on Church Street in Phoenicia. To the far right is the Odd Fellows Hall, which is now home to the Shandaken Theatrical Society. The building was constructed in 1887 for the society's meetings and

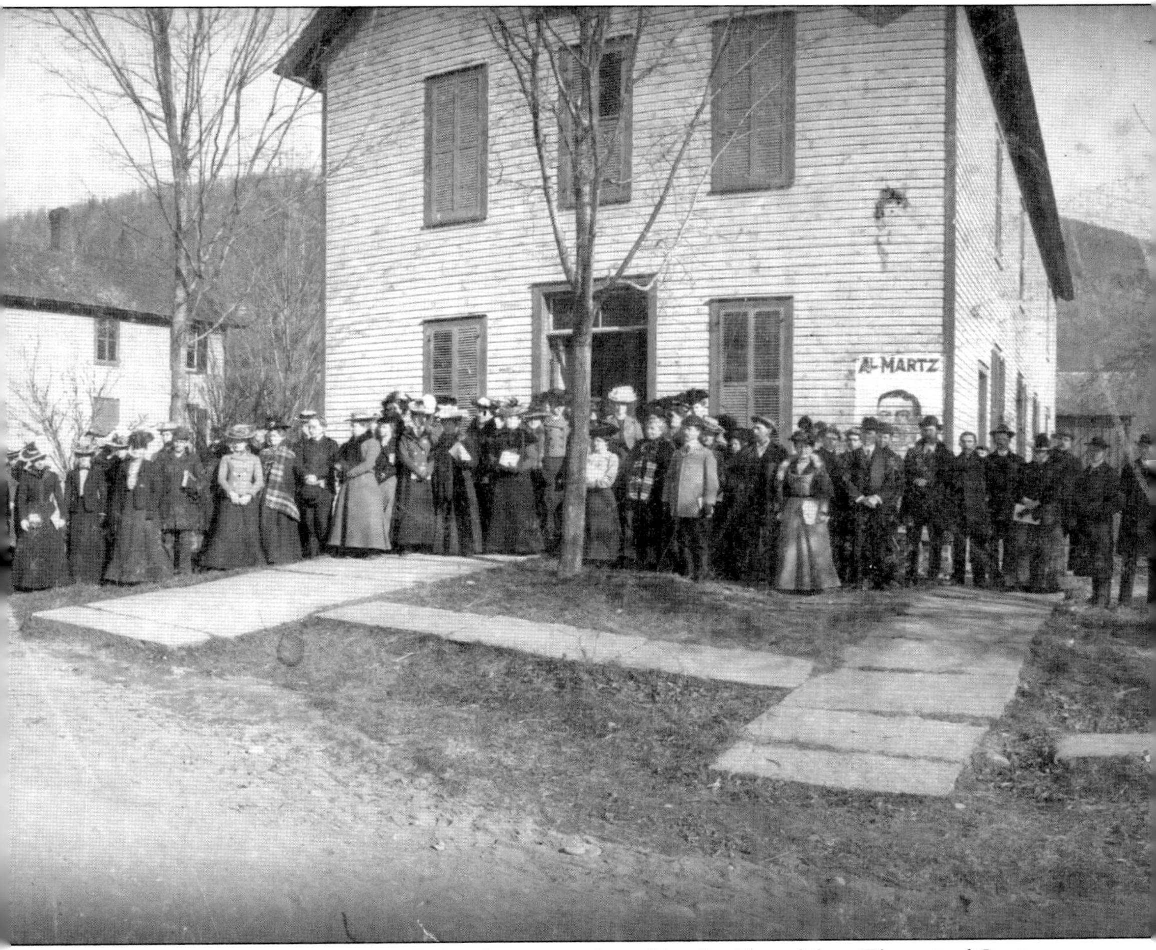

philanthropically driven activities. Before being purchased by the Shandaken Theatrical Society it was also used as an auction house and a movie theatre.

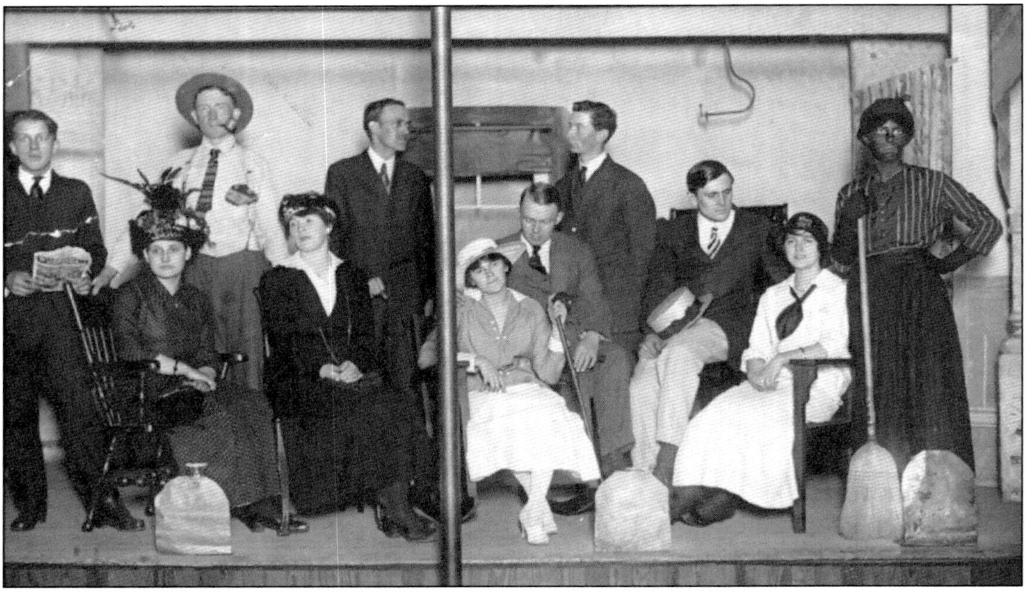

Many productions were performed on the stage of the Odd Fellows Hall in Phoenicia for entertainment as well as fund-raising. The cast of one such production poses for a publicity still. They are, from left to right, as follows: George Loundsberry, Kenneth Ennist, Tommy McGrath, Flavius Dibble, Lou Gosso, Carroll Simpson, Kay Simpson Ennist, Ida Voss Bruckner, Marie Lang, Francis Hill, and Lorna Van Demark.

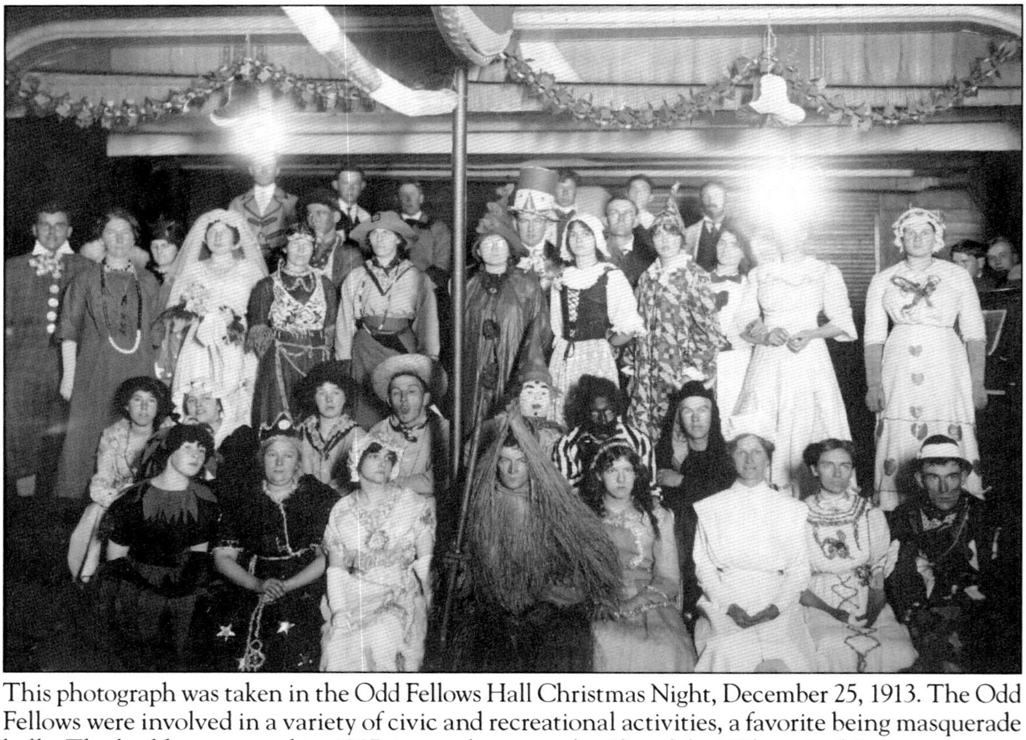

This photograph was taken in the Odd Fellows Hall Christmas Night, December 25, 1913. The Odd Fellows were involved in a variety of civic and recreational activities, a favorite being masquerade balls. The building, erected in 1887, is now home to the Shandaken Theatrical Society.

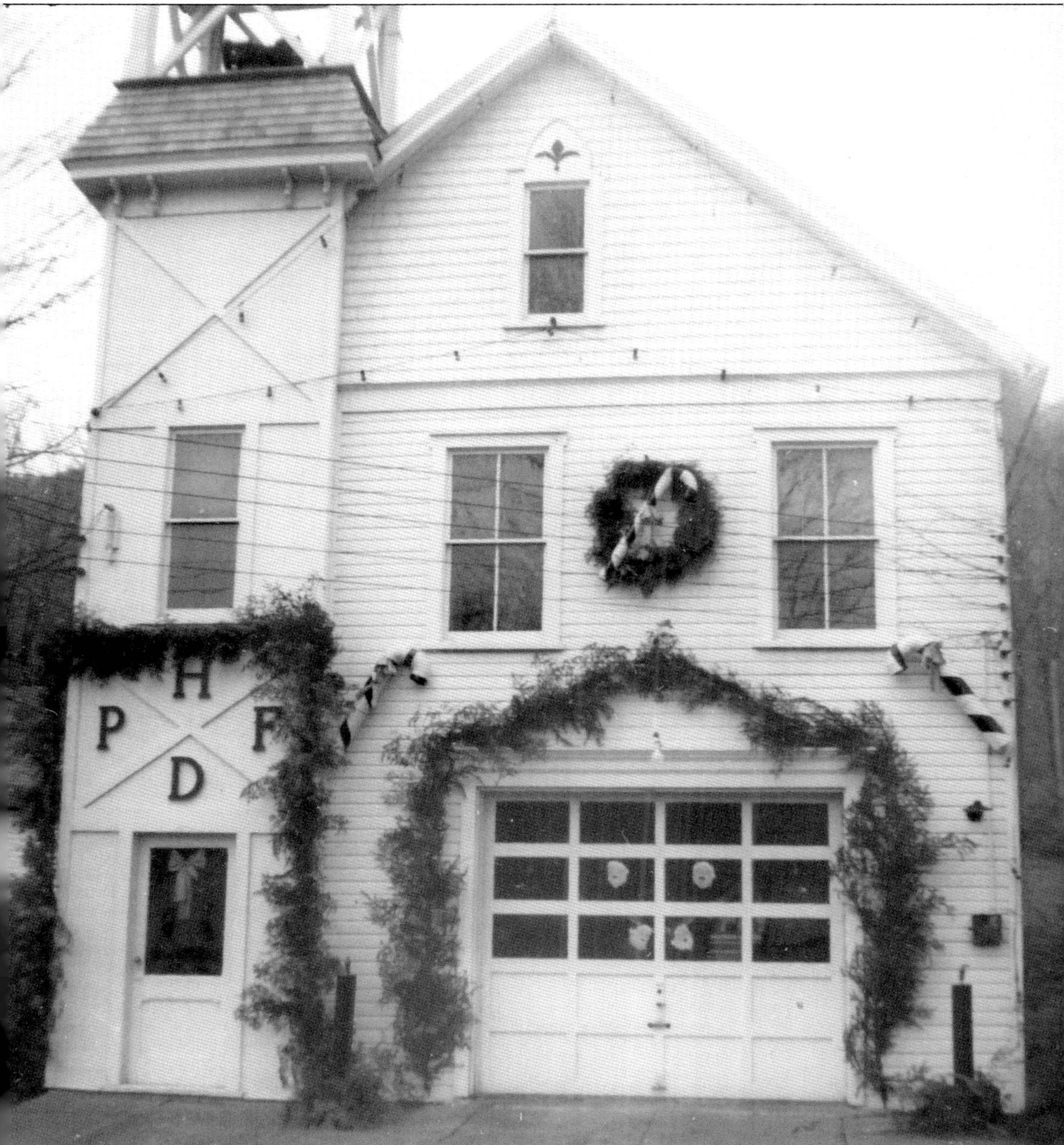

This photograph shows the Pine Hill Firehouse decorated for the holidays in 1954. The department operated out of this building until the 1990s when they moved to larger quarters just east of these on Main Street in Pine Hill. The building still retains its outer identity, despite being converted to a private residence.

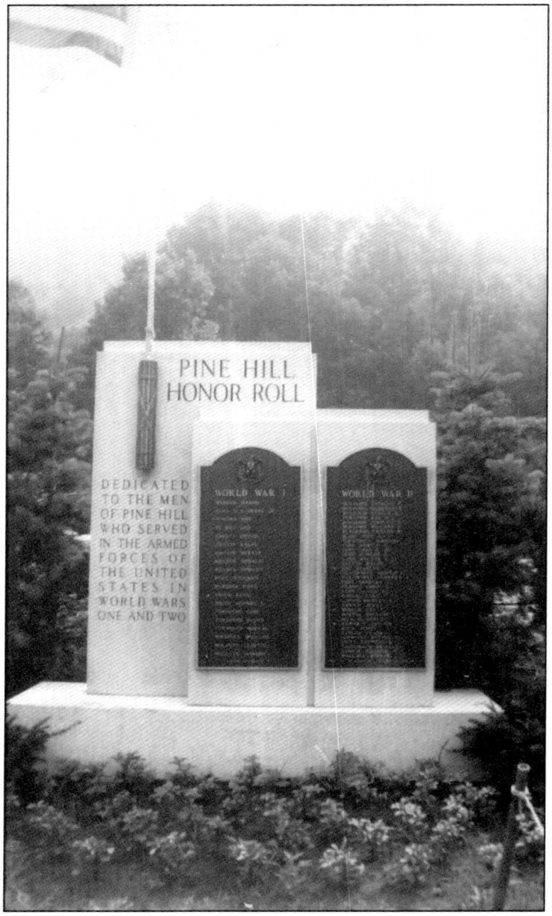

The Pine Hill Honor Roll pays tribute to those who served the country in war. The monument was designed so that additional stones could be added as required.

A parade on Phoenicia's Main Street, whether for Memorial Day, Fourth of July, or Veterans Day, always drew a crowd. Here in the 1950s, the Main Street shops are the Conway Pyrofax Gas Service, Holzers Market and the Central Hotel.

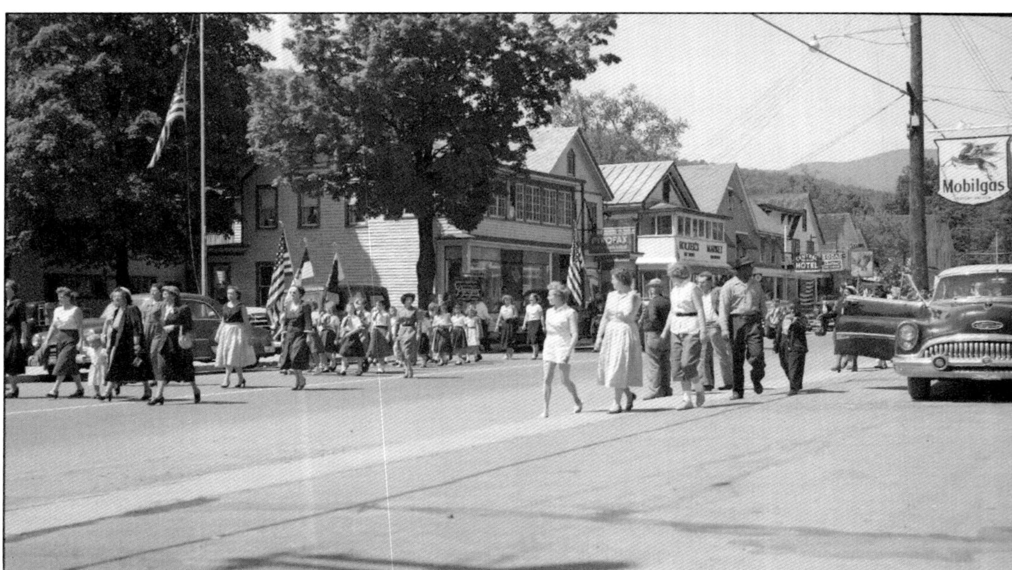

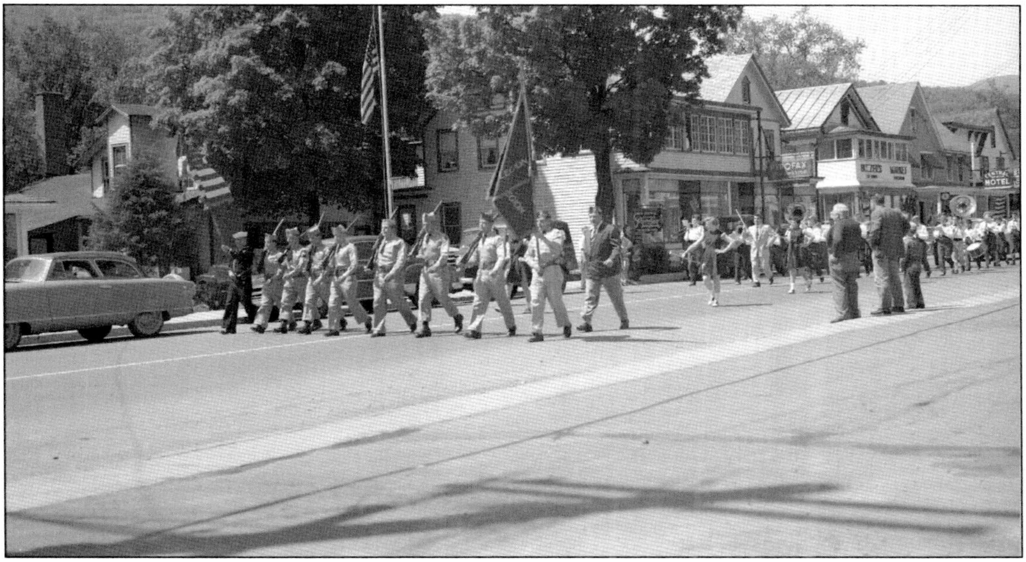

The American Legion parades down Main Street in Phoenicia followed by the high school band.

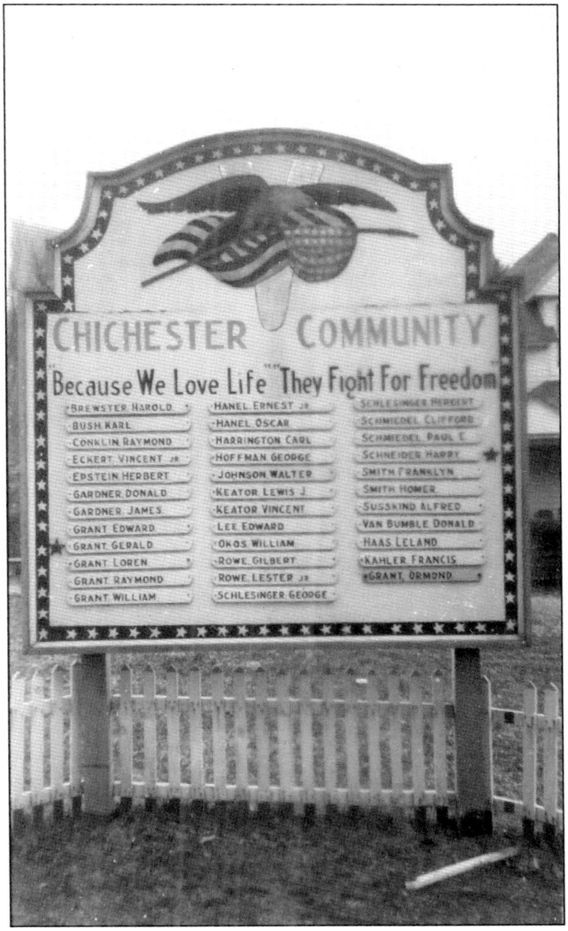

The Chichester Honor Roll for War Veterans bore the names of many longtime local families including Grant, Rowe, Hoffman, Gardner, and Smith.

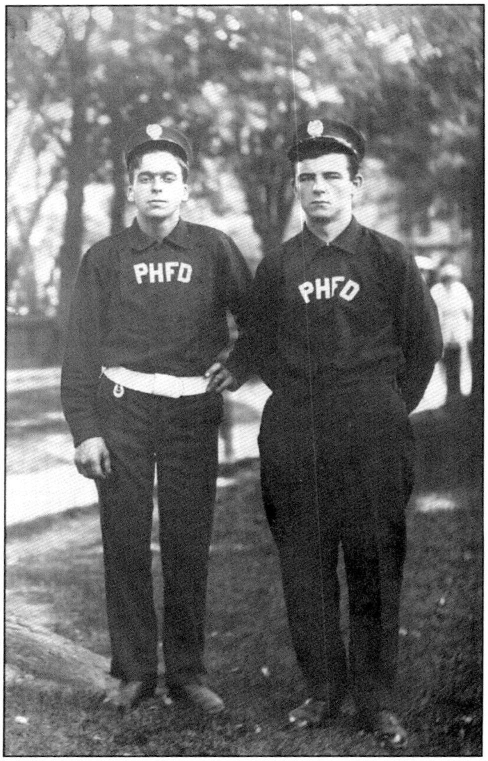

This is a portrait of Pine Hill fireman George Barrett and Henry Judson.

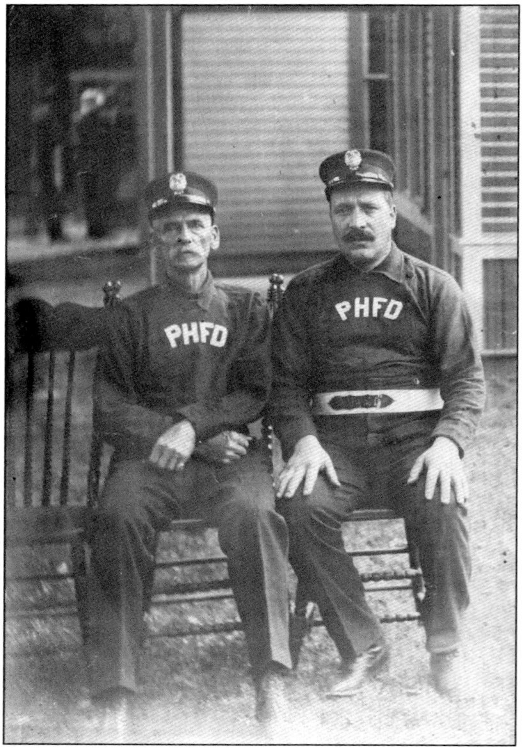

In this portrait, Pine Hill fireman Joseph Harrington is on the left.

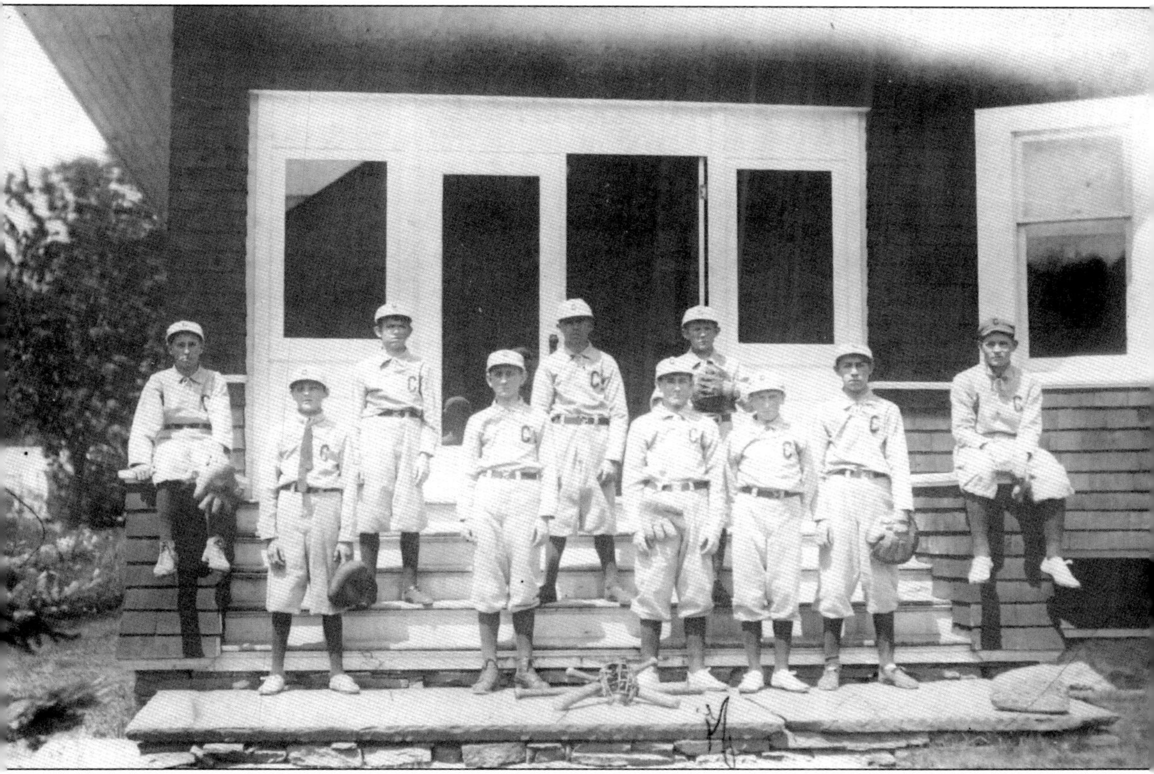

Baseball was a very popular sport, and every town had a team and favorite players. Cooperstown was to the north a few hours and Babe Ruth was known to stay at the Phoenicia Hotel. This photograph of the Chichester Baseball Club was taken in 1910. From left to right are as follows: Reginald Bennett, Arthur Kahler, Ralph Grant, Alfred Lane, Arthur Hill, Claude Hill, Everett Grant, Earl Bennett, Albert Schmiede, and Willie Casey.

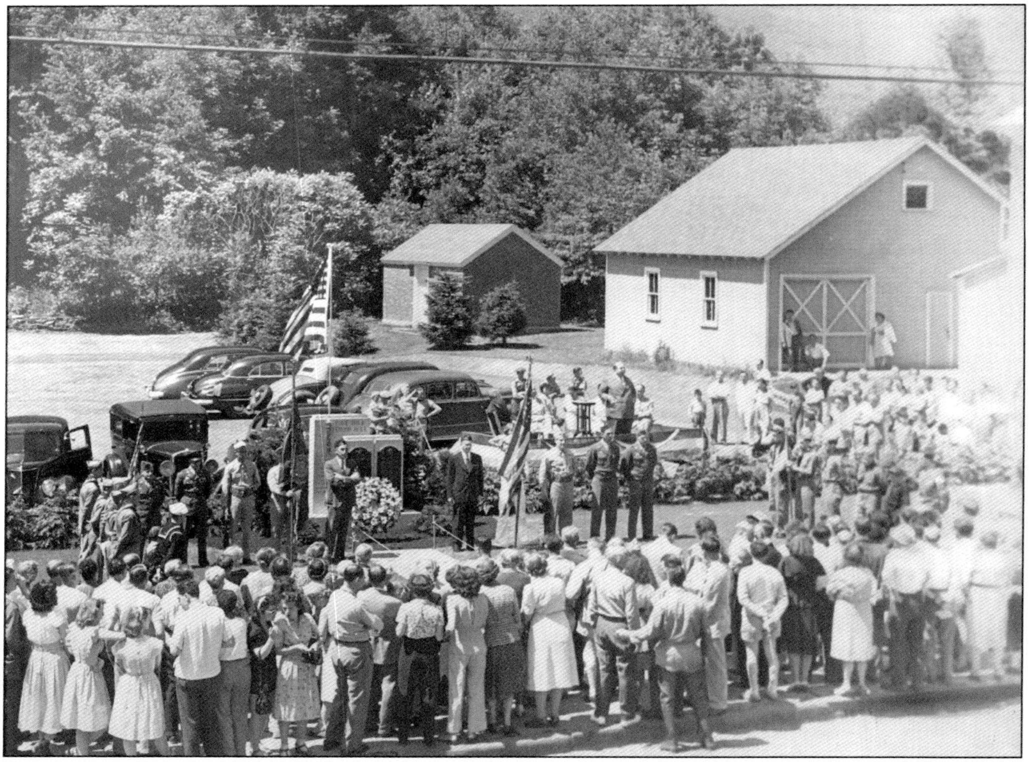

This photograph shows the unveiling of Pine Hill Honor Roll on July 4, 1947, by the Phoenicia Post Number 950 of the American Legion. Doctor Frederick Voss was the commander.

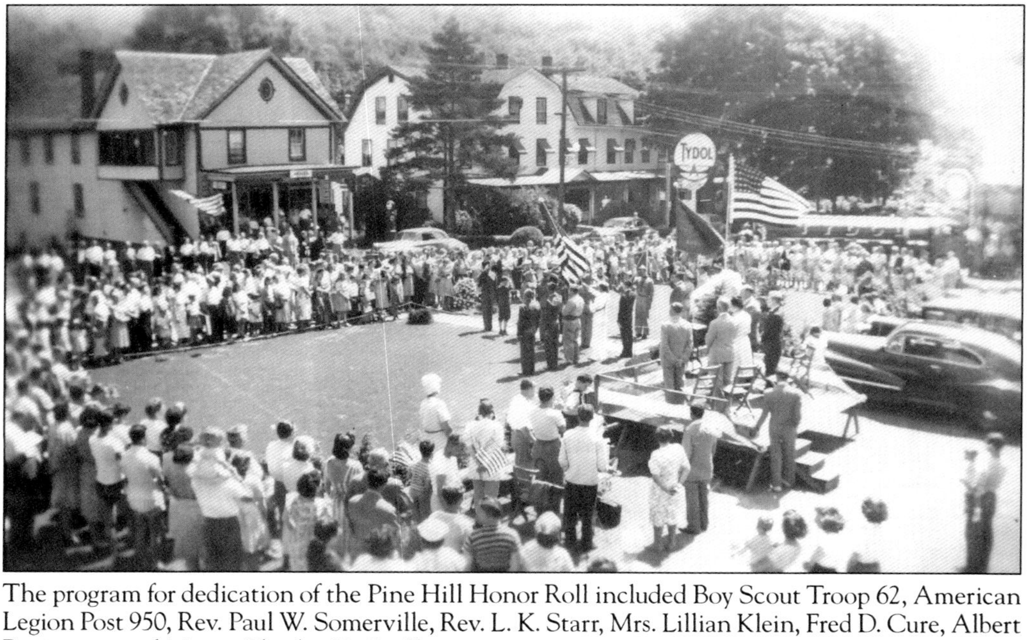

The program for dedication of the Pine Hill Honor Roll included Boy Scout Troop 62, American Legion Post 950, Rev. Paul W. Somerville, Rev. L. K. Starr, Mrs. Lillian Klein, Fred D. Cure, Albert Benjamin, and Mayor Charles H. Griffin.

Five

Notable Residents and Regular Folks

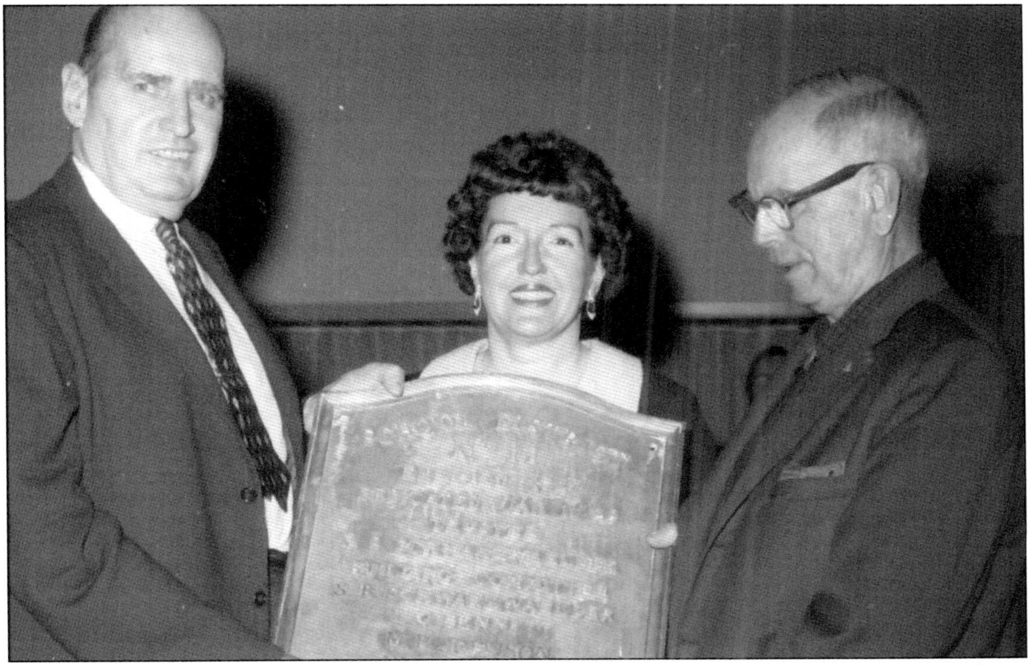

Marion Umhey was the only female supervisor to be elected to the post in Shandaken as of this publication. She was also the first female to be elected to the Legislature of Ulster County, New York. She also owned a local newspaper, the *Ulster County Townsman*, for many years. She is shown here with former supervisor Raymond Dunn and town historian Edward West presenting a plaque to commemorate the District 11 Schoolhouse.

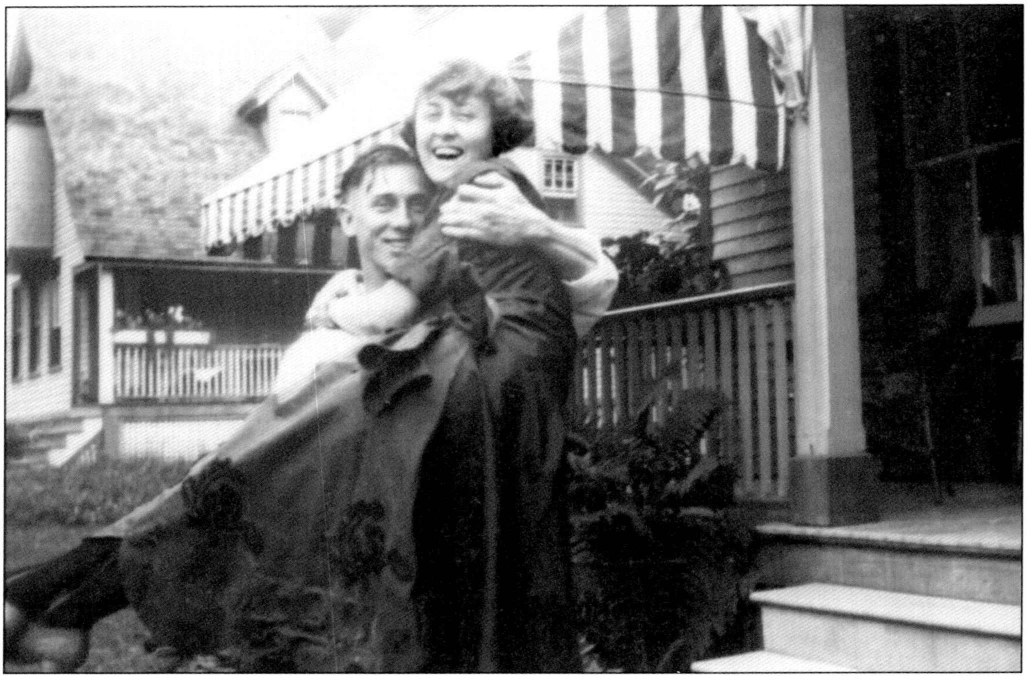

Reginald and Bess Bennett share a happy moment during a visit when "Bess came home from Kingston for the weekend." Their brother, Stanley, is credited with being the photographer.

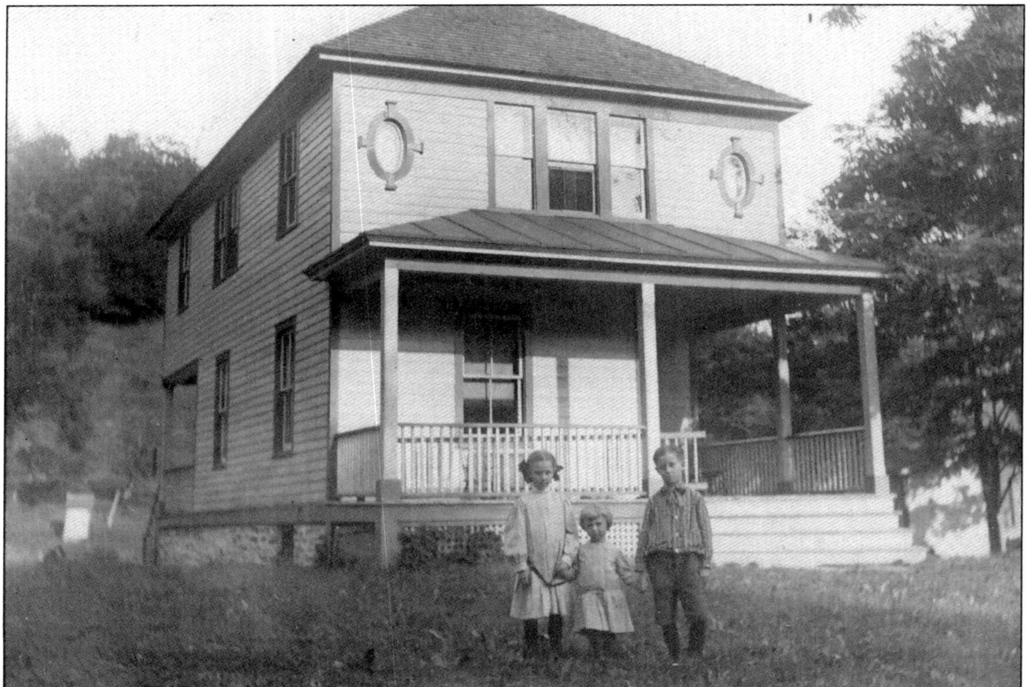

Pictured in front of Crow Hill, the Bennett home in Chichester, are Reginald, Bess, and Stanley Bennett.

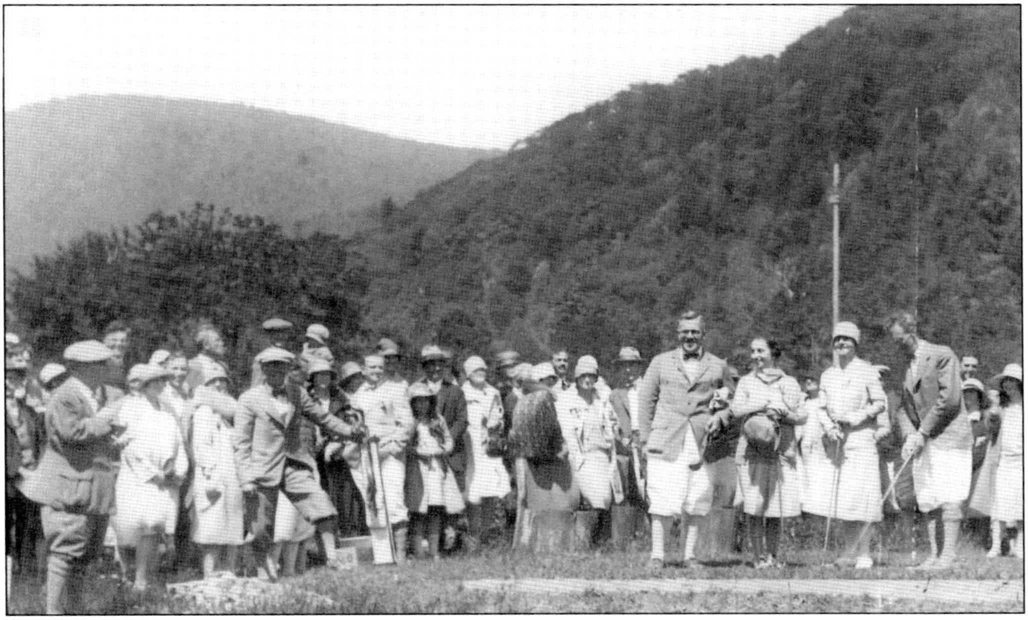

This photograph was taken opening day at the Rip Van Winkle Country Club in Pine Hill in 1926. Third from right in the front row is famous opera singer Amelita Galli Curci, who had a home in Highmount. In the back row, the youngest person at the gathering is Margaret "Peggy" Ousterhoudt, held by her father, Frank Ousterhoudt. Just below them, fourth from left in the first row, are Anton Otto Fischer, Mary Sigsbie Fischer, and Katrina Fischer.

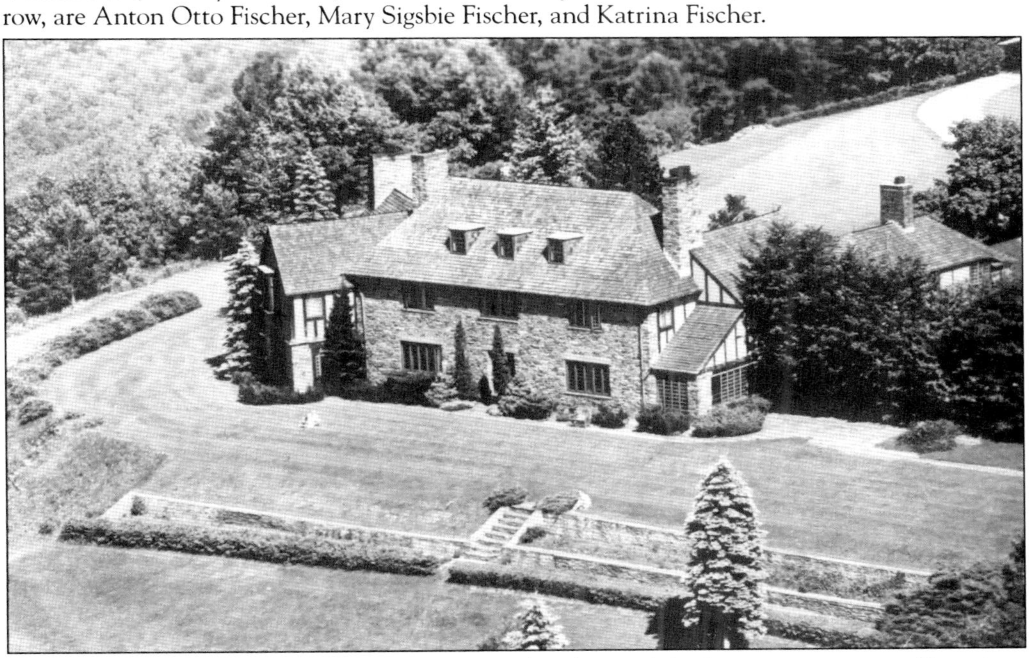

Amelita Galli-Curci was a gifted soprano, considered one of the best opera singers of her time. In 1922, she built this impressive estate called Sul Monte in Highmount, where she summered for many years until she sold the estate in 1937. She sung from the balcony, to the delight of her neighbors.

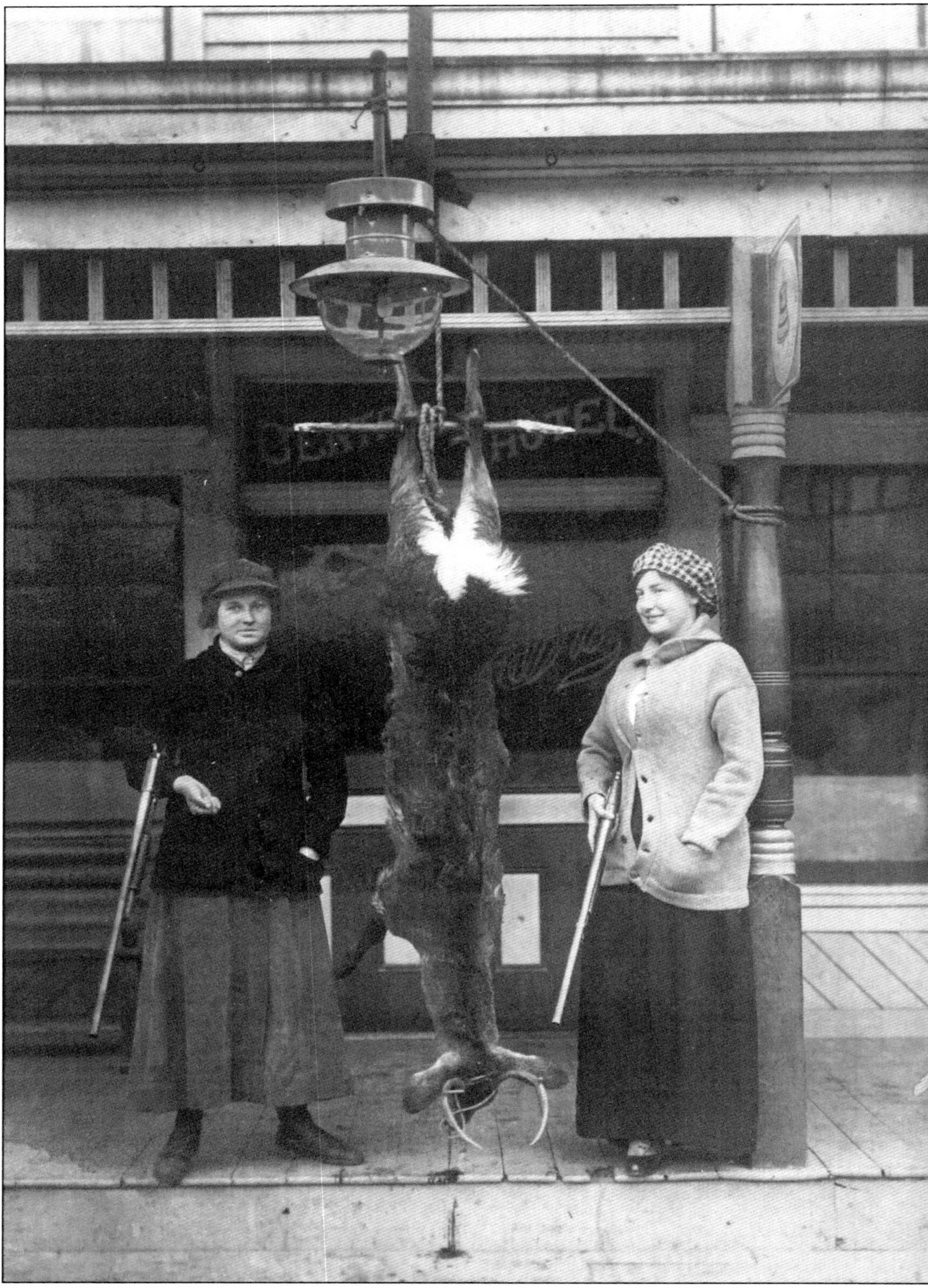

Violet Ford and Marian Kline, niece of Pop Whispell, pose with their trophy in front of the Central Hotel in Phoenicia. The building is still in use today as Ricciadella's Restaurant.

Mason and Donald Gossoo of Pine Hill catch a bobcat in a steel trap in January 1937. The lads first thought they had caught the neighbor's pet cat, but when they went to release it the bobcat turned on them in defense. The frightened boys ran to the home of their uncle, who returned to the catch with them, bringing along a shotgun.

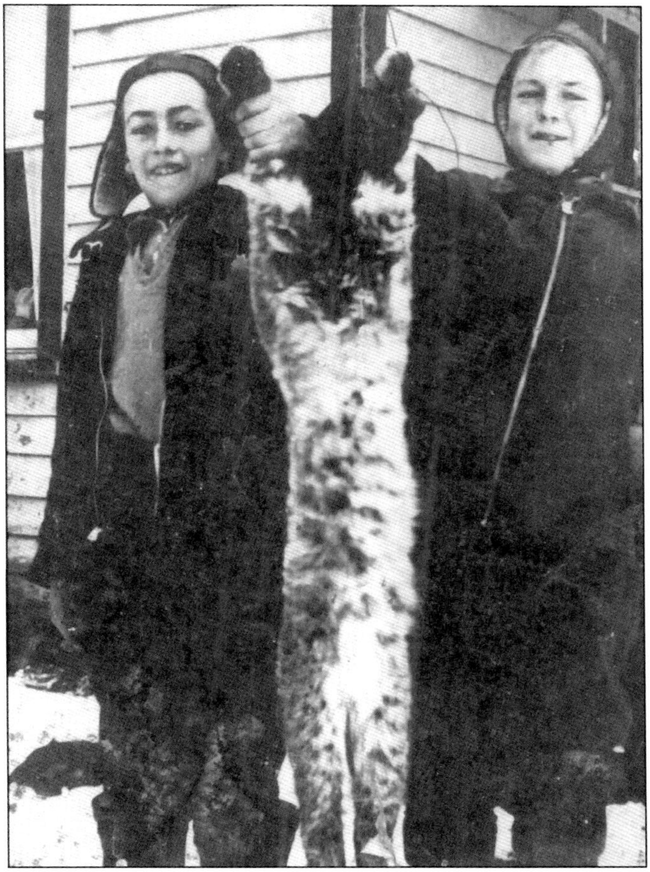

This is a photograph of successful bear hunters in Shandaken, dated December 7, 1911. Hunting was not only a source of food in the area but was also a lure for tourist and pest control.

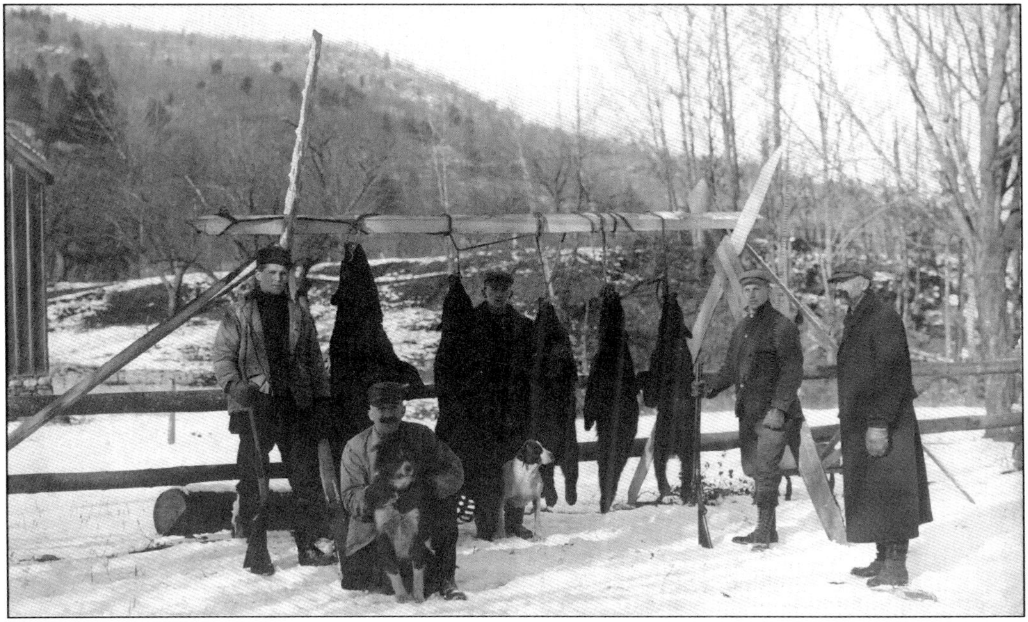

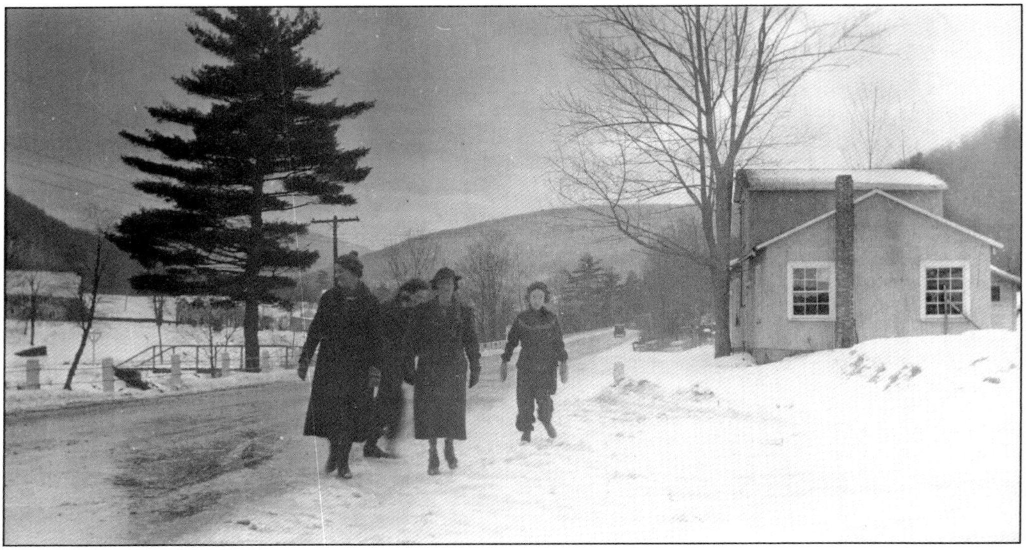

Walking on a snow-covered State Route 28 are Grace Ousterhoudt, Peggy Ousterhoudt, Edna Hummell, and Margaret Hummell.

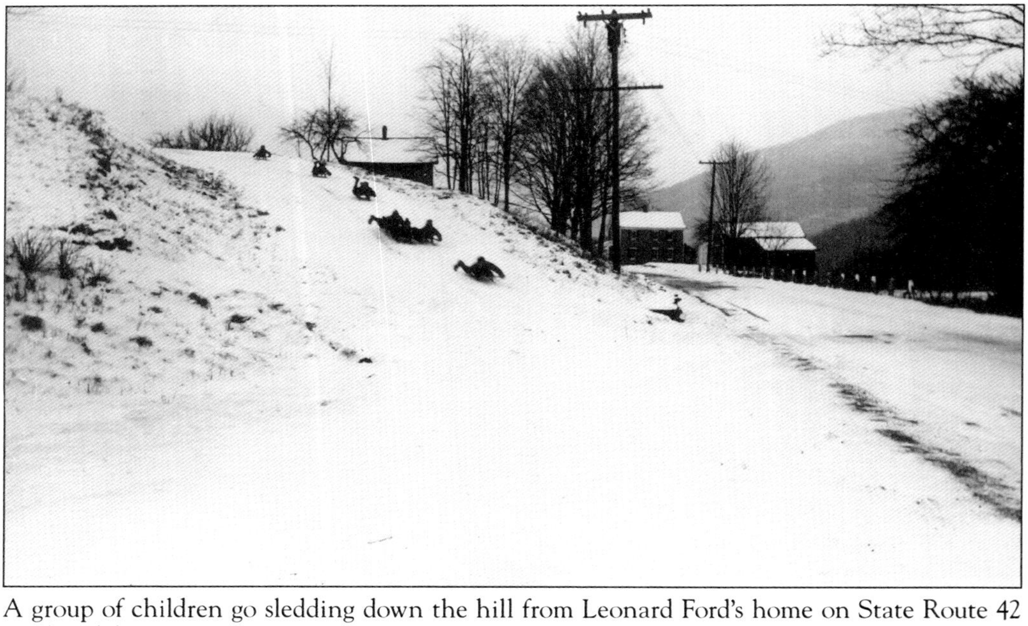

A group of children go sledding down the hill from Leonard Ford's home on State Route 42 in Shandaken.

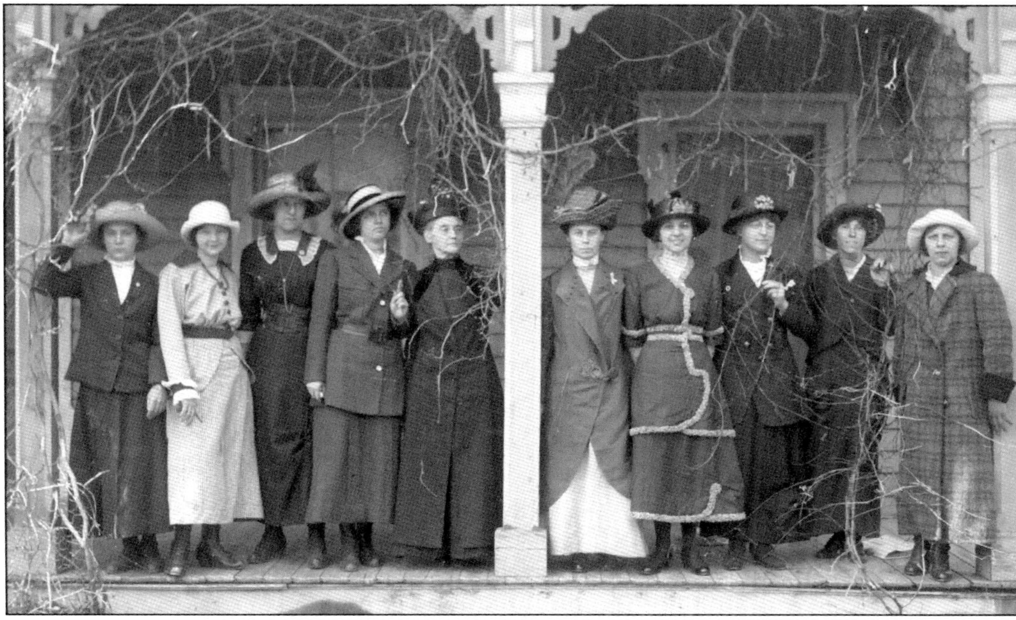

These ladies on an outing with Mrs. Boice, who was in no doubt their chaperone (as was required in the day), are, from left to right, Betty Gosso, Mary Molyneaux, Edna ? Cole, Francis Hill, Mrs. Boice, Nellie Bennett, Helen Gulnick, Blanche Hallenbeck Smith, Elsie Rider Schultz, and Myrtle Ennist Gailes.

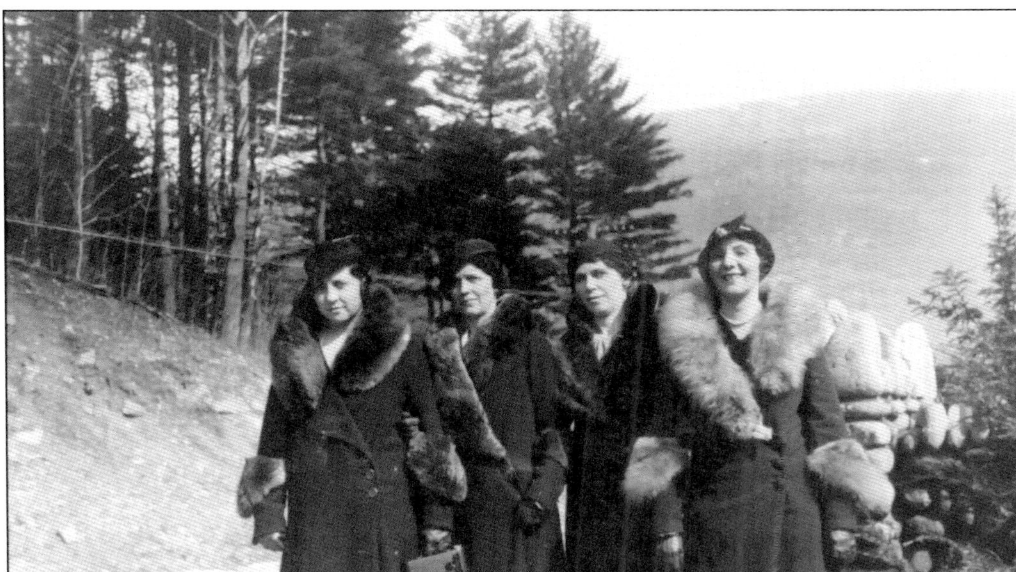

Francis Hill and her friends Mary Van Steenberg, Francis Hill, Lorna Van DeMark, and Helen Gulneck are dressed for an excursion in their finest coats.

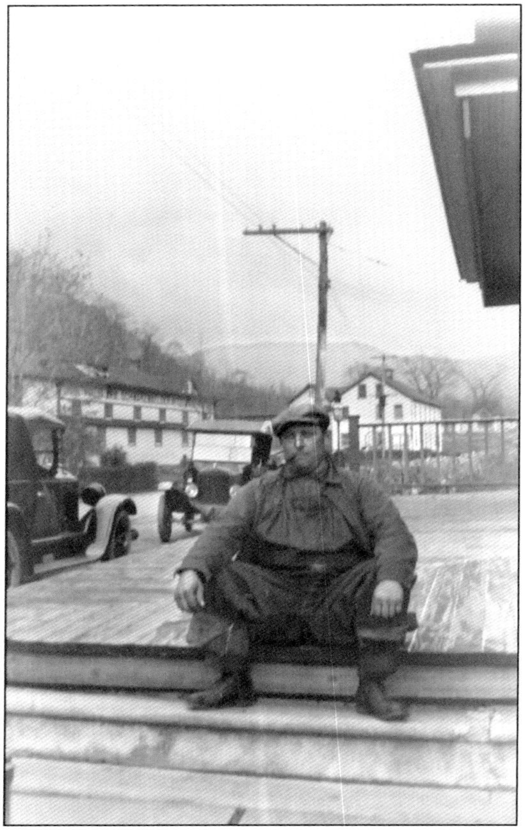

This photograph shows Herman Hill seated on the porch of the Chichester Store. He was a well-known bootlegger who, incensed he did not inherit the farm of a relative, burned the barn with the help of his employee. They were both sentenced to jail time. When he was not involved in nefarious deeds, he also played on the Chichester baseball team.

Cornish Harrington poses for a picture with his dog.

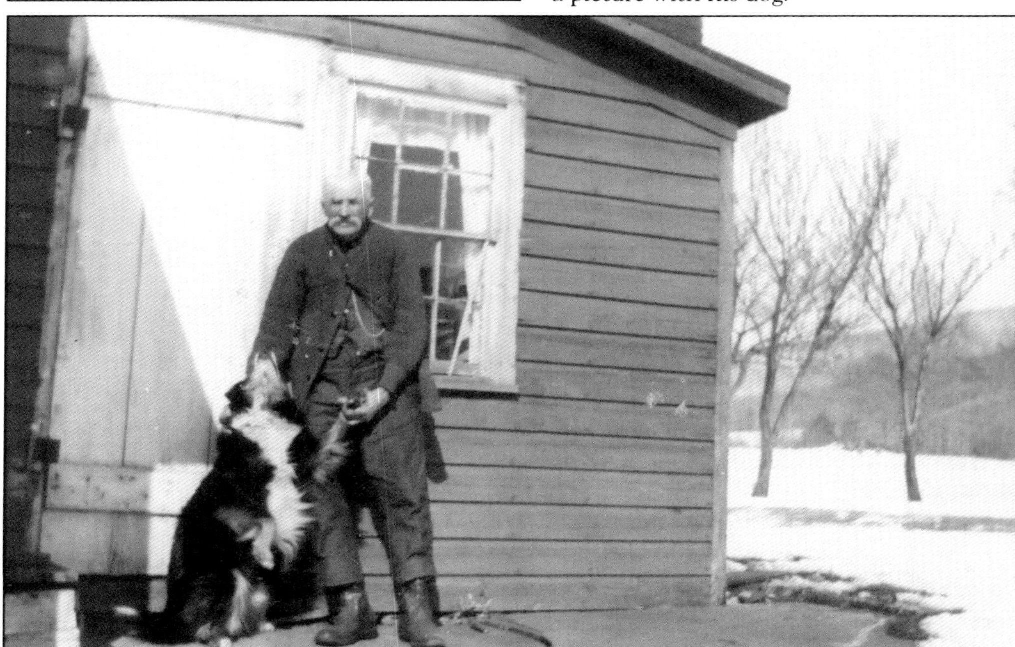

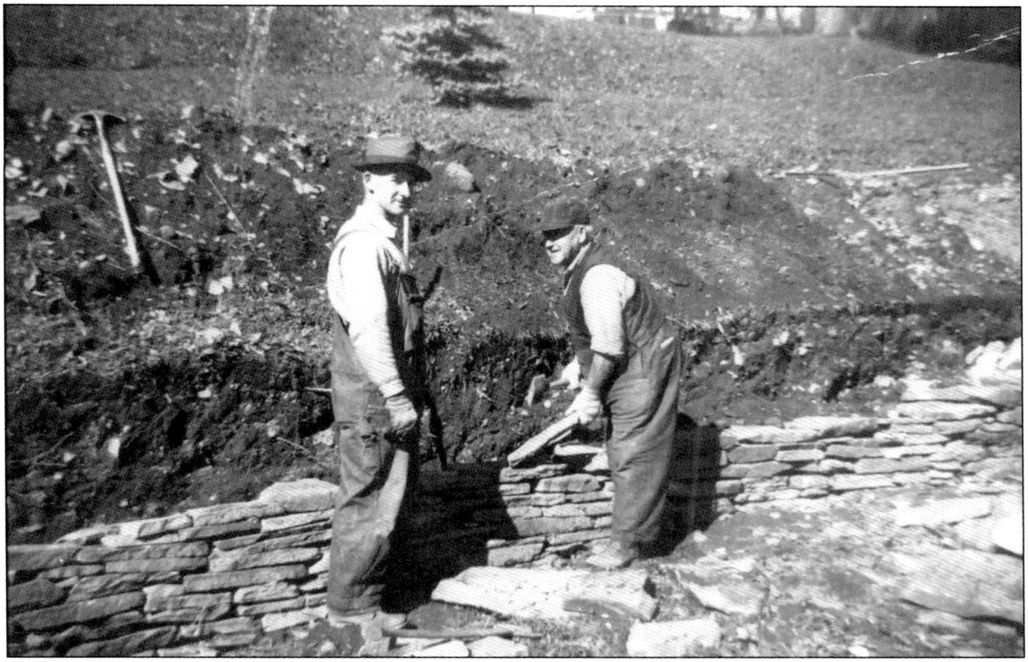

James Smith and Leo Dubois pause while carrying out a common Catskill activity, rock wall building.

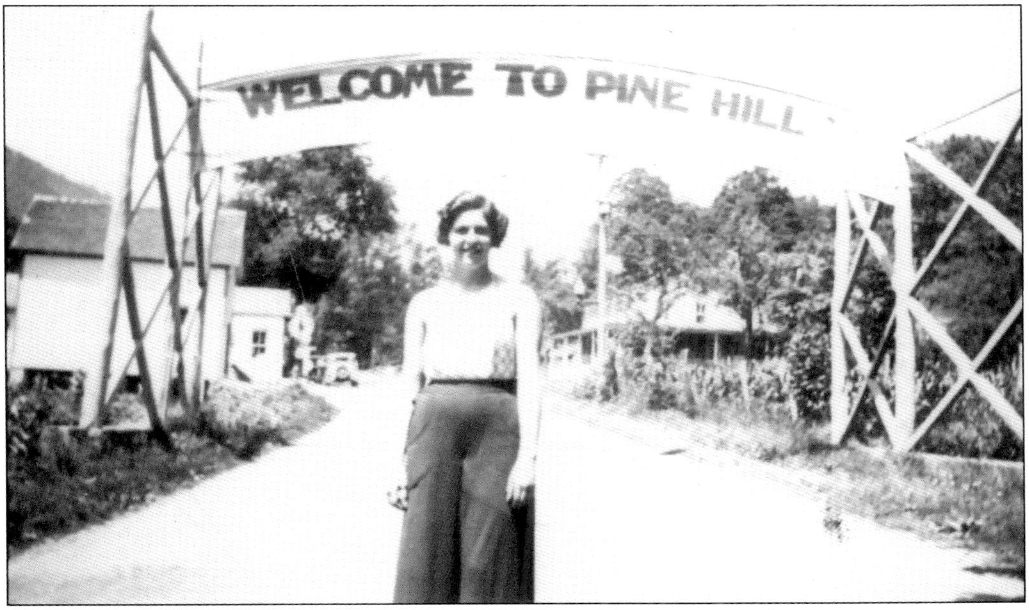

Polly, a summer visitor, poses in front of the welcoming sign in Pine Hill.

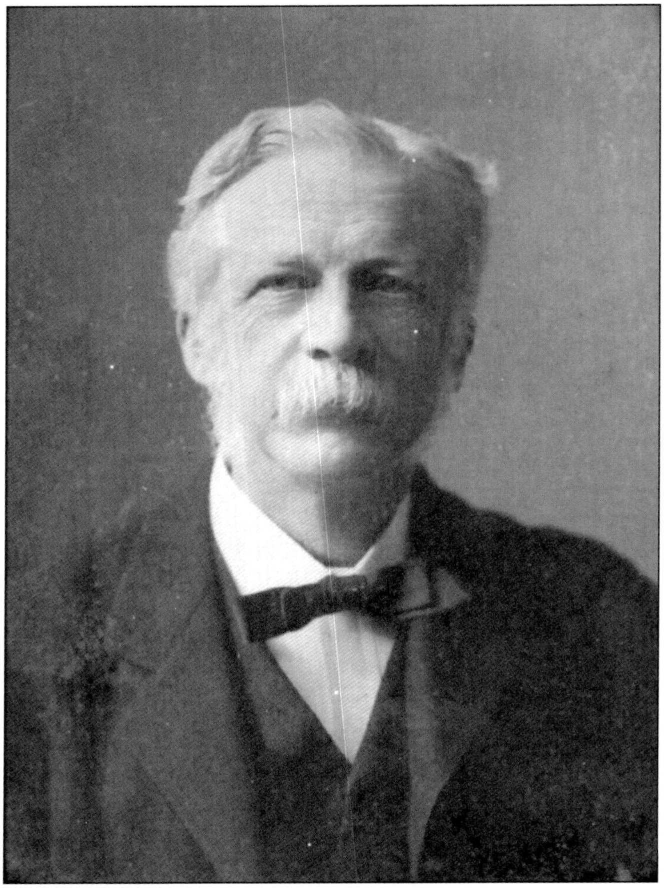

This is a photograph of Dr. Henry Samuel Morton Sr.

The Morton Memorial Library on Elm Street in Pine Hill is one of several libraries built by the Morton family and dedicated to loved ones. This building, to be dedicated to Clara Morton, was in its planning stages when Henry S. Morton died in 1902. It was completed by his sons Henry S. Morton Jr. and Quincy L. Morton in memory of both parents. The library was chartered on April 26, 1906.

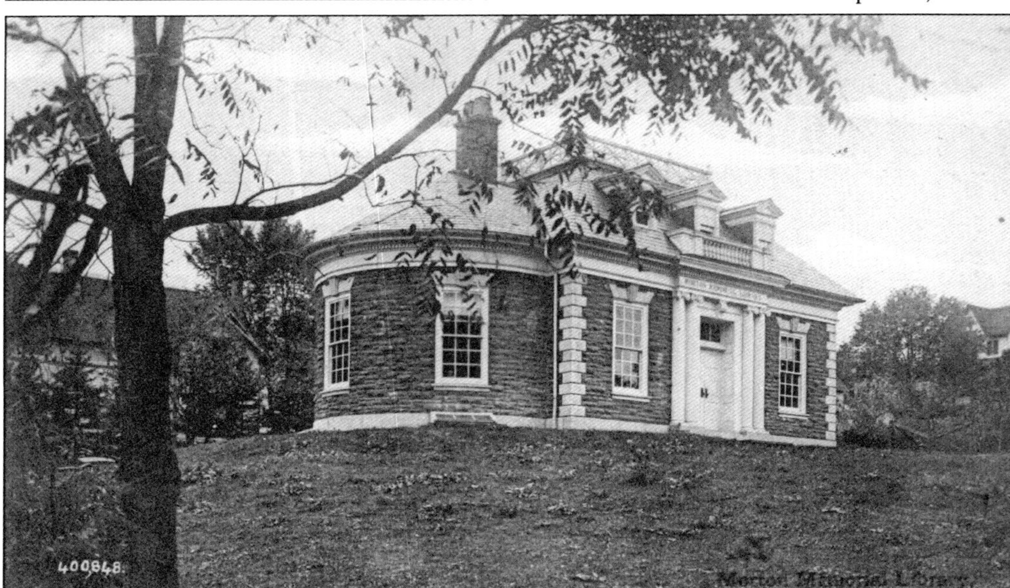

This is a photograph of Clara Dodge Morton.

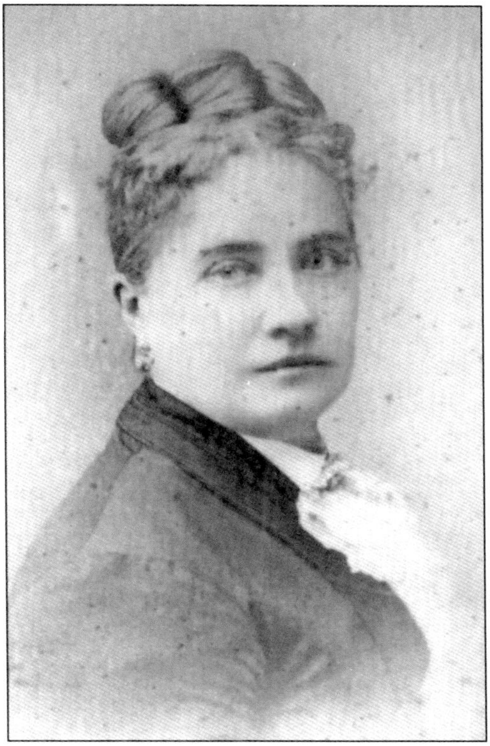

The children of Sarah and Henry S. Morton Jr., Henry, Clara, and Bronson are seen here posing on the porch of Upenuff, the summer residence of the Morton family on Birchcreek Road in Pine Hill.

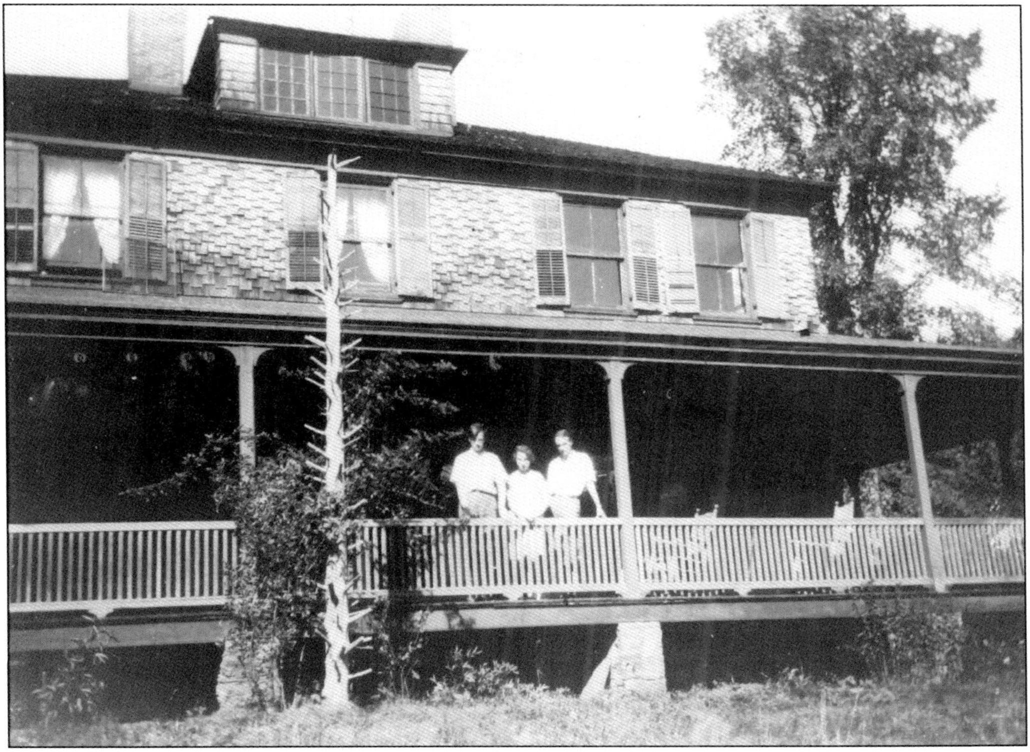

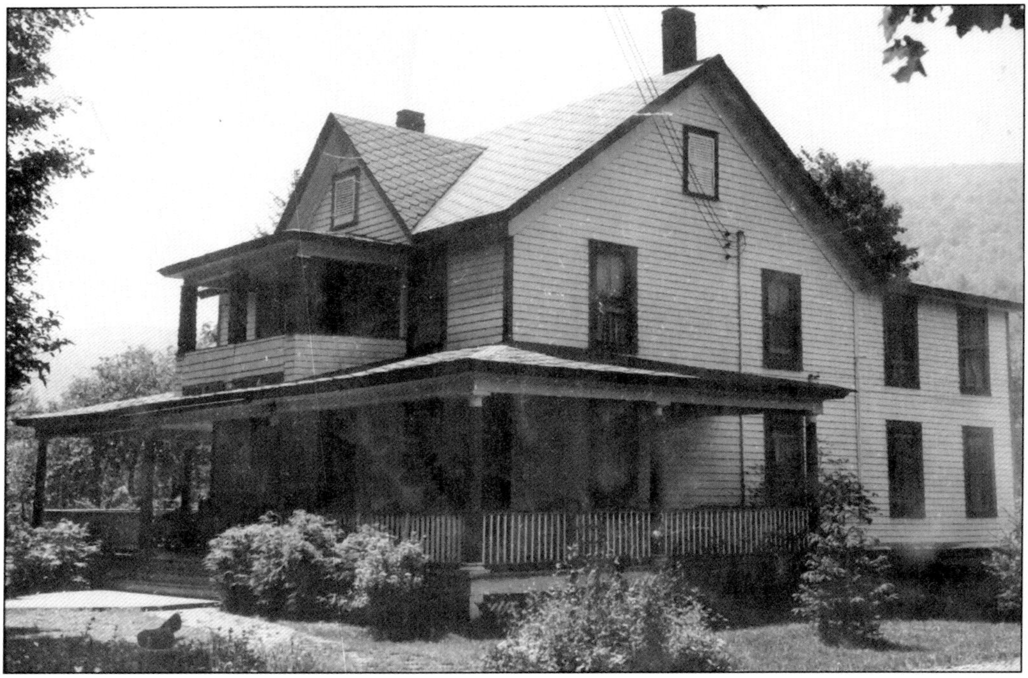

The farm of the Piccolo Midgets was purchased by Raymond Smith and developed into a cabin complex for tourists.

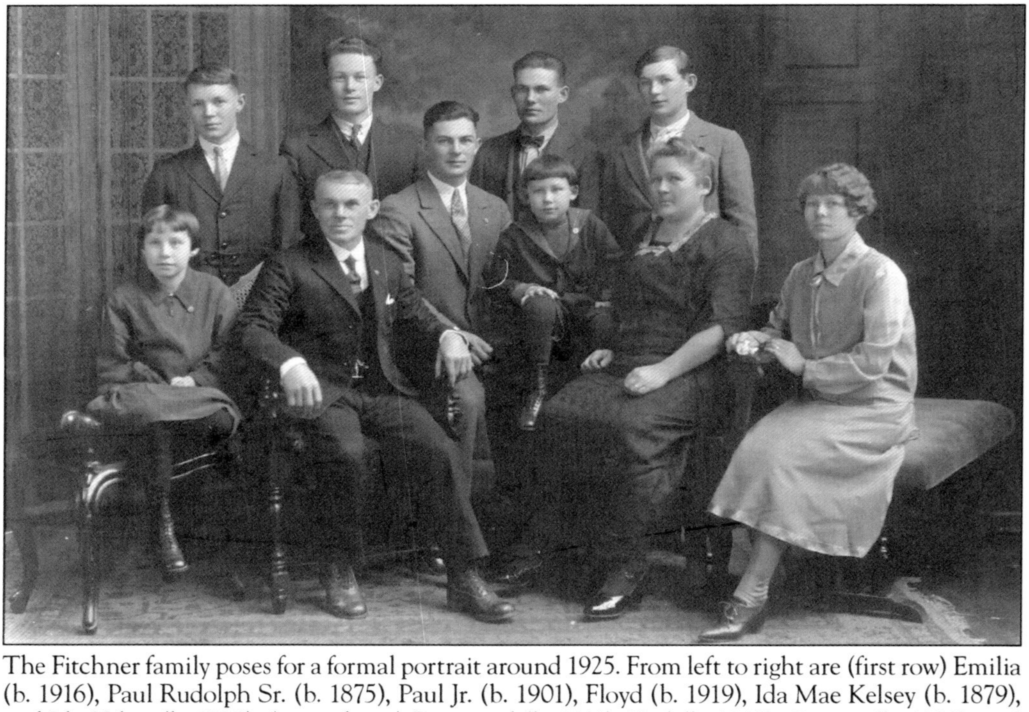

The Fitchner family poses for a formal portrait around 1925. From left to right are (first row) Emilia (b. 1916), Paul Rudolph Sr. (b. 1875), Paul Jr. (b. 1901), Floyd (b. 1919), Ida Mae Kelsey (b. 1879), and Ida Hilna (b. 1899); (second row) Raymond (b. 1911), Karl (b. 1903), George (b. 1909), and Frederick (b. 1909).

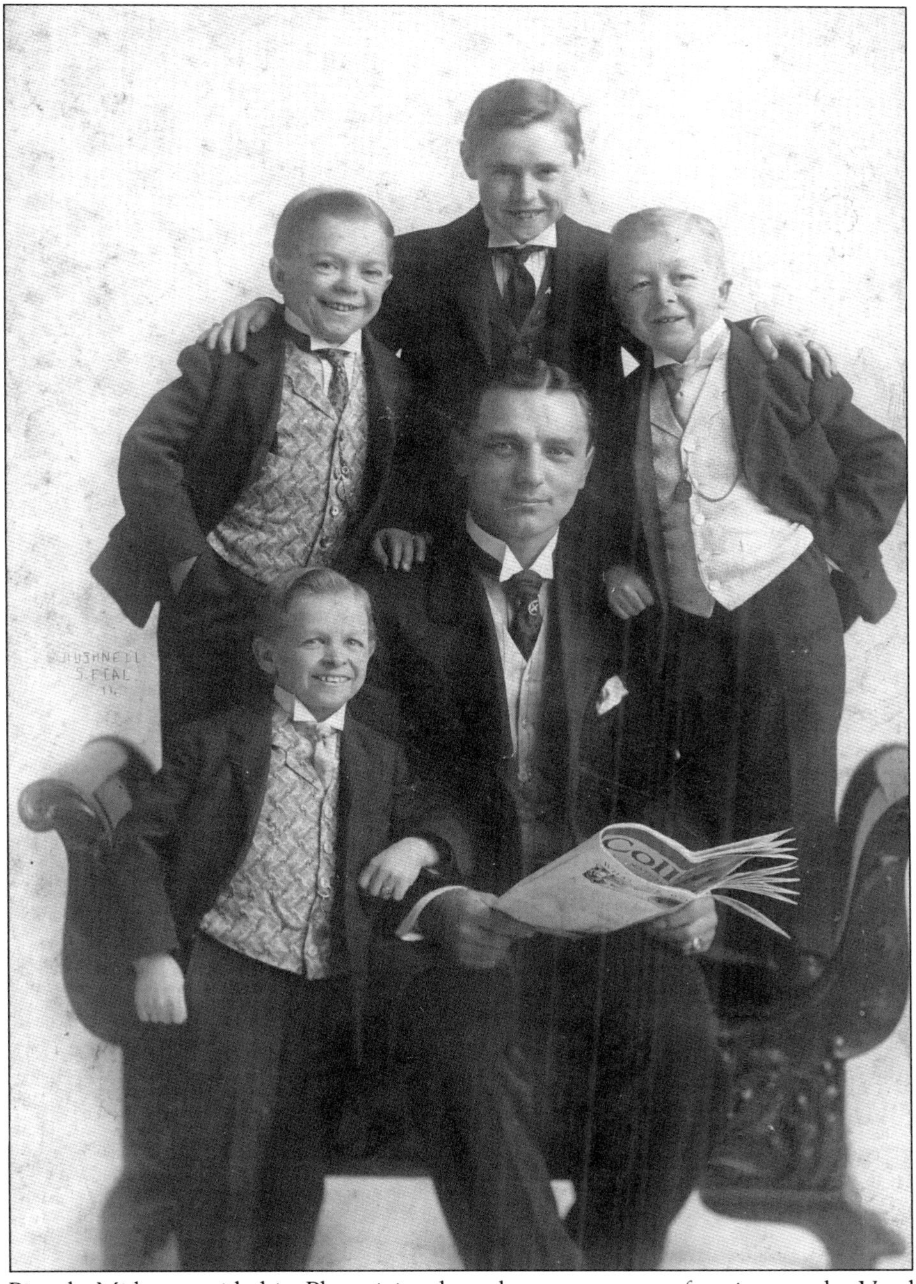

The Piccolo Midgets resided in Phoenicia when they were not performing on the Vaudeville circuit. They arrived in America from Germany in 1904 and were sworn in as American citizens on December 11, 1911, in Kingston, New York. The newspaper reported not only their names and country of origin but their ages, heights, and weights as well. They are Alexander Paul Richard Ebert, 32, height 3 feet 6 inches, weight 55 pounds; Otto Frederick Schemmel, 29, height 3 feet 1 inch, weight 44 pounds; Otto Therme, 32, height 3 feet 2 inches, weight 45 pounds; and Adolph Karl Meyer Schemmel, height 3 feet 1 inch, weight 44 pounds. They are shown in this publicity photograph with their manager, Alex Ebert.

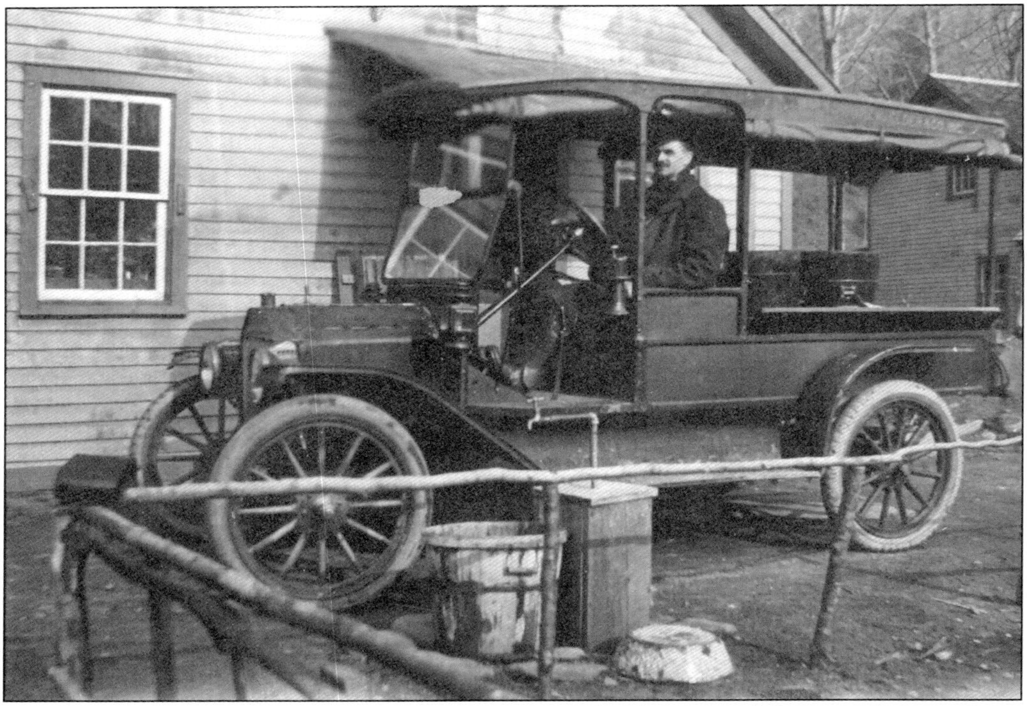

This is a photograph of C. Smith on April 8, 1919, posed in his automobile. Just a few years later, in 1923, the Phoenicia Garage advertised band new Fords for $295, with starter and demountable rims for $85 extra.

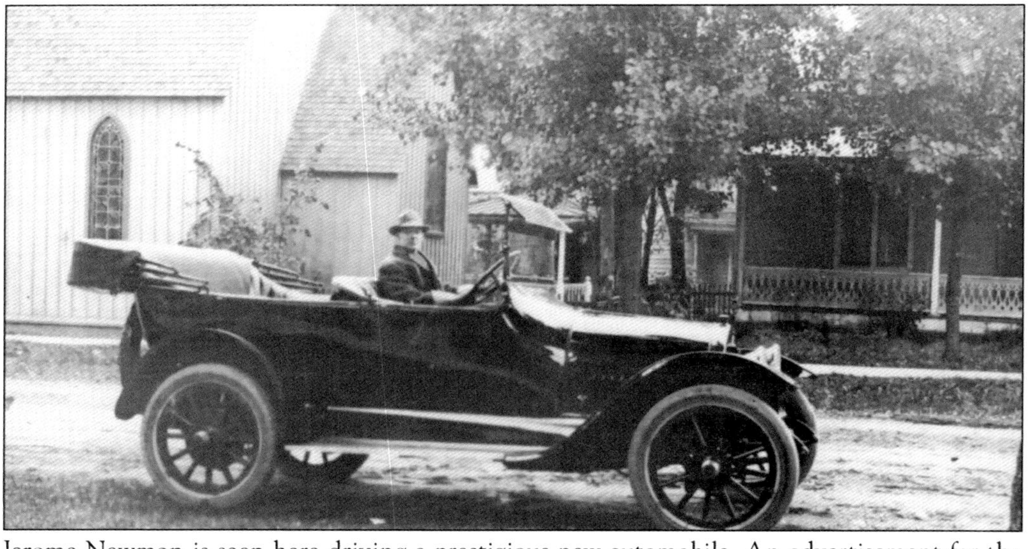

Jerome Newman is seen here driving a prestigious new automobile. An advertisement for the Globe hotel listed a J. A. Newman as the proprietor. Ironically, it was the popularity of just such an automobile that gave tourists a choice in transportation modes and destinations, which led to the decline of tourism in the Catskills after the initial peak around 1913.

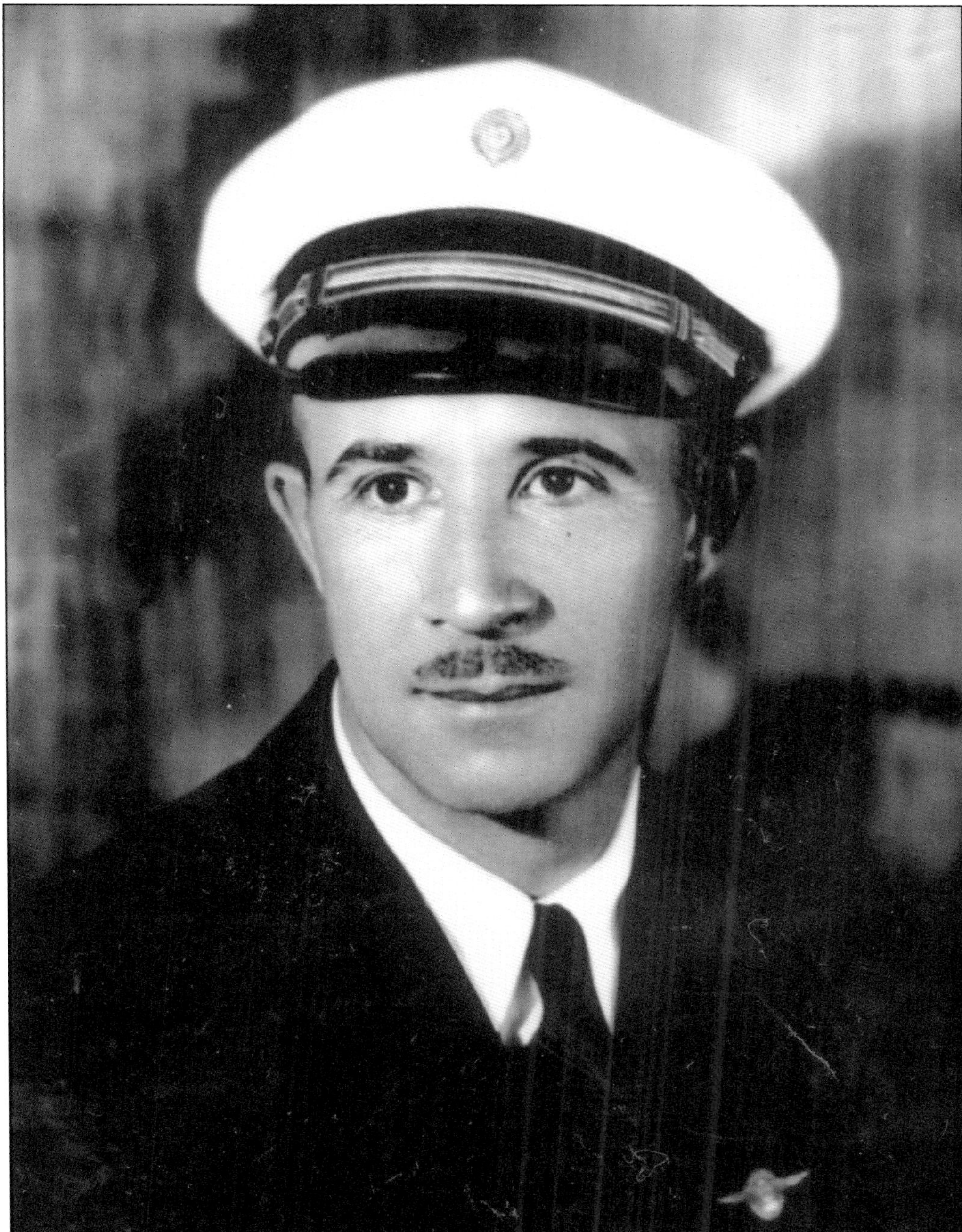

Capt. Basil Rowe was born on Fox Hollow Road in Shandaken in 1896. He flew in both World War II and the Korean War. An aviation pioneer, he was a friend of Charles Lindbergh and ended his career as a Number One Pilot for Pan American airways. He wrote an autobiography of his life titled *Under My Wings* and was even featured in Ripley's Believe It or Not for flying miles the equivalent to 223 trips around the world. He passed away in 1974. There is a plaque to honor him on Fox Hollow Road.

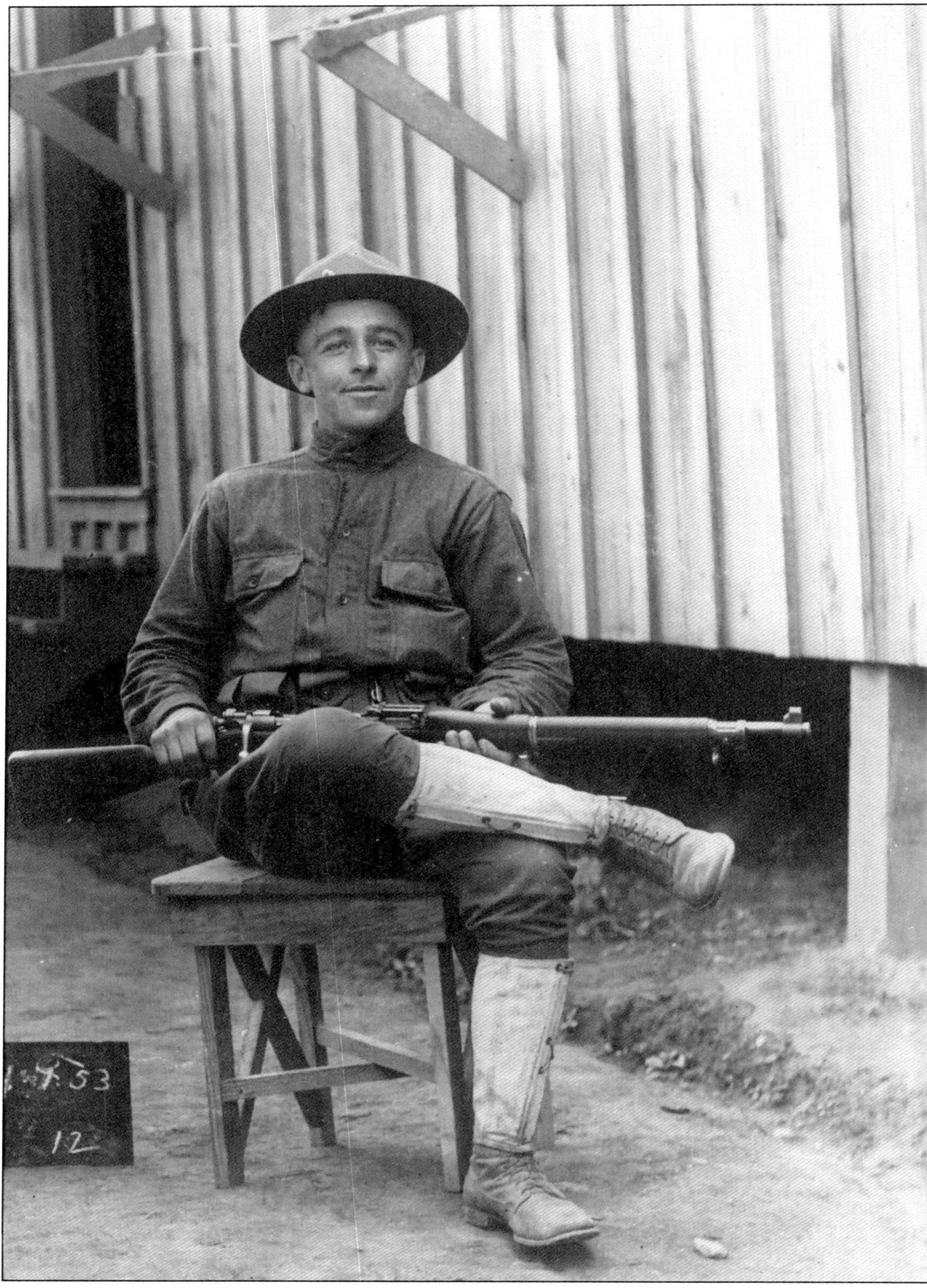

This candid picture of Leo Du Bois was taken in 1913 when he served his country in World War I. His granddaughter Mary Rogers Todd was very proud of her grandfather, who is handsomely attired in the uniform of the day.

Six

The Railroad and Tourism

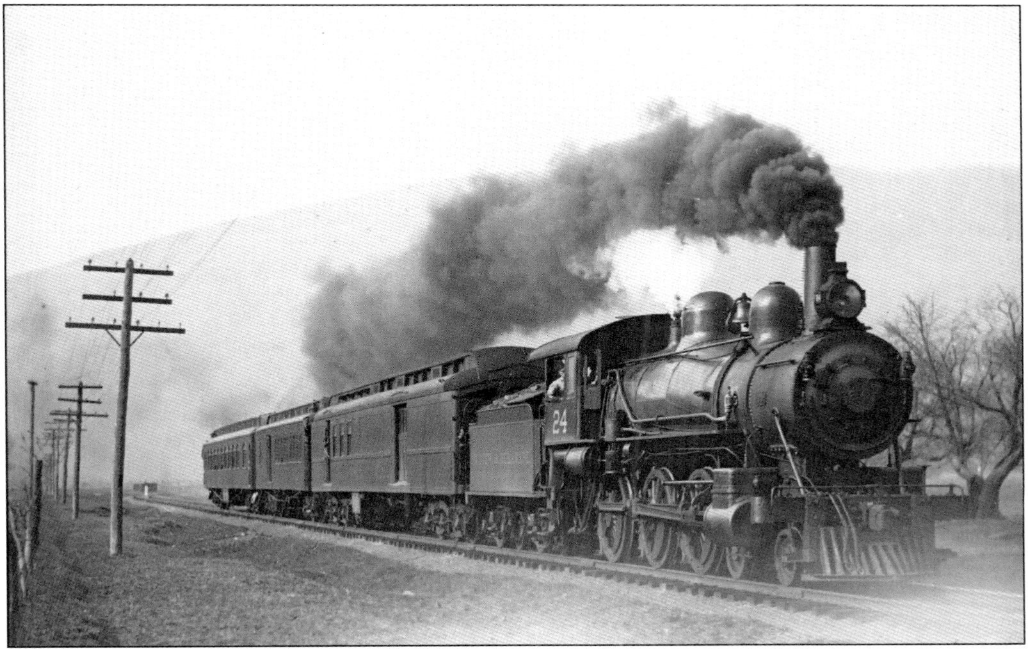

The railroad first came to Phoenicia in 1870 and then Pine Hill in 1871. Tourism was widely promoted by the railroad interest, who wanted to haul passengers as well as freight. The photograph shows this engine passing in the flats between Mount Pleasant and Phoenicia, yet the 1914 engine roster of the railroad skips over this number. Regardless, it is a perfect representation of the engines that serviced the line until diesel engines took over.

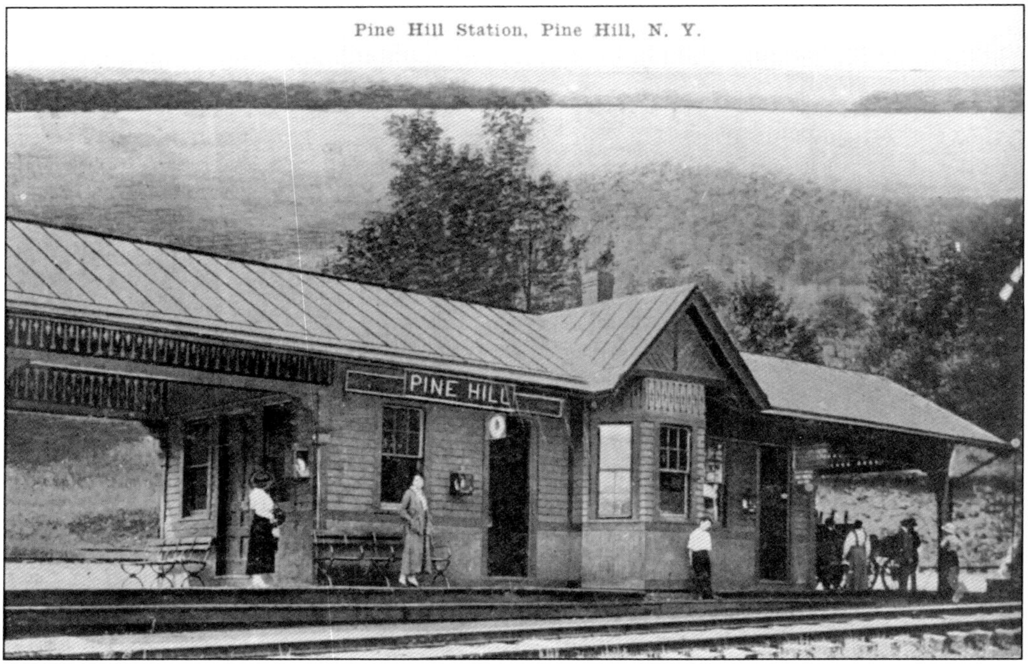

Pine Hill Station was situated on the slope of Belleayre Mountain above Pine Hill. Once a lively stop on the line, the downward trend began in the 1920s and continued into the 1930s as automobiles became popular and commonplace.

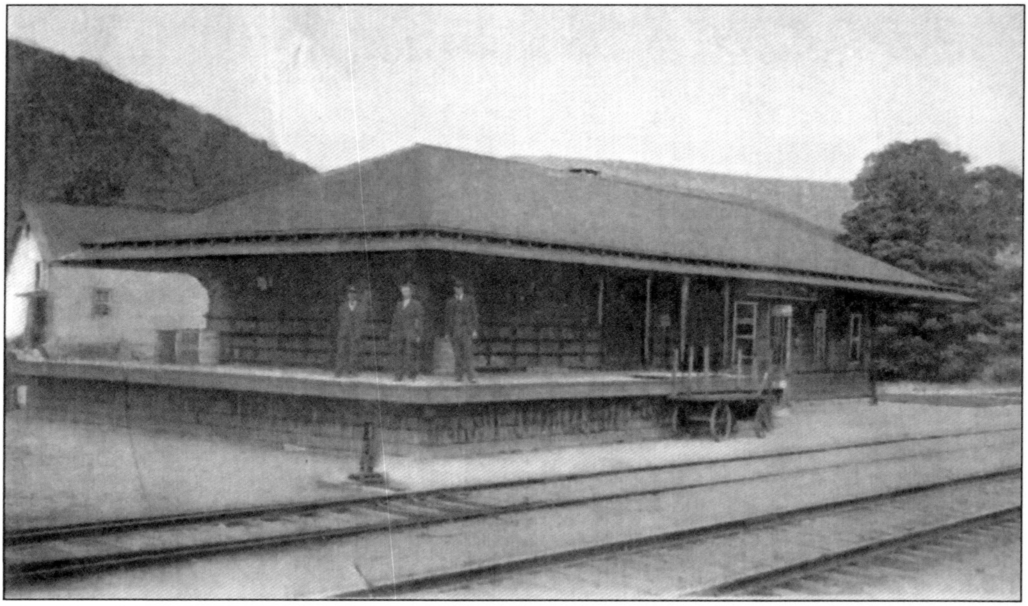

The Shandaken Station replaced the Allaben after a dispute with the Shandaken town officials as to where the new station would be located. The town took the position that the Allaben Station was part of a bustle of activity on State Route 28. There was a bluestone yard, a grocery store, garage, and several hotels and boardinghouses. One night, using locomotives and cables, the railroad tore down the old station, making way for construction of the new station.

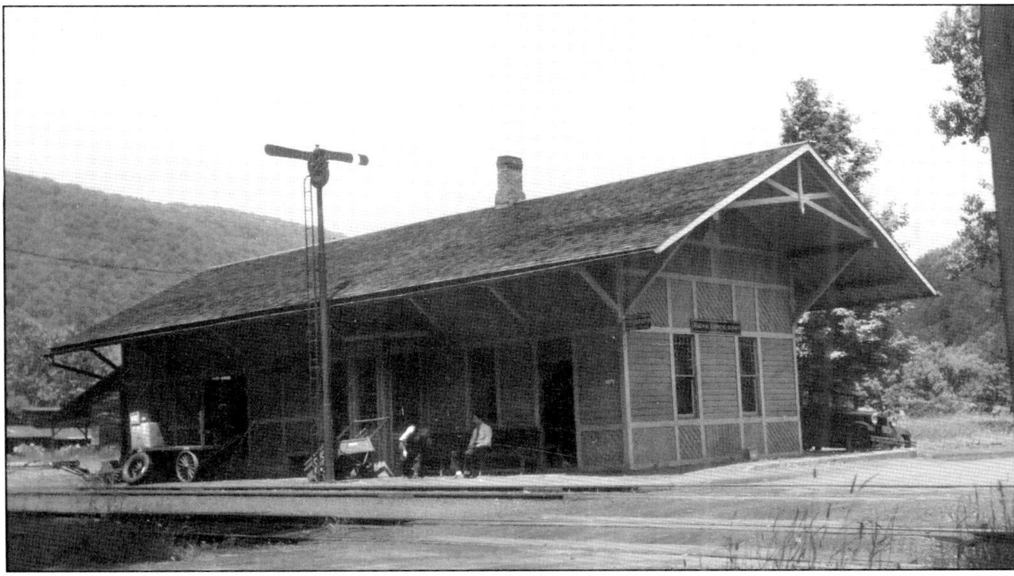

The Big Indian Station not only served the local boardinghouses and hotels but provided a junction for those who were travel further up the valley to Oliverea.

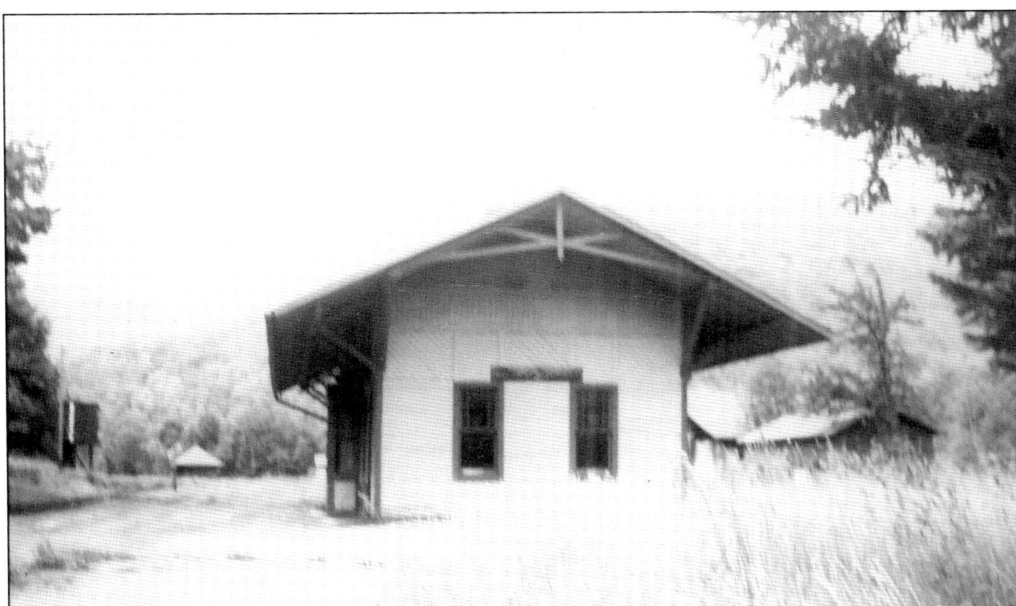

The Big Indian Freight House held wares between trains. The water tower that serviced the trains can be seen to the left. The tower was located across from Tom Blythe's store, now Morra's Market. With little money for new equipment, the same steam engines that serviced the line in the early 1900s were still engaged in the late 1940s.

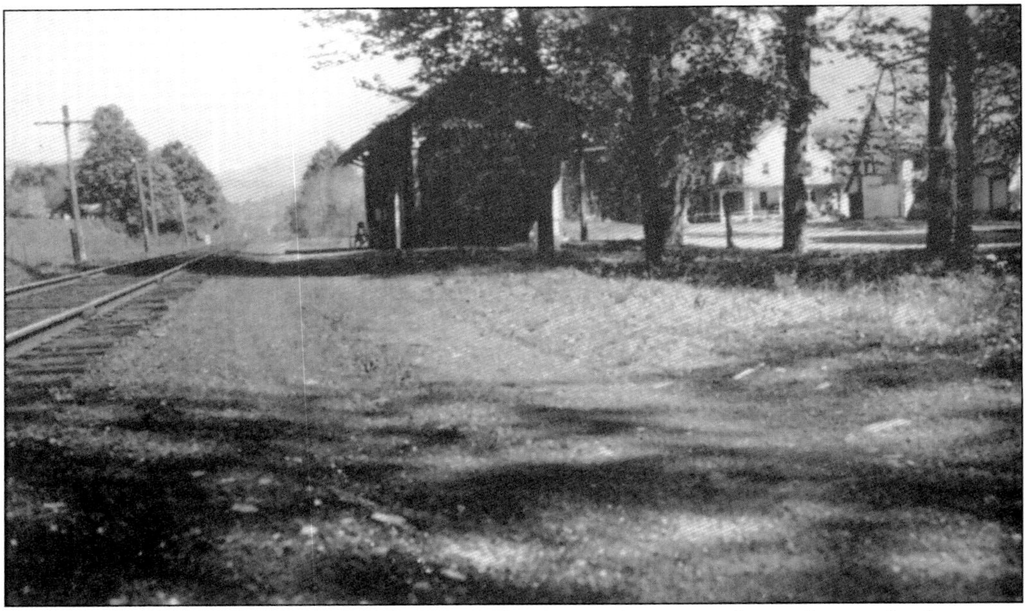

Mount Pleasant Station, known as Longyear Station early on, was located near the Longyear Farm in Mount Pleasant. It serviced dozens of boardinghouses in the area. The first trains to make the trip took two hours to cover the 23-mile span from Kingston.

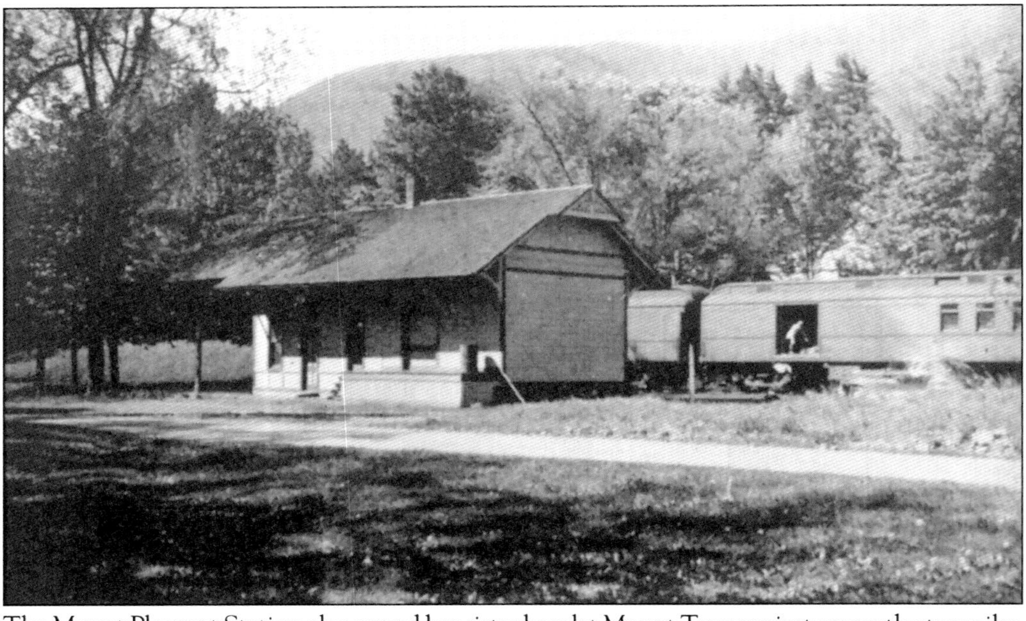

The Mount Pleasant Station also served her sister hamlet Mount Tremper just across the turnpike, later to become State Route 28. The hamlet was called Ladew Corners, The Corners, and finally Mount Tremper after Jacob Tremper.

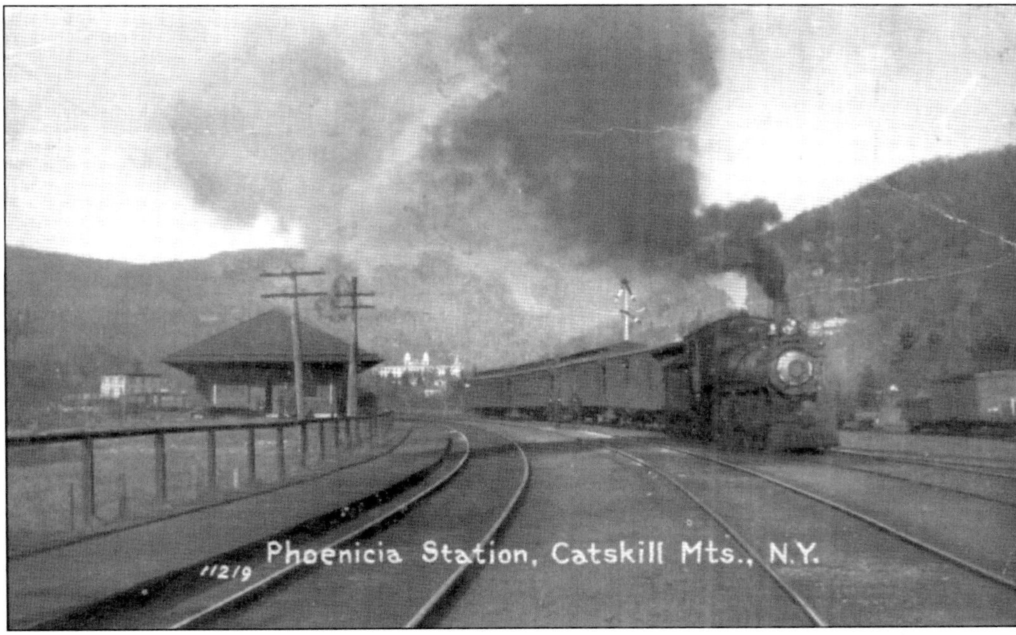

Phoenicia Station is now home to the Empire State Railway Museum and is listed on the National Register of Historic Places. Regarded as one of the most important stops on the line, here passengers could disembark for Phoenicia or Woodland, or connect to the Stony Clove Branch for points north.

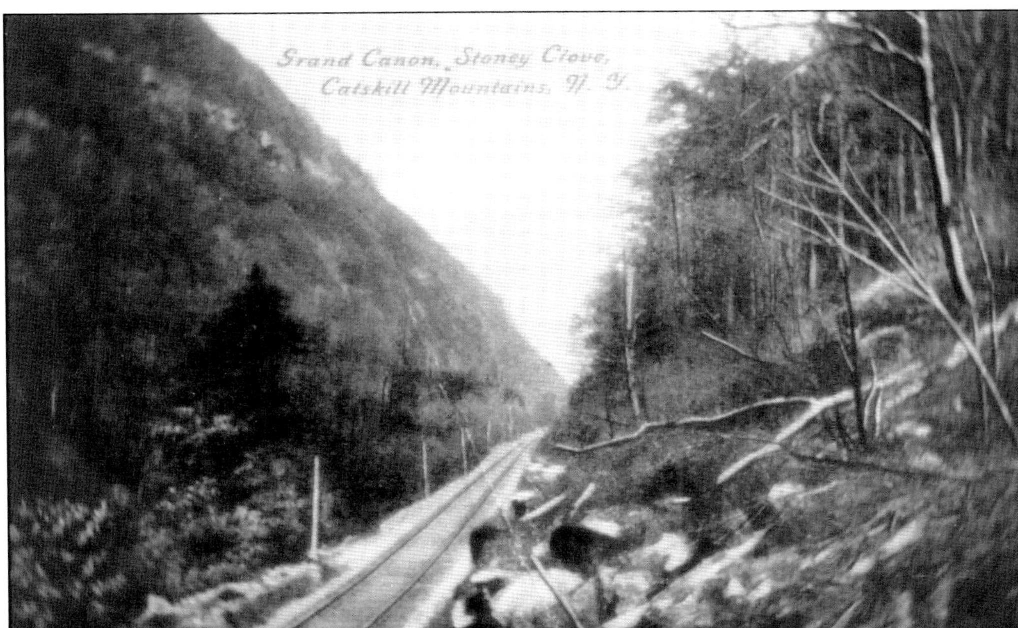

The railroad tracks in Stony Clove Notch brought passengers and freight up to the Greene County hamlets of Hunter and Tannersville. They were torn up in the 1950s for scrap metal.

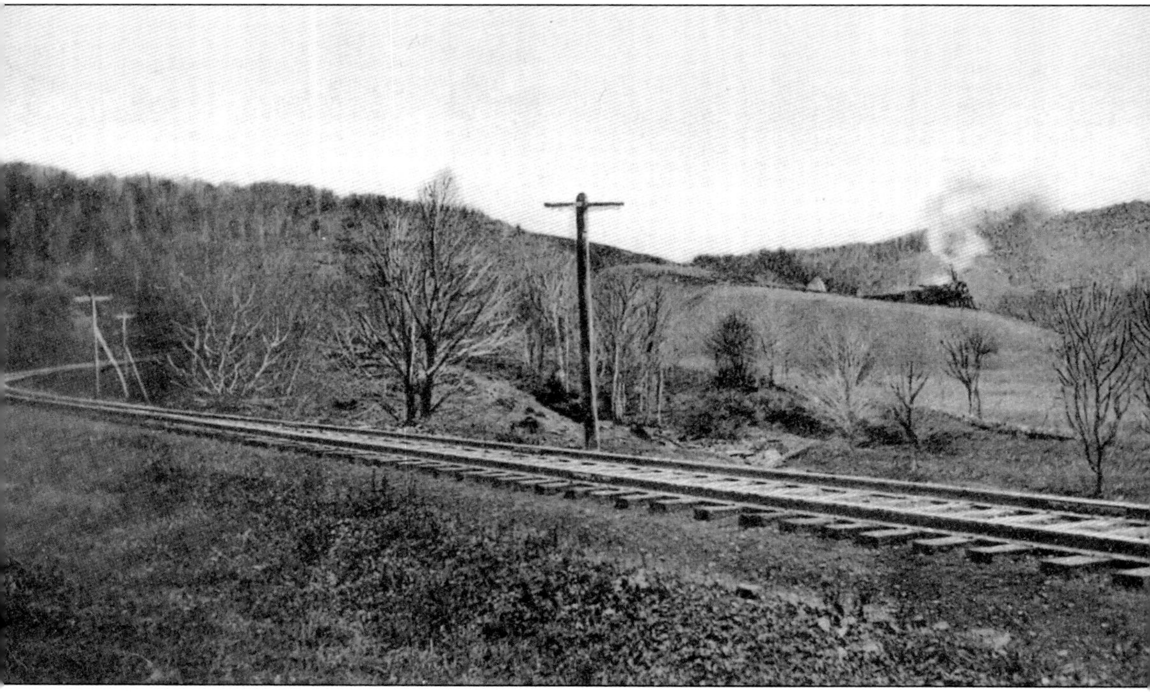

The Pine Hill Horse shoe curve was laid due to the railroad's failure to obtain permission to blast a tunnel through the mountain. The railroad instead devised a double horseshoe curve to

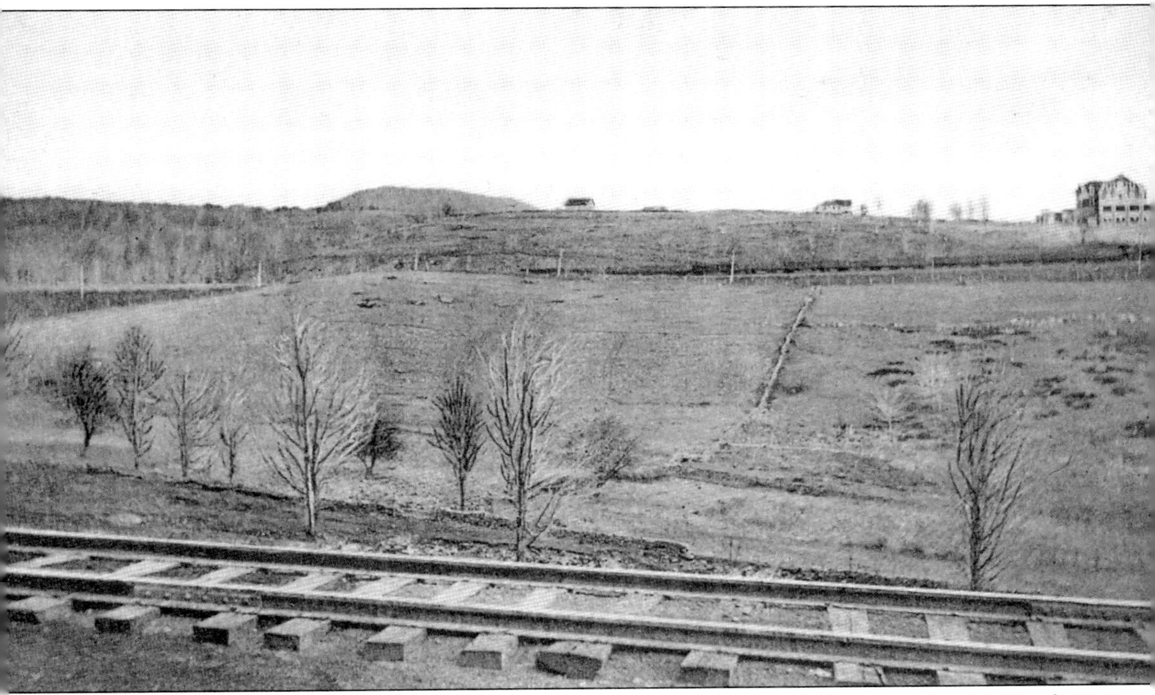

ascend the steep terrain. The distance to the summit was approximately 227 feet, yet the arcs of the tracks would triple that expanse.

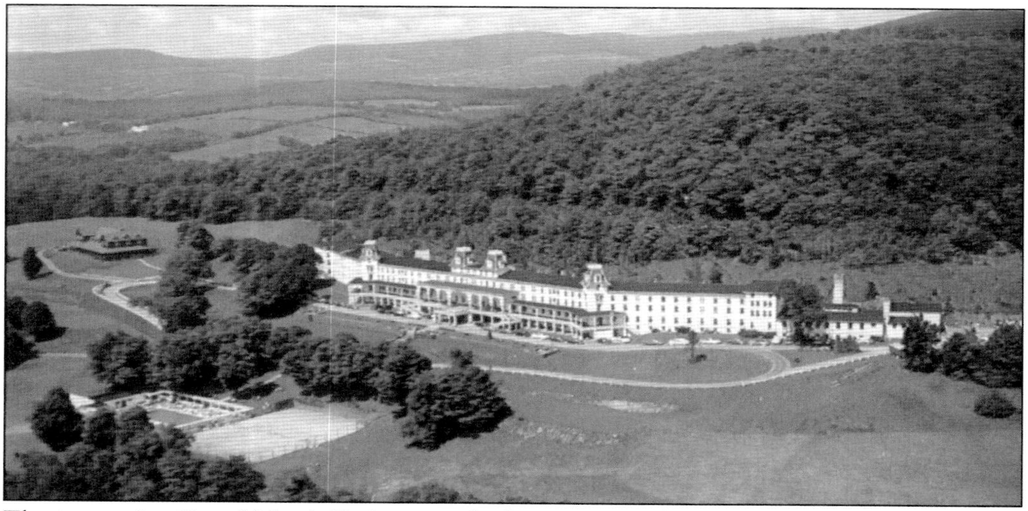

The impressive Grand Hotel, Highmount, built in 1881, could accommodate 400 guests. The Grand Hotel was a full eighth of a mile long and straddled the Delaware and Ulster County lines. It reportedly had a bar mounted on railroad tracks that could be rolled from one county to the other to escape fines during Prohibition.

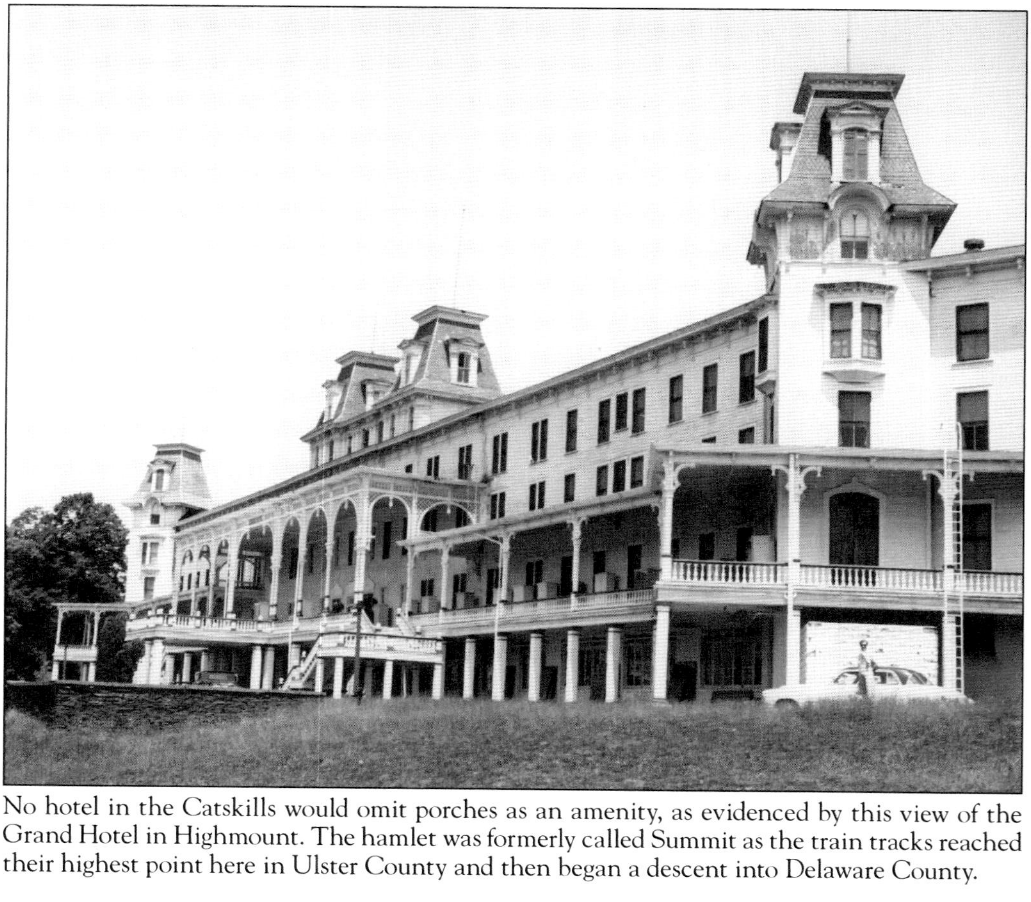

No hotel in the Catskills would omit porches as an amenity, as evidenced by this view of the Grand Hotel in Highmount. The hamlet was formerly called Summit as the train tracks reached their highest point here in Ulster County and then began a descent into Delaware County.

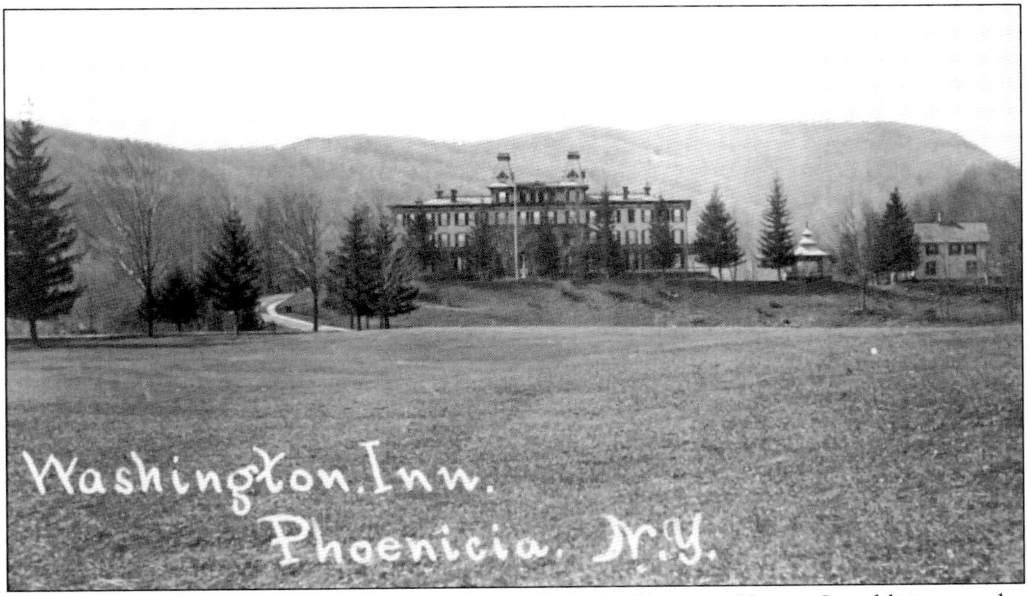

Built in 1878, the Washington Inn was first called the Tremper House. In addition to the extraordinary inn, it boasted cottages and rustic houses for 250 guests. The spacious dining room could seat 300, with separate facilities for private maids and children. The inn burned in 1908.

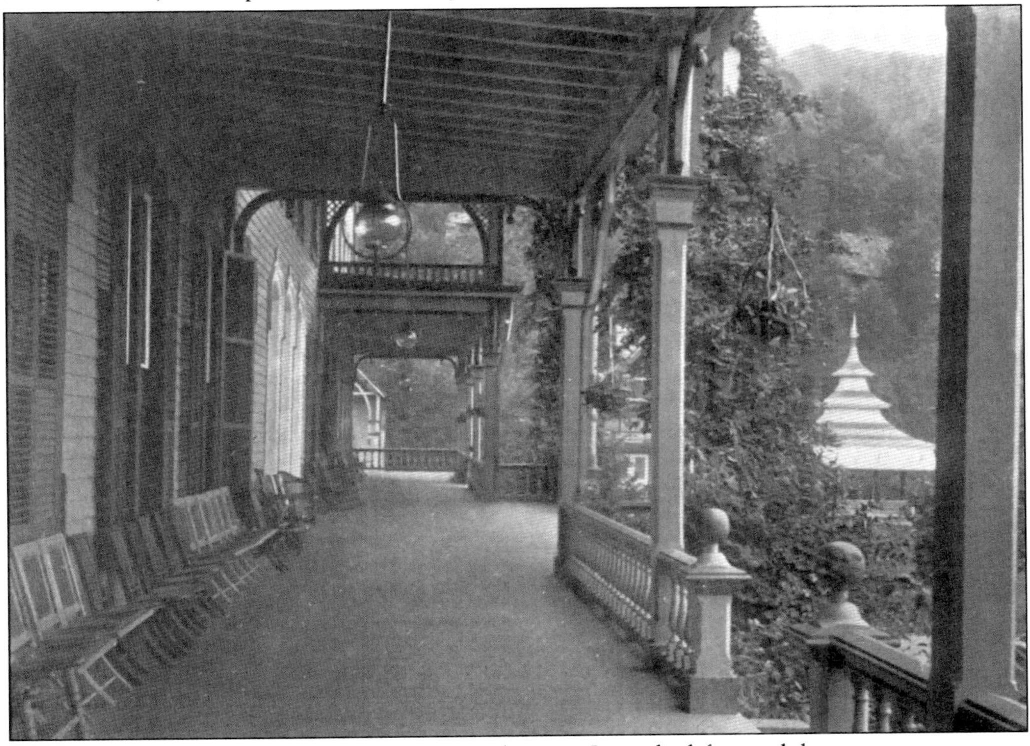

This photograph is a detail of a porch of the Washington Inn, which boasted that every room was an outdoor room with perfect ventilation. Hot and cold running water, private baths, sanitary plumbing, steam heat, gas and electric lighting, and an elevator were among the comforts advertised.

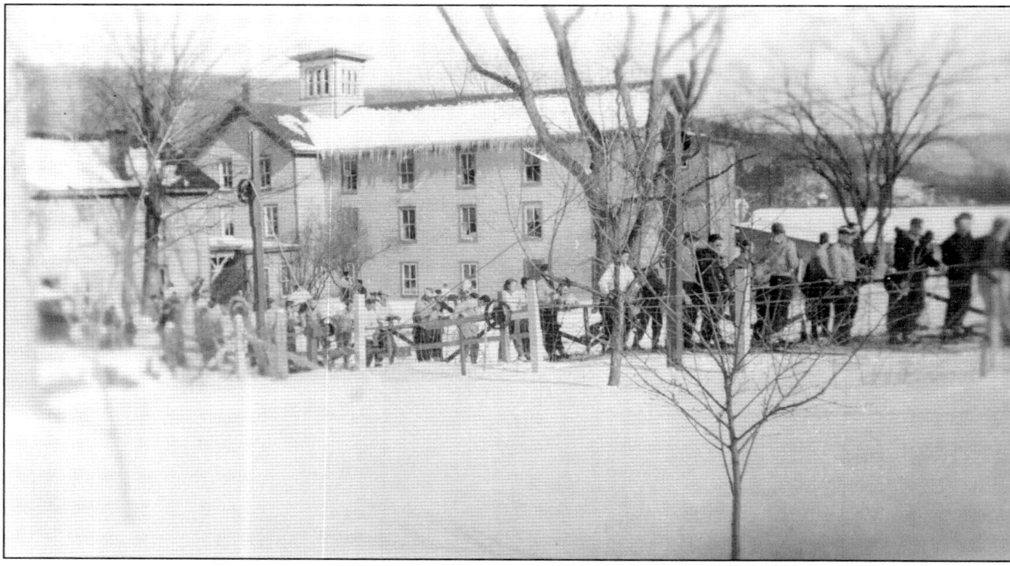

The first skiing in Pine Hill was at the Colonial Inn. Proprietor Ralph Dalton rigged up a tow rope, so the guests could ski down the hill behind the inn. He was also instrumental in creating the Belleayre Ski Area. The Colonial Inn still caters to skiers, hunters, and summer visitors today.

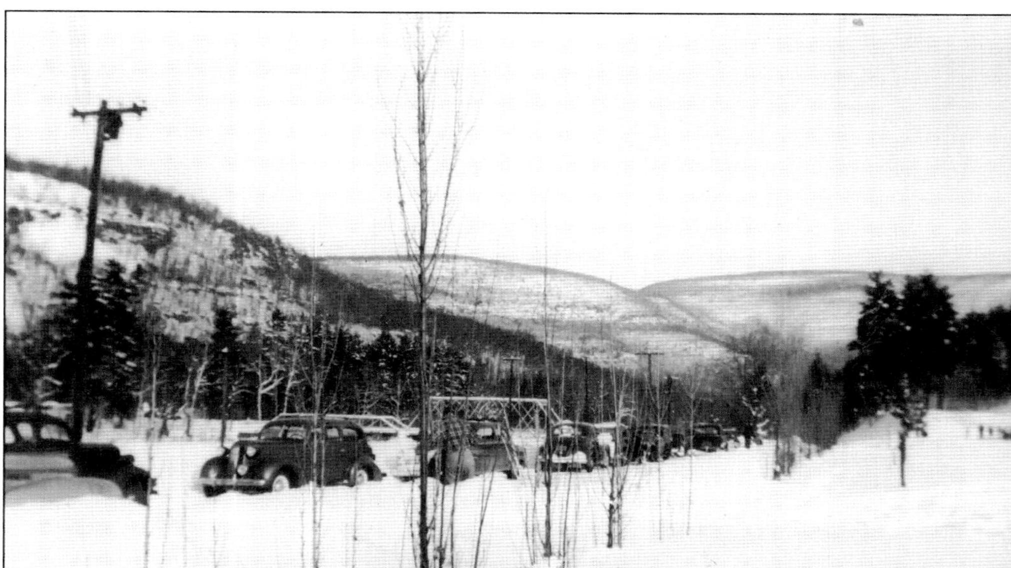

Skiing at Simpsons first started in 1935 by brothers Mickey and Carroll Simpson. They combined a parcel of their own land with that of New York State and were able to use the resources of the Civilian Conservation Corps to create the slopes. The inventive brothers and friends fashioned the first rope out of parts from an old Buick, which was reportedly the first rope tow in New York State.

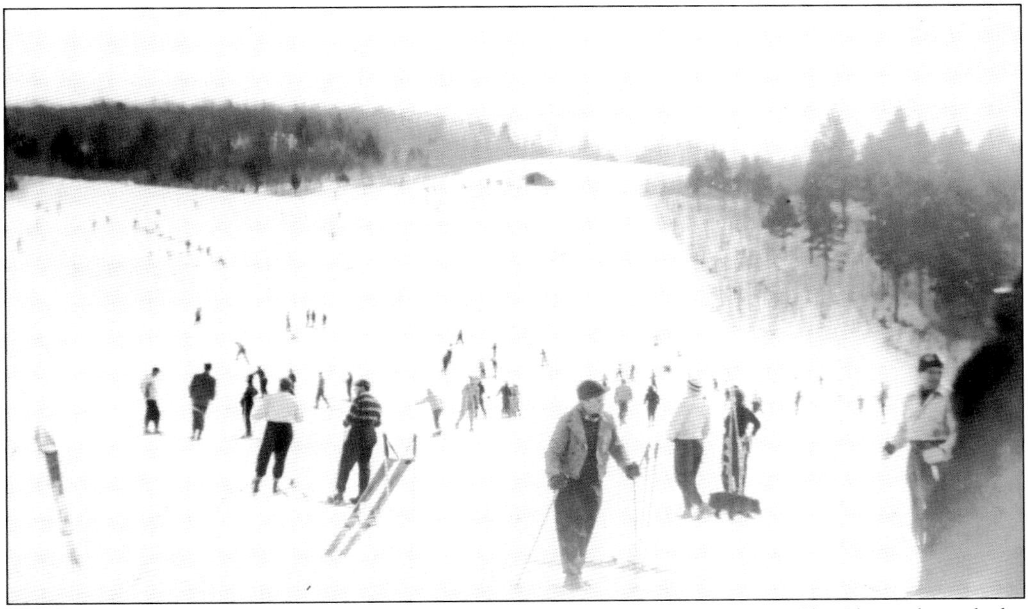

Opening day was February 11, 1935. Skiers were delivered to Simpsons Ski Slope directly by the railroad beginning in 1936. The train would remain slope side all day so that patrons would have use of the cars, including the dining cars and a special Ski Shop car sponsored by Saks Fifth Avenue.

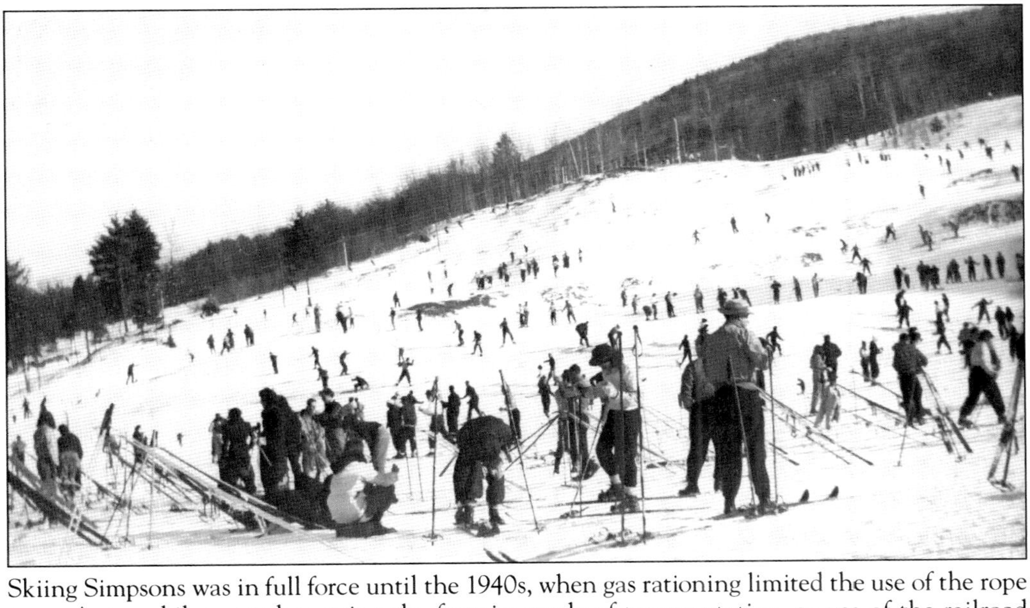

Skiing Simpsons was in full force until the 1940s, when gas rationing limited the use of the rope tows. Automobiles were becoming the favorite mode of transportation, so use of the railroad was limited. New York opened Belleayre Mountain in 1949 and with it the state's first chair lift. Despite the competition, Simpsons was able to stay in business until 1979.

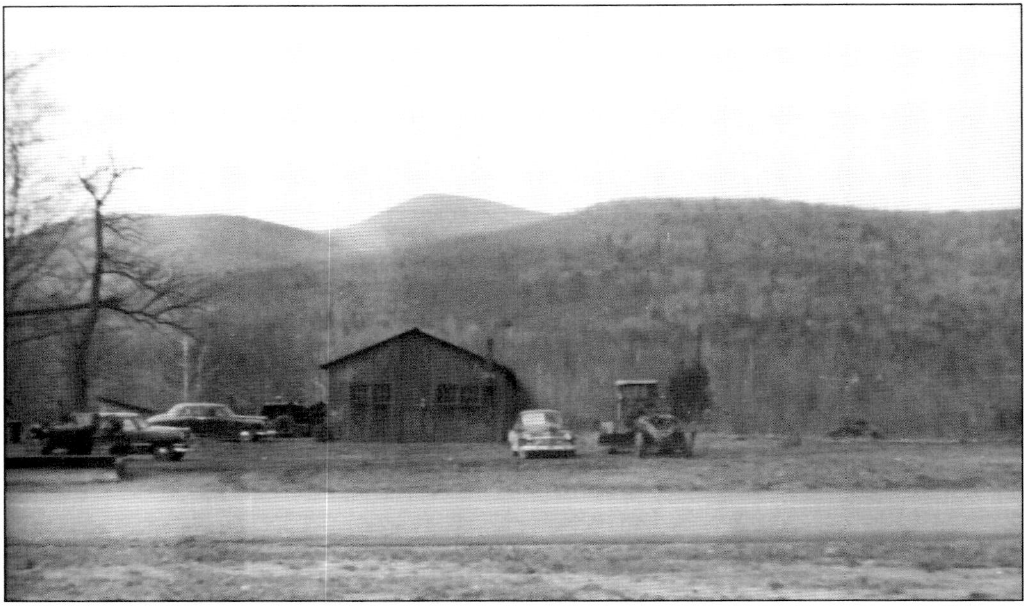

The New York State Department of Environmental Conservation began work on Belleayre Mountain Ski area to spur economic development of the region when, in 1947, the people of the State of New from York voted overwhelmingly to approve an amendment to the state constitution. Shown here is the first lodge that was erected for opening in the winter of 1949–1950. It was replaced in 1953 with the new Ski Hut and became part on the maintenance department.

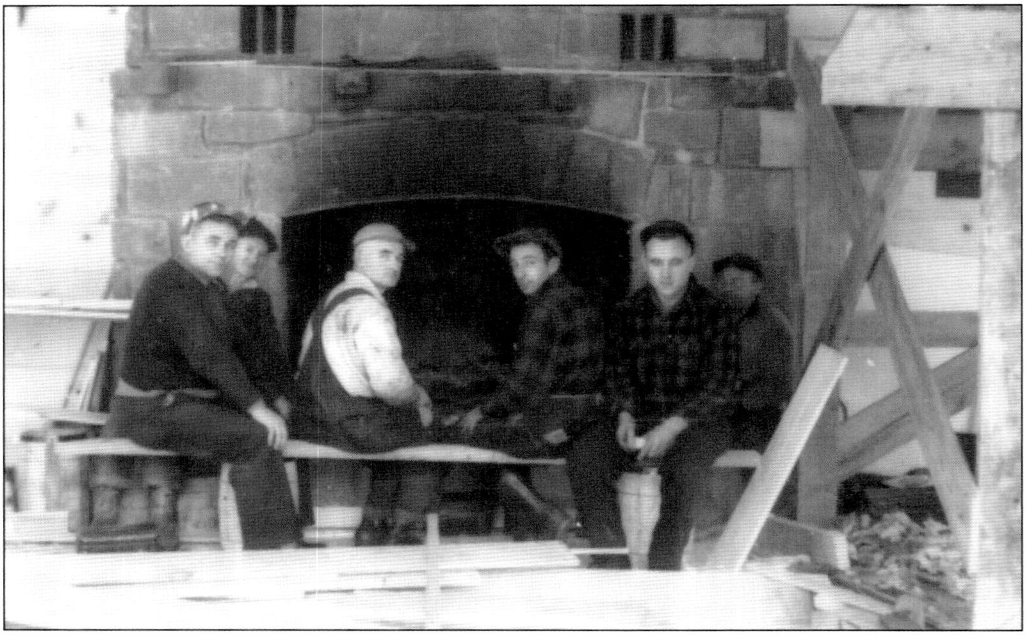

Built with a legislative appropriation of $260,000 to the New York State Conservation Department, Bellayre Mountain opened in the winter of 1949–1950. Workers taking a warming break during the building of Belleayre Ski Hut, from left to right, are Ed Ocker, Hector Colisimo, ? Smith, ? Persons, and ? Babcock.

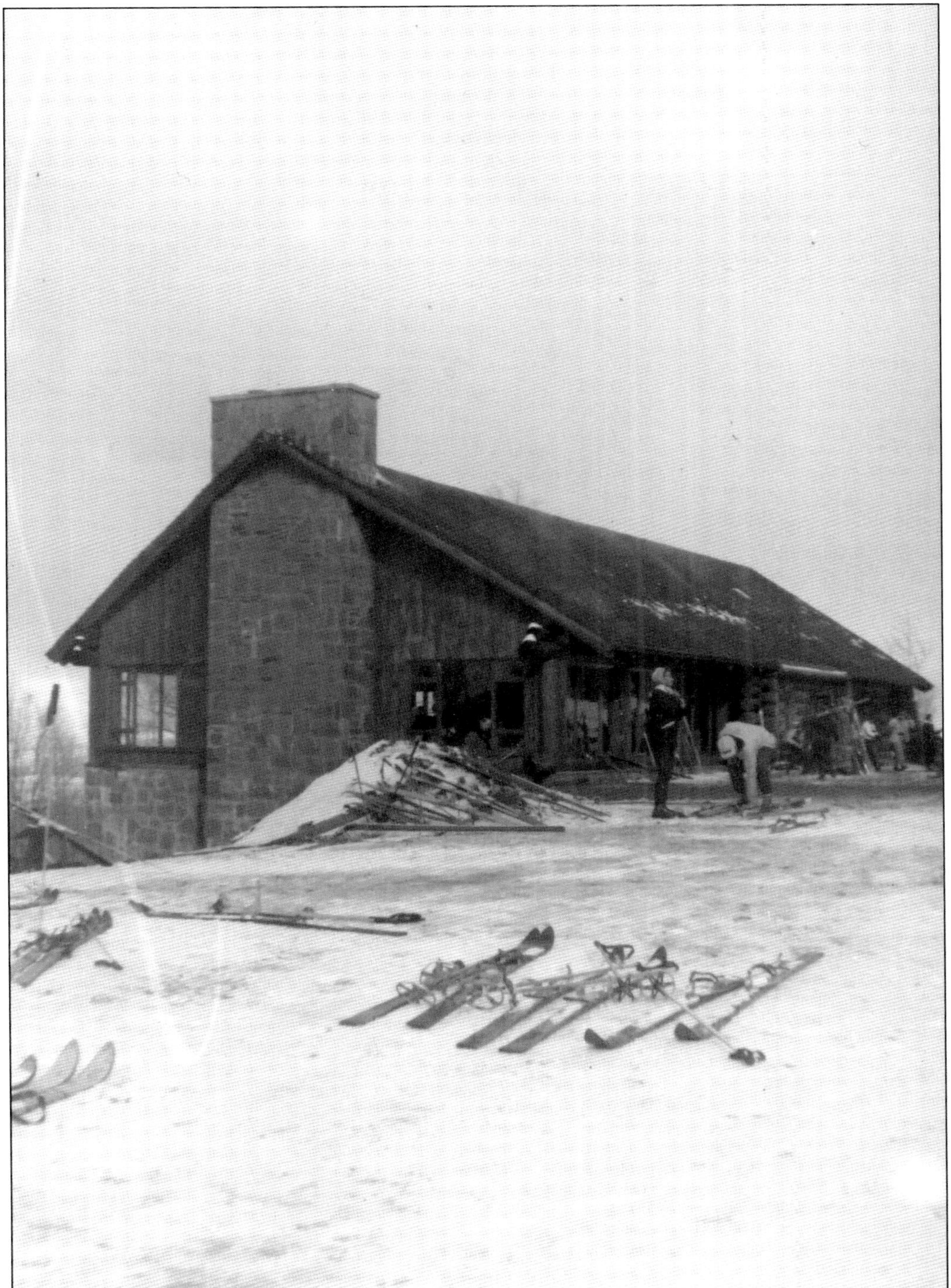

Replacing the smaller shelter hastily built for the opening of the ski area, in the beginning this modest lodge was known as the new Belleayre Ski Hut. An all-day lift ticket was $3.50, with single rides available for just 75¢.

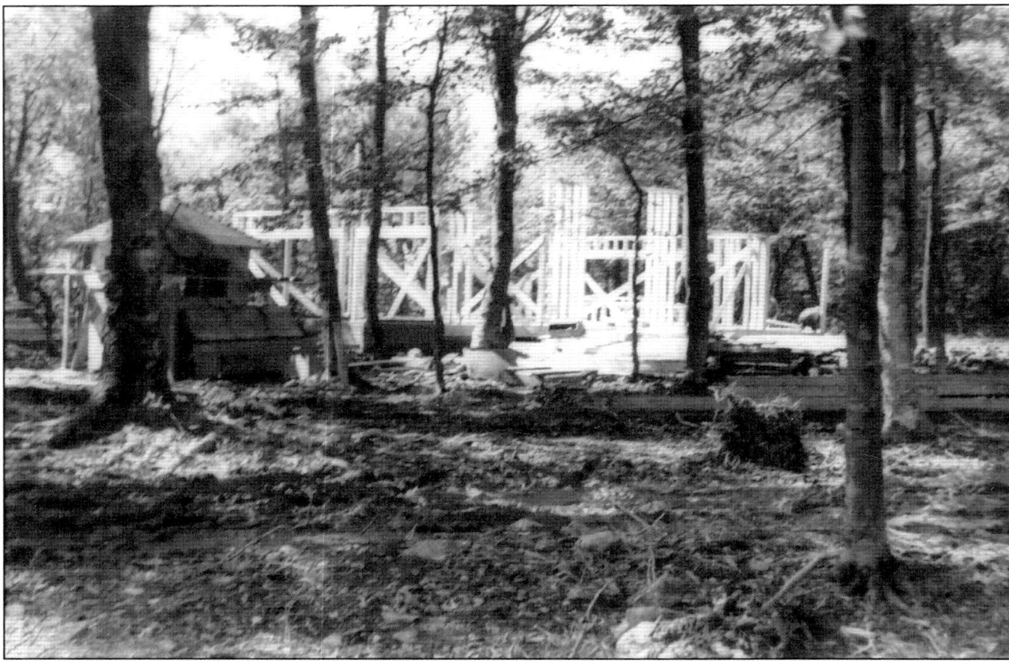

The Summit Shelter is pictured on the top of Belleayre Mountain during construction. Located at an elevation of 3,325 feet, the hut offered not only a place to warm up and catch a bite but also spectacular views of the Catskill Mountains.

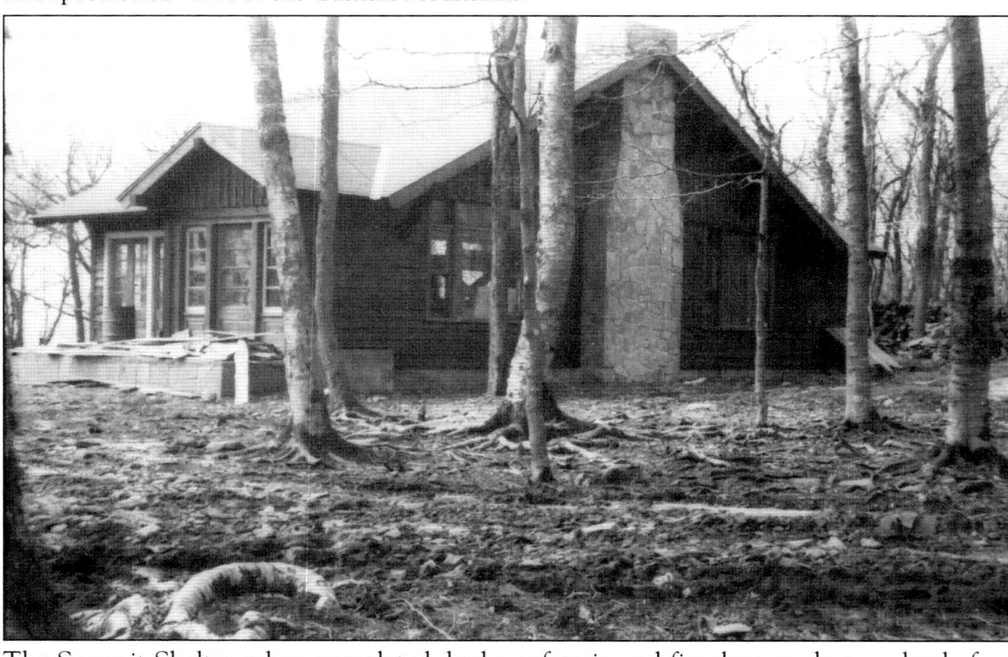

The Summit Shelter, when completed, had a cafeteria and fireplace made completely from native bluestone that was able to take logs up to four foot long. At the base of the mountain, a small 20-foot-by-60-foot base shelter was erected. Brochures explained that the ski facilities took preference over elaborate buildings at that time.

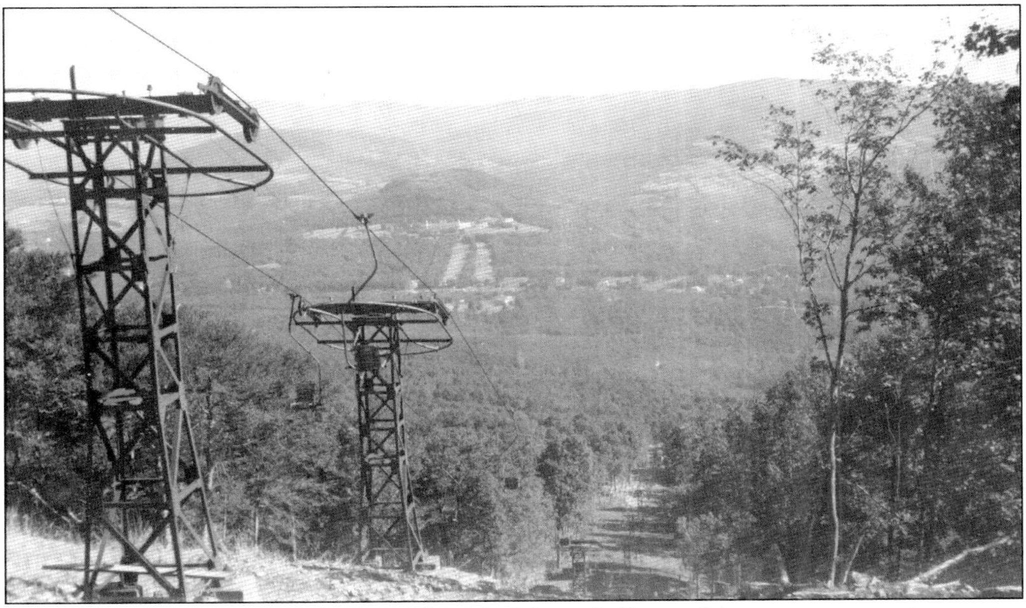

The completion of New York State's first ski lift on Belleayre Mountain was an impressive achievement. Across State Route 28 in the distance is the Grand Hotel. From the summit of Belleayre Mountain, the plateau where the Grand Hotel once stood is still visible, as well as the two private ski runs in the foreground.

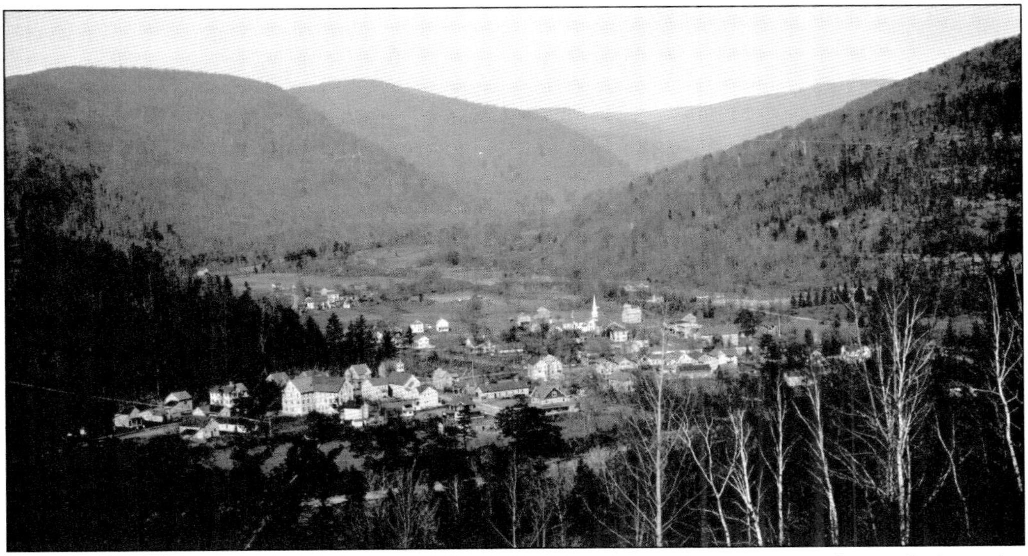

This view of Phoenicia shows the Waldorf Hotel that was built in 1906. It was located where the pavilion at Al's restaurant stands today. Just to the right the suspension bridge on Main Street can be seen just before the intersection of State Route 214. This structure was eventually replaced with a concrete span and rebuilt again in the 1990s. The impressive steeple of the Methodist church is also visible in the center.

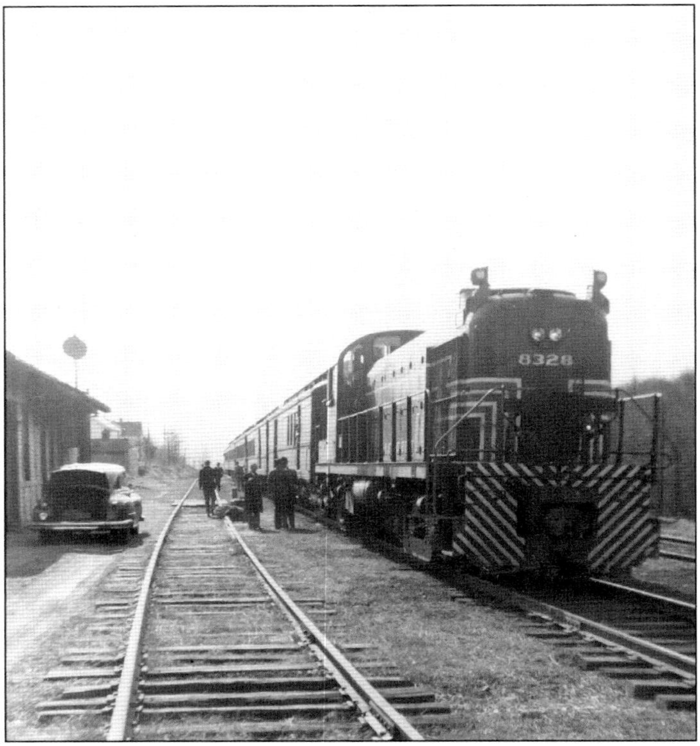

For 106 years, the Catskill Mountain Branch of the Ulster and Delaware Railroad made its way through the mountains. The last passenger train along the Ulster and Delaware line ran in April of 1954. After that, a freight train was run on the line three times a week. Freight service was eventually halted on October 3, 1976.

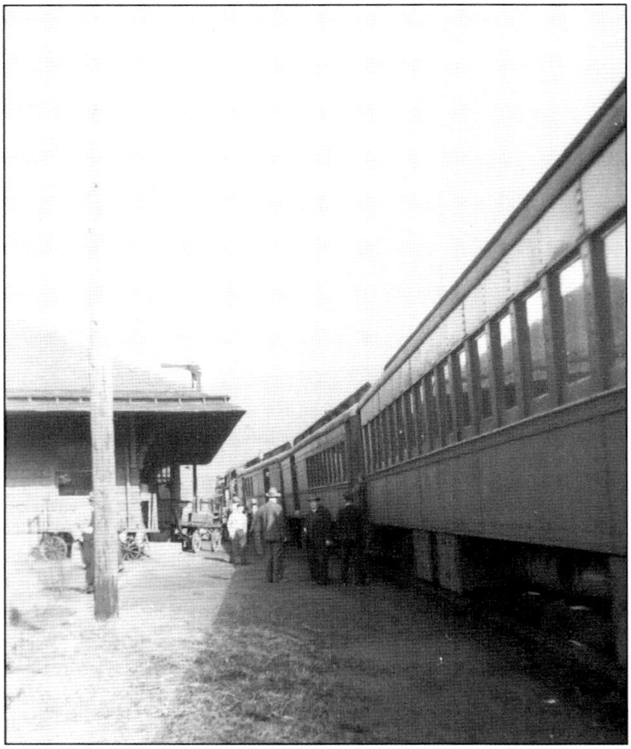

In 1948, diesels took over the line, but it was not enough to keep the passenger service viable. In July 1952, a 15-car train excursion was booked from Kingston to Stamford sponsored by several civic organizations, the longest passenger train run on the branch. In March 1954, a group of Margaretville elementary students took a nostalgic ride on the line just days before the service ended.

Seven

The Hamlets

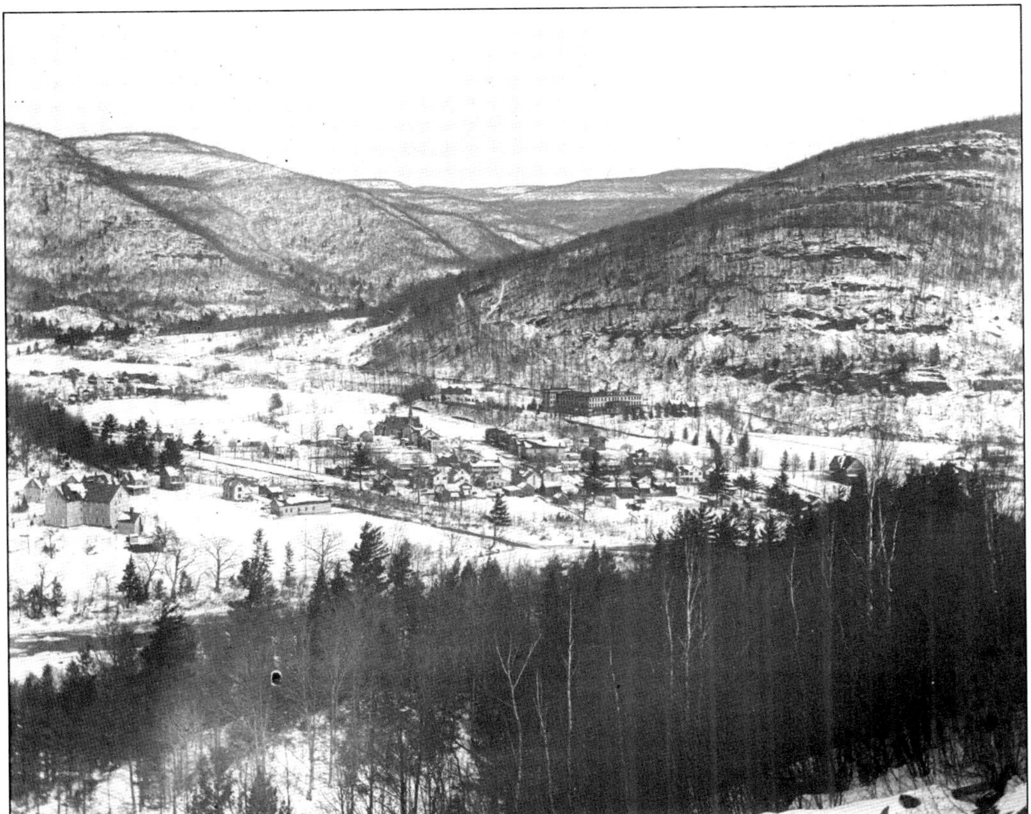

A charming portrait of Phoenicia taken prior to 1908 shows the Tremper House to the right, at the base of the mountain also named Tremper.

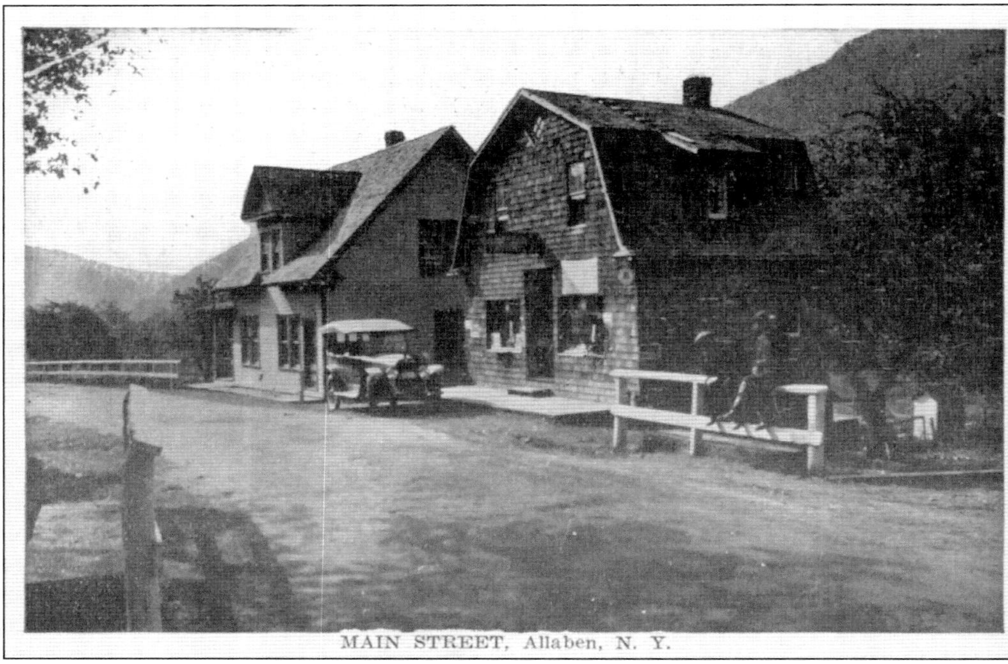

This postcard of Main Street in Allaben shows the post office that was destroyed by fire in the 1940s. E. Haynes owned the grocery store that was also caught up in the blaze.

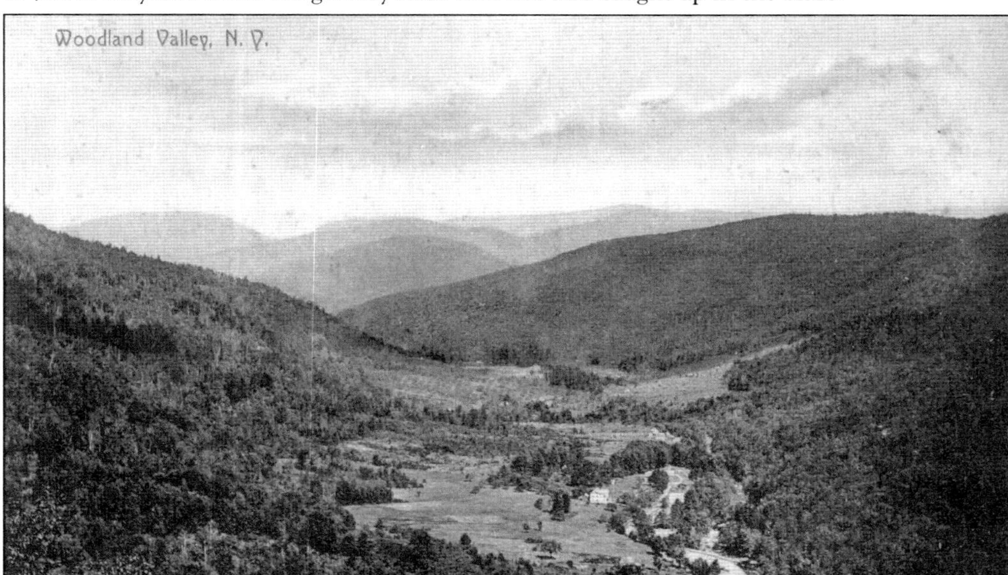

Woodland Valley was first known as Snyders Hollow after Col. H. Snyder started a tannery there in 1851. Beginning at a notch between Romer and Garfield Mountains, the 9-mile-long road ends at the base of Slide Mountain. A publication by the Phoenicia Improvement Association in 1906 advertised an excursion entitled "Around the Block," enticing visitors to take a horse-drawn wagon through Woodland Valley, over Slide Mountain, and back to the state road through the Big Indian Valley.

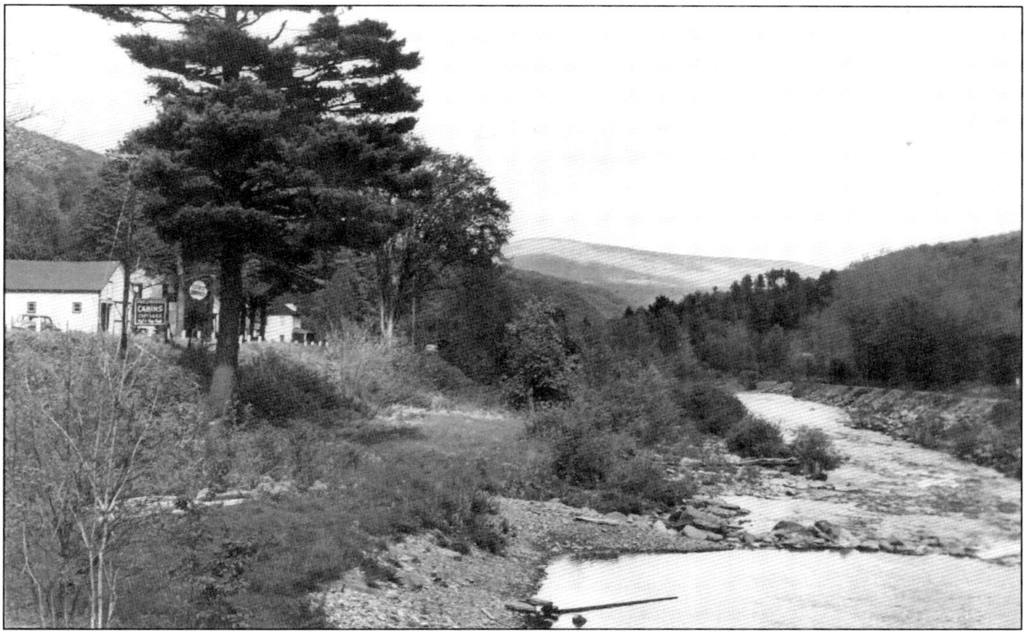

A cabin community is nestled along the Esopus Creek in Shandaken. The railroad was the first form of transportation to bring the masses to the once-isolated communities of the Catskills. The birth of the automobile similarly helped to develop the cabin communities that sprang up during the 1950s and 1960s.

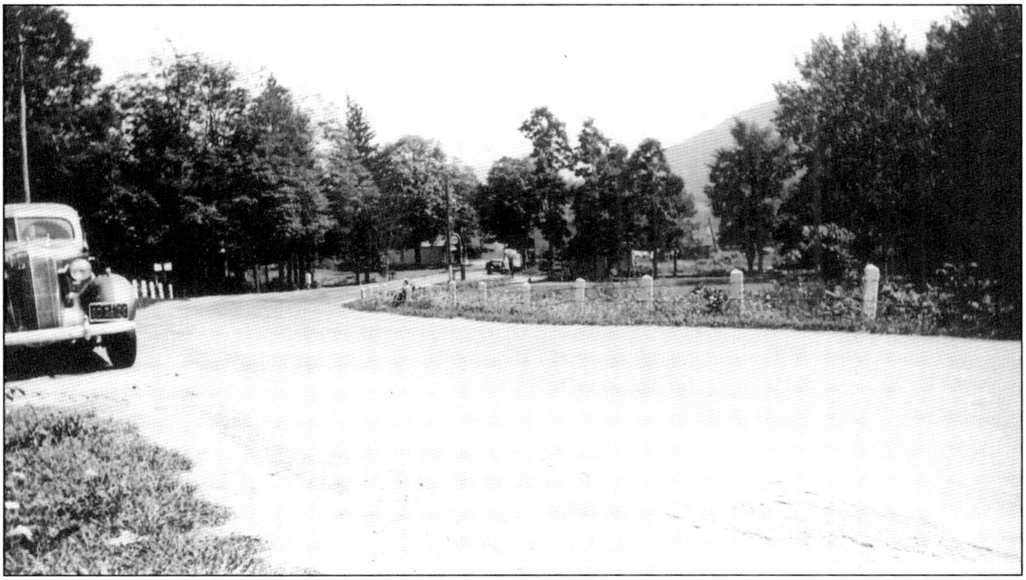

This picturesque curve on the new road (now old State Route 28 and renamed Creekside Drive), just before arriving in Shandaken from Big Indian, was typical of that observed by motorist cruising in the Catskills in the 1940s.

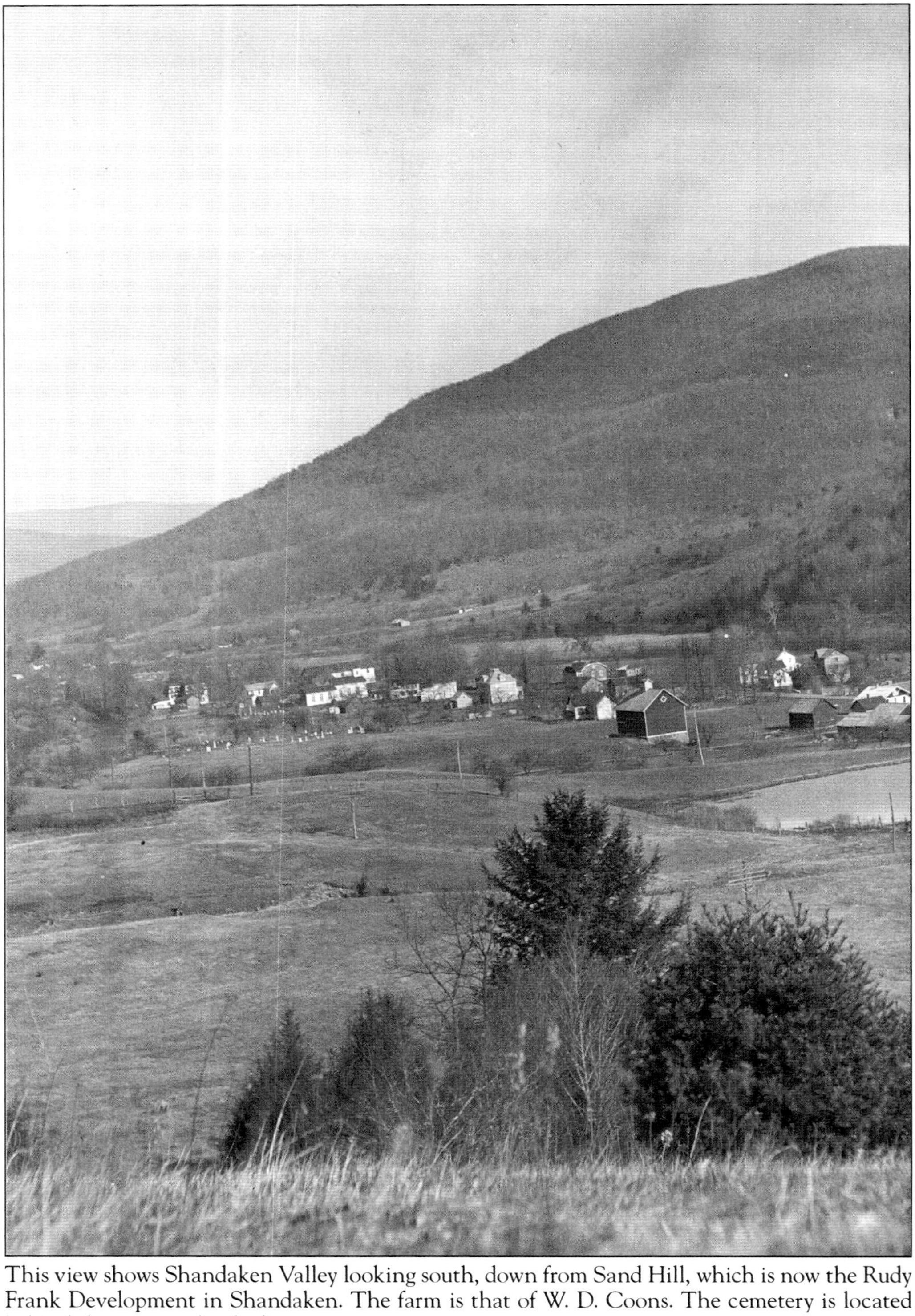

This view shows Shandaken Valley looking south, down from Sand Hill, which is now the Rudy Frank Development in Shandaken. The farm is that of W. D. Coons. The cemetery is located behind the present-day firehouse.

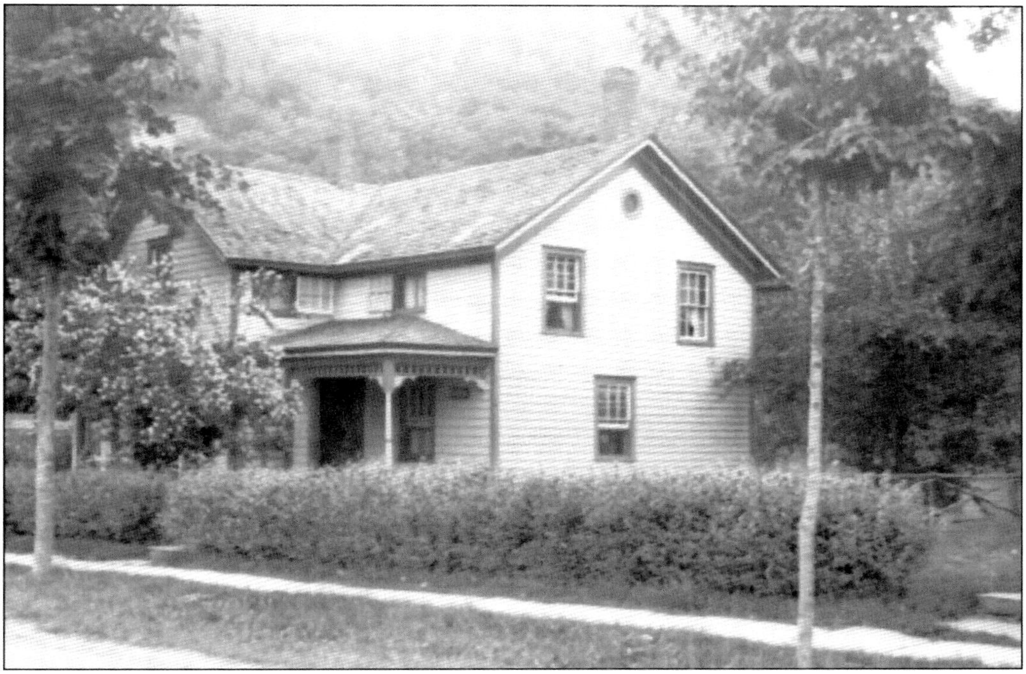

A well-manicured home located at 23 Main Street in Chichester was photographed by A. J. Lea around 1910. Lea was a prominent photographer in the area and the official photographer for the Schwartzwalder Factory.

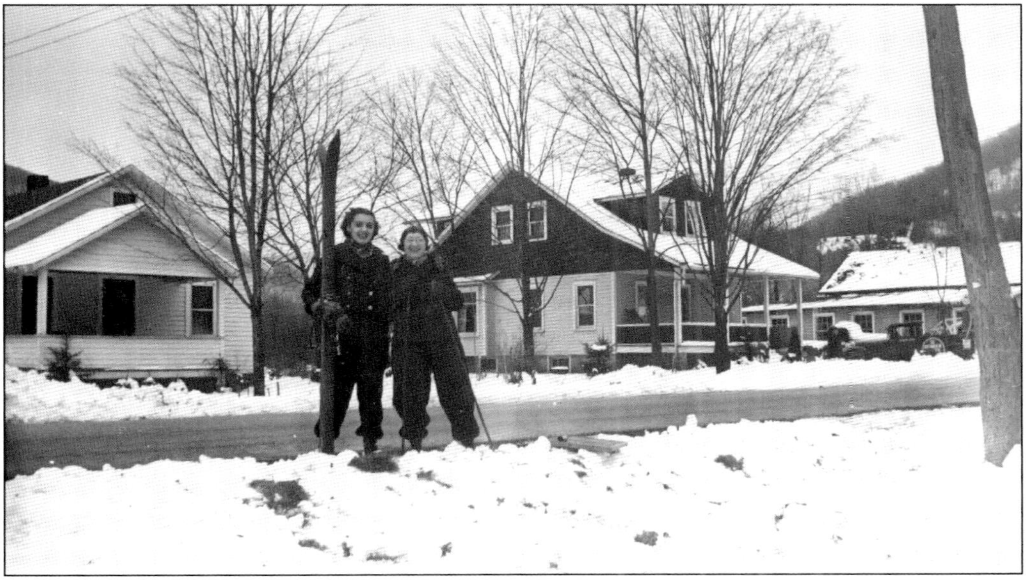

Carolyn Ford and Esther McLaughlin are looking excited to head out for a day of skiing. The buildings in the background on State Route 28 in Shandaken once all belonged to the Hummell family. In the background, from left to right are the home of Mrs. Hummell, the home of Ward and Edna Hummell, and Hummell and Fords Garage.

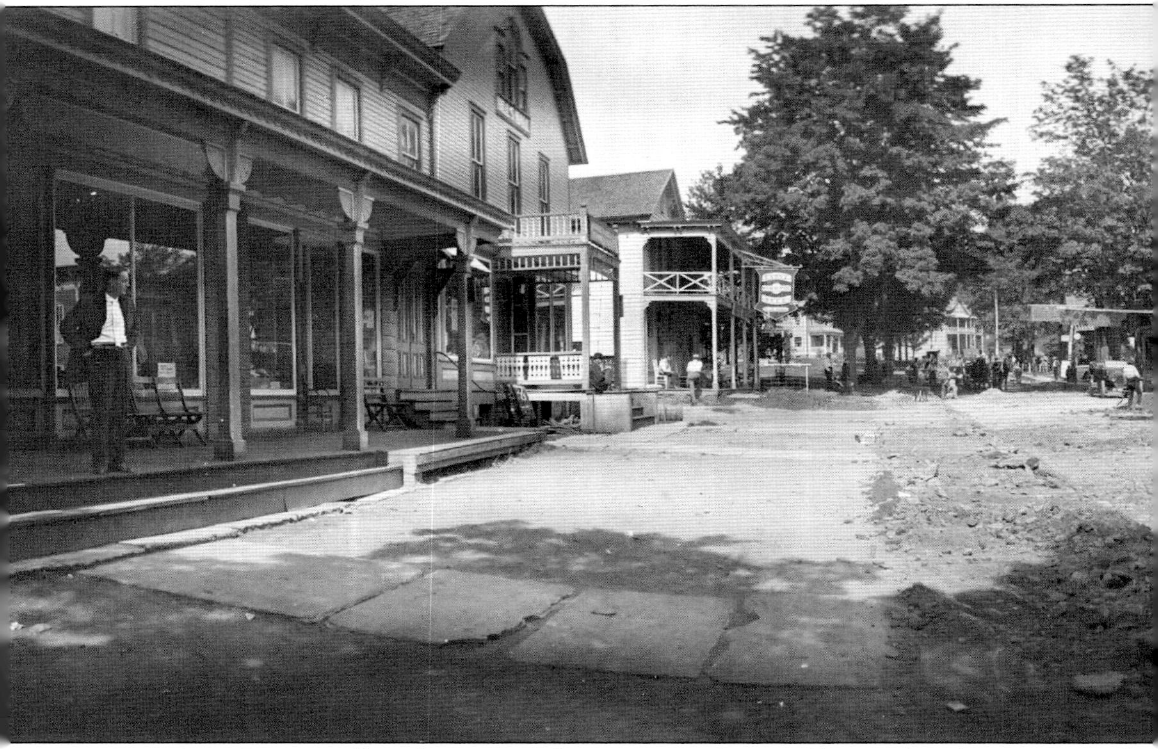

In 1912, workers are rolling the ruts out of Main Street of Pine Hill, as road work was an eternal activity the road crews of before modern paving. The first building on the left is I. D. Hills Store. The third building from the left, advertising Pabst Beer, is now the site of the Pine Hill Honor Roll for war veterans. The porch of the current Boyer residence is visible, as is that of the old Corner Store, now a private residence. The nose of a steam roller is visible on the far right across from the

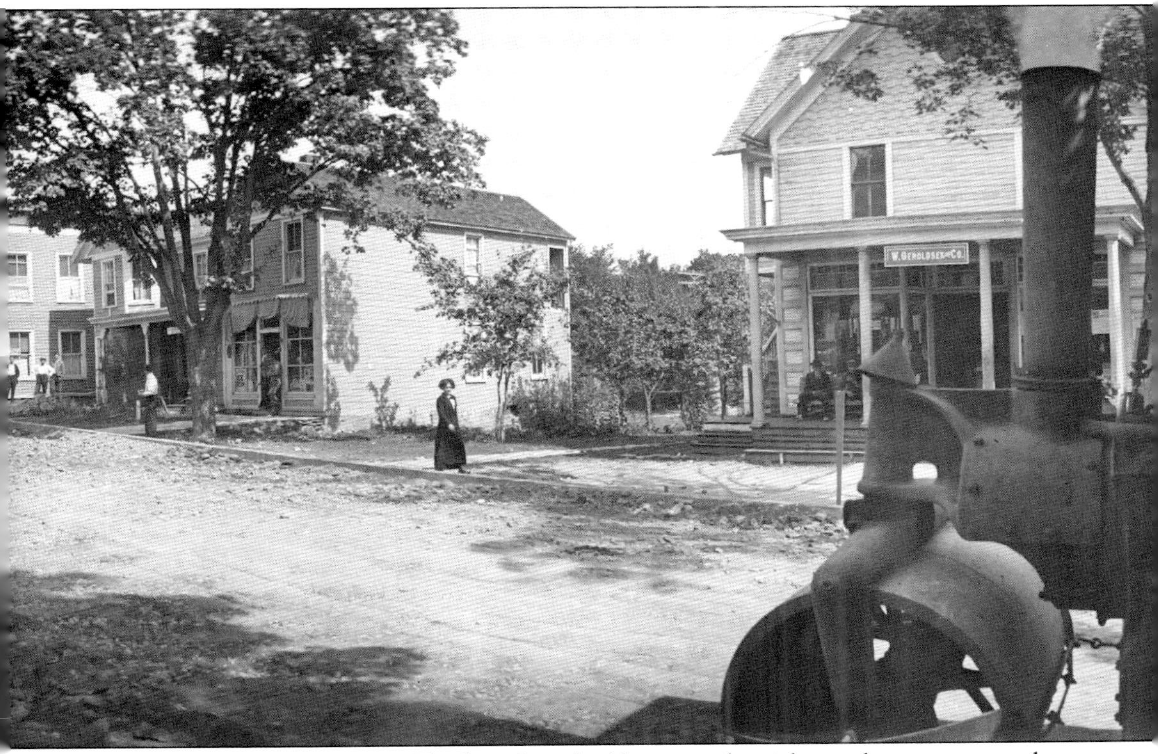

shop of Geroldsek and Company. The last three buildings on the right are long gone, yet the second building—which now houses the Pine Hill Post Office, several shops, and apartments—was restored by Bernard and Florence Hamling to how it looked in 1912. No longer obscured by the trees, the next building is the Zephyr, which was a souvenir shop and later the Village tavern.

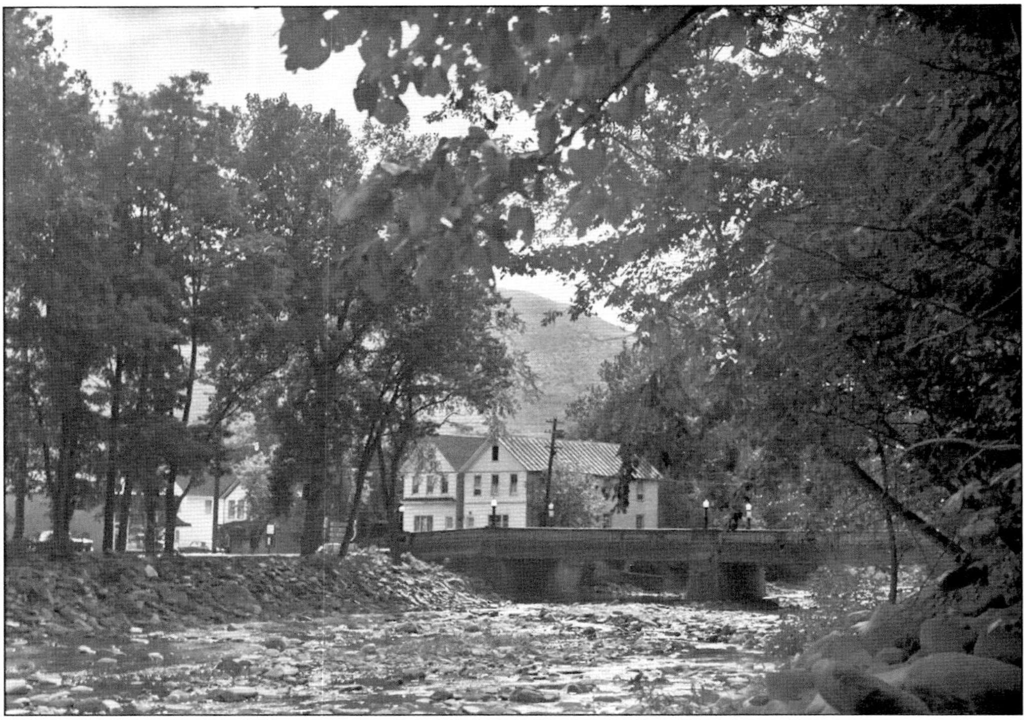

The suspension bridge that spanned the Esopus between State Route 28 and State Route 214 in Phoenicia was replaced with an updated structure lined with light poles. It, too, was modernized in the 1990s and the lights removed. One of the poles that were salvaged was preserved and is now in the Town of Shandaken Historical Museum.

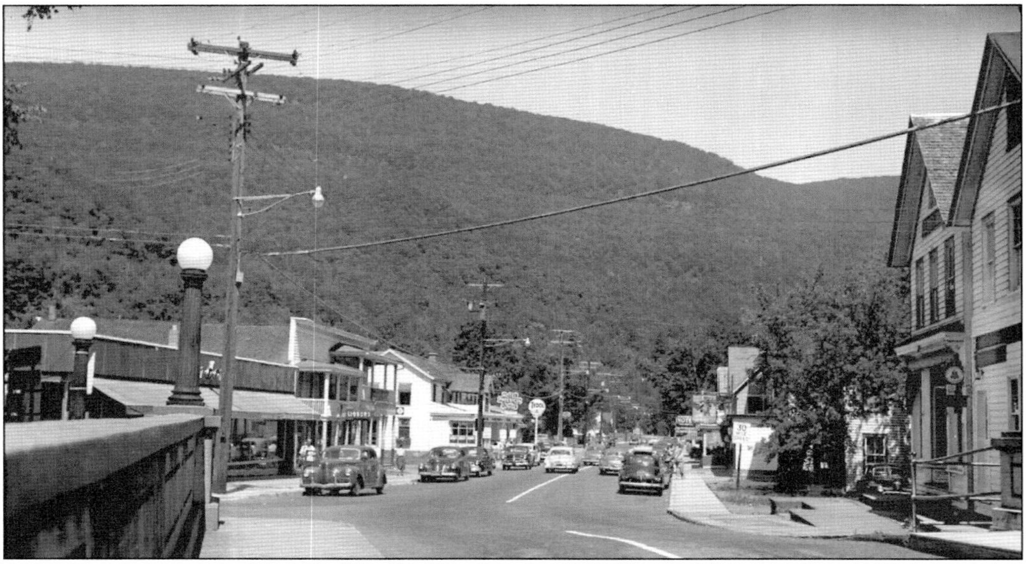

A timeless view of Main Street, Phoenicia, was captured looking north from the bridge. The Phoenicia Pharmacy is the first building on the left. With the exception of the Phoenicia Hotel being lost to a fire, the streetscape has not changed much as of today.

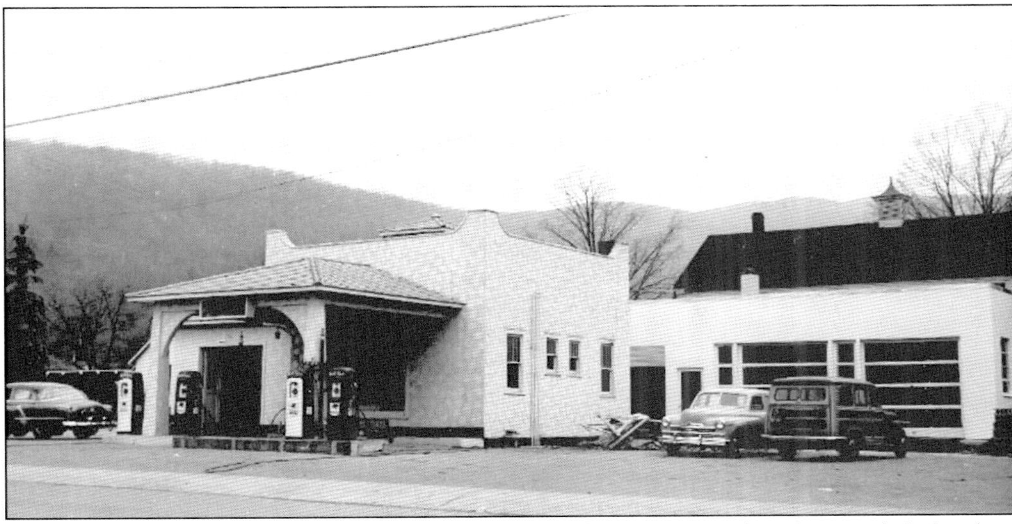

The original Alamo Gas Station building is in the forefront awaiting demolition, while finishing touches are put on the modern Texaco in the rear.

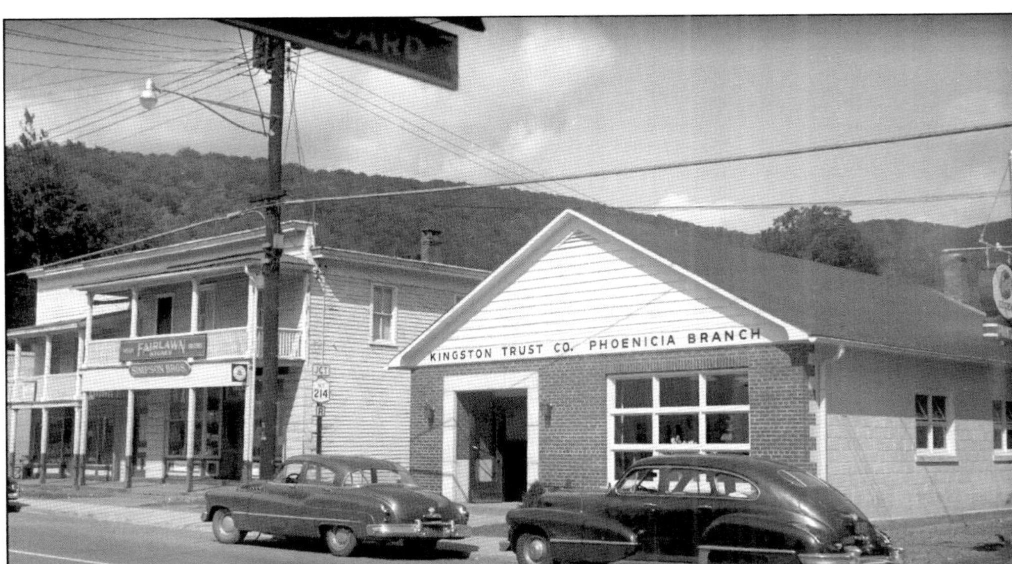

The brick building, right, on Main Street Phoenicia still houses a community bank. On the left, the old Simpson Brothers store is the longtime home of Sweet Sue's restaurant.

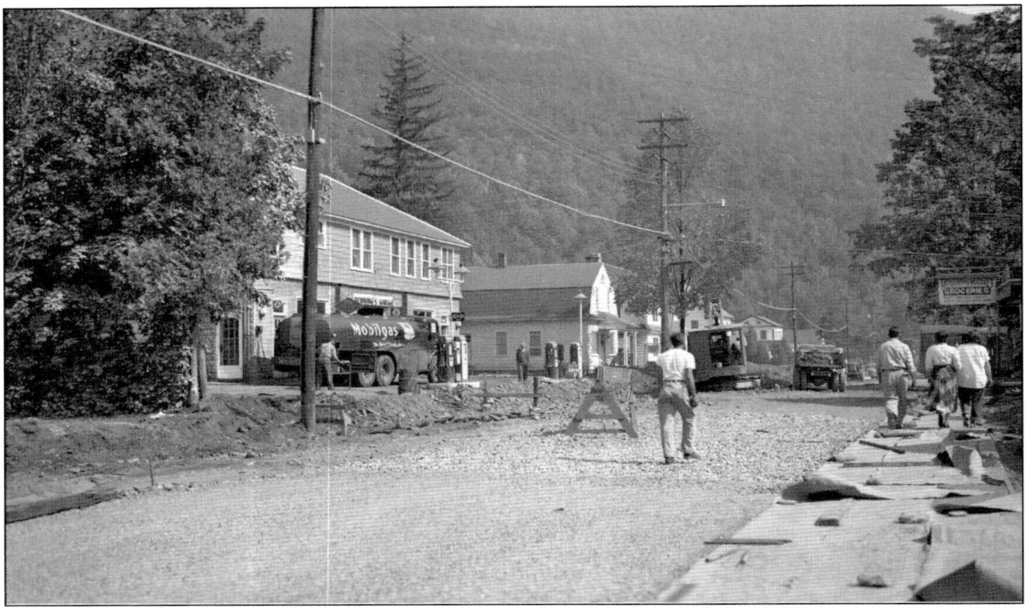

The 1950s brought progress to Phoenicia in the form of roadwork that widened the street. Looking east on the left is now the Phoenicia supermarket and the Gormley Funeral Home. Across the street on the far right is McGraths Market.

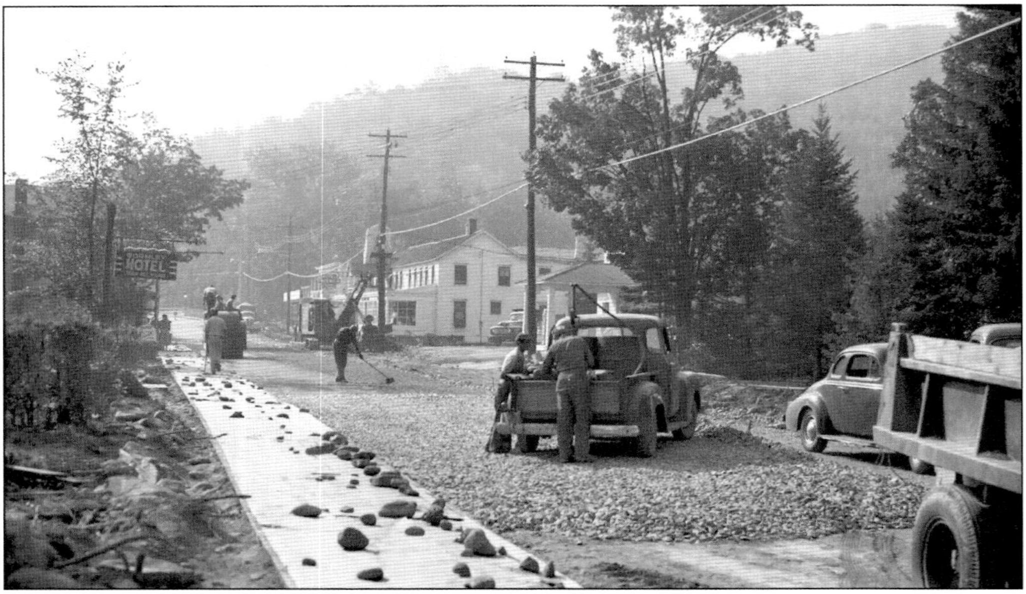

All of the Maple trees lining the road were removed before the widening and repaving of Main Street in Phoenicia in the early 1950s.

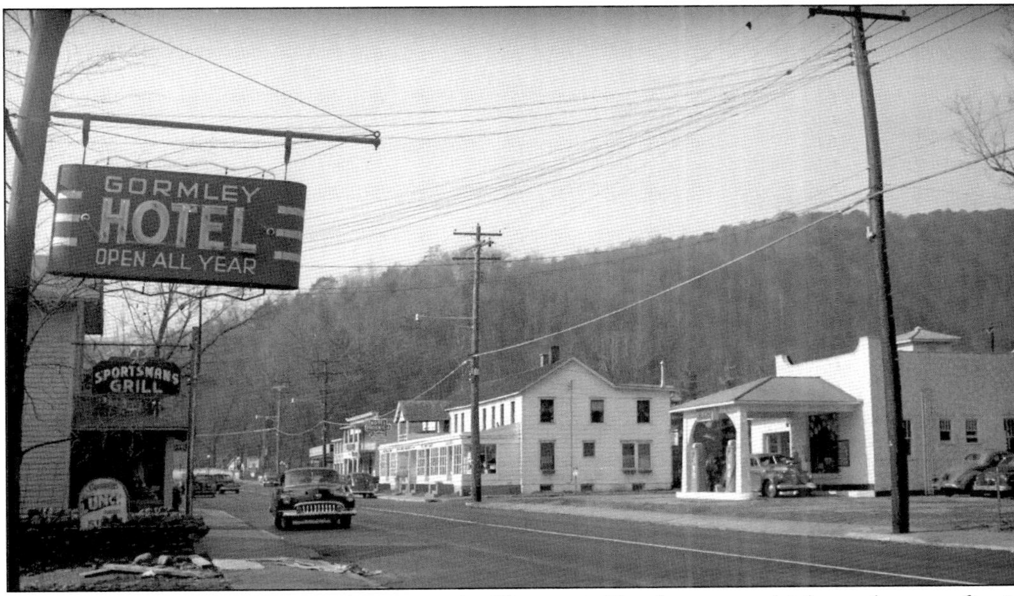

A finished modern streetscape showcases the Phoenicia Hotel, center, which was lost to a fire in 2008. On the far left is the Sportsman's Grill, now Brio's.

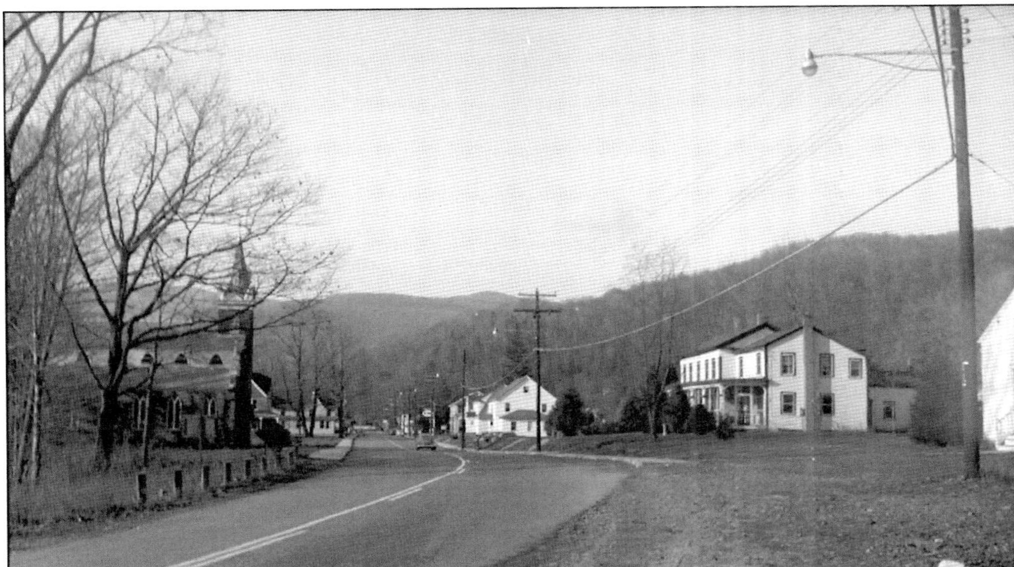

The St. Francis DeSales Church is on the left in this portrait of a newly paved Main Street in Phoenicia. The parsonage is directly across the street.

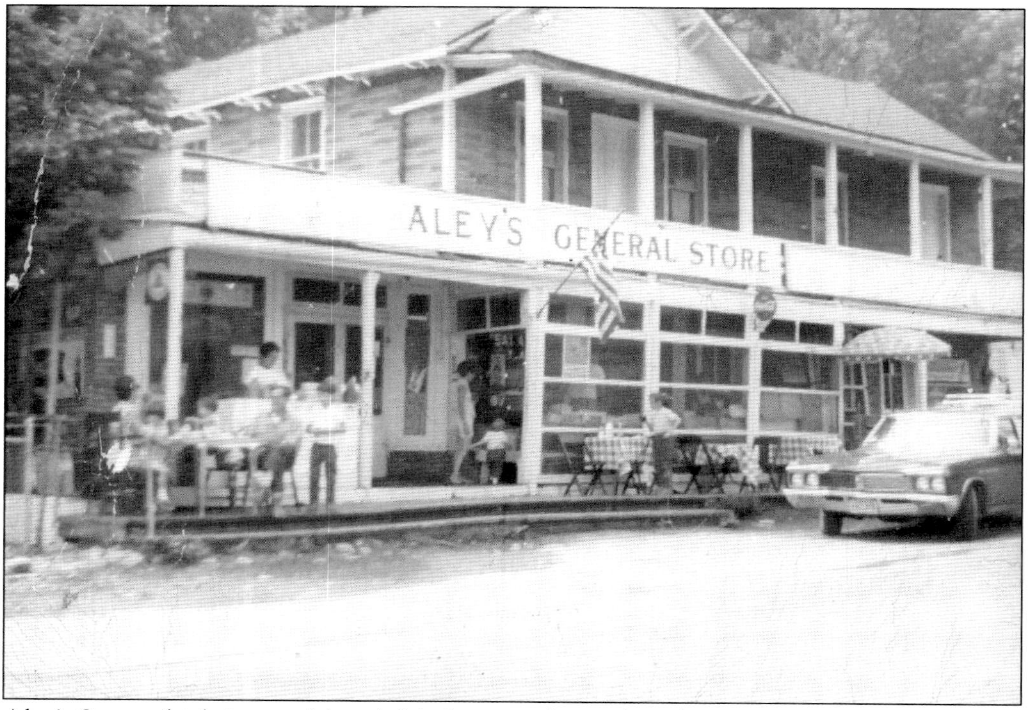

Aley's Store which is now Morra's Market, was located at the intersection of State Route 28 and County Route 42 in Big Indian. Legend has it that this building was a stop on the Underground Railroad.

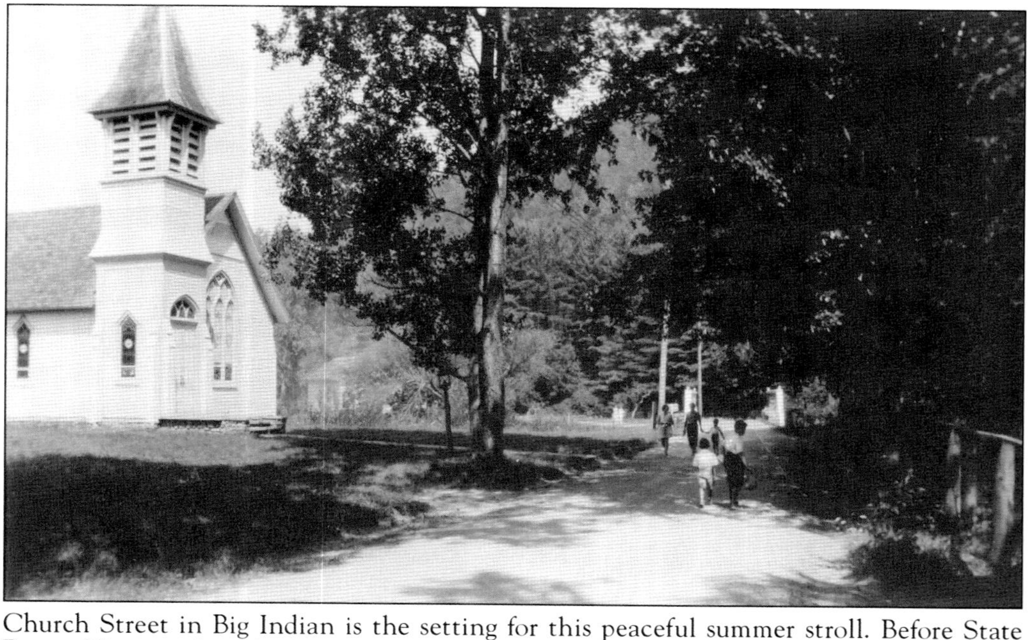

Church Street in Big Indian is the setting for this peaceful summer stroll. Before State Route 28 was realigned, a bridge connected Church Street to the old State Route 28 (renamed Creekside Drive).

Eight

Mountains and Streams

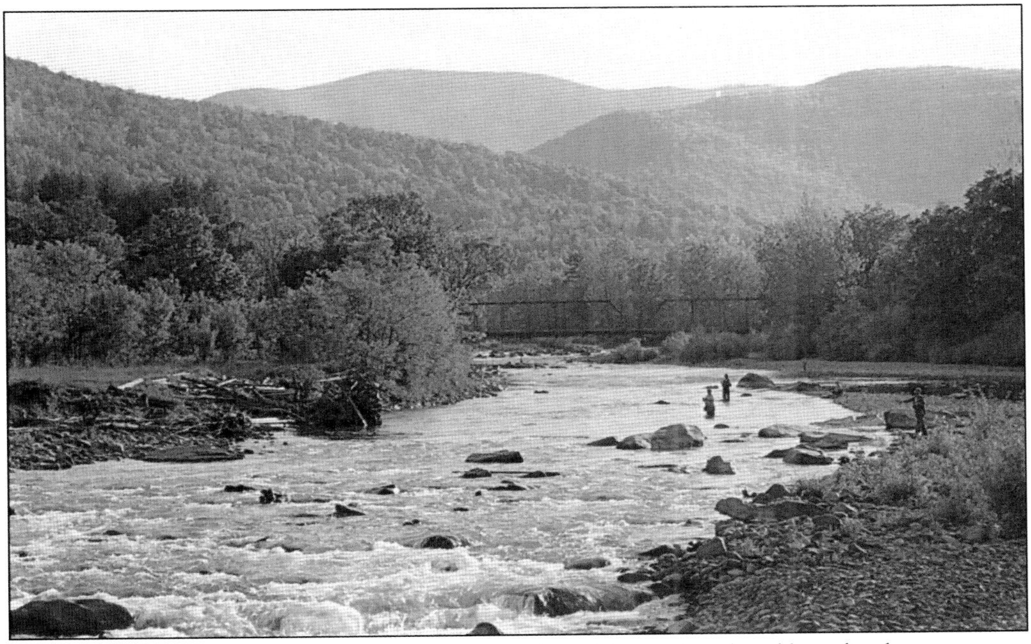

Fishing on the Esopus was an activity strongly endorsed by the hotel and boardinghouse owners in their advertising. Here fly-fishing was born and continues to this day.

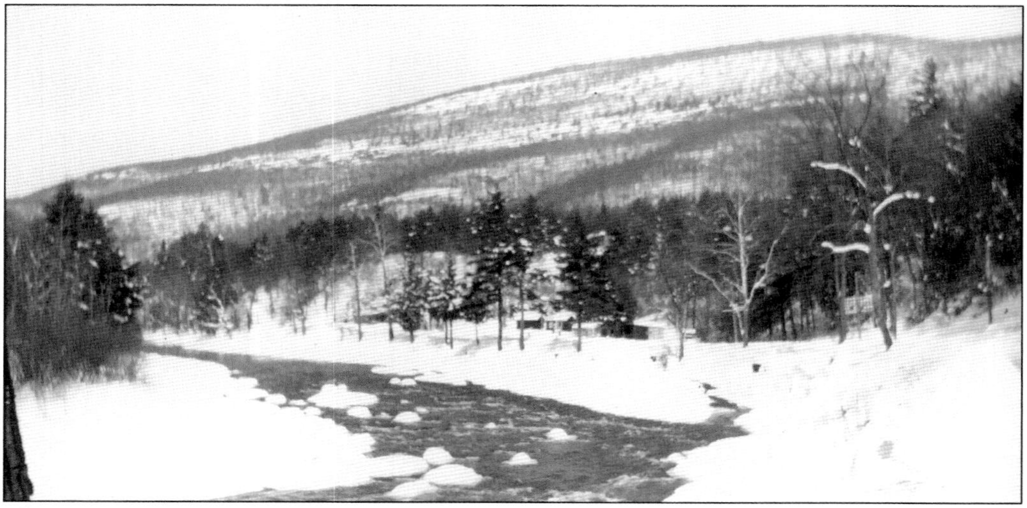

The Stony Clove Creek bed was settled soon after Phoenicia was established as a village. As the mountain paths developed into crude roads, settlers claimed the acreage. The valley was called Edgewood, until the Chichester brothers came and developed the hamlet.

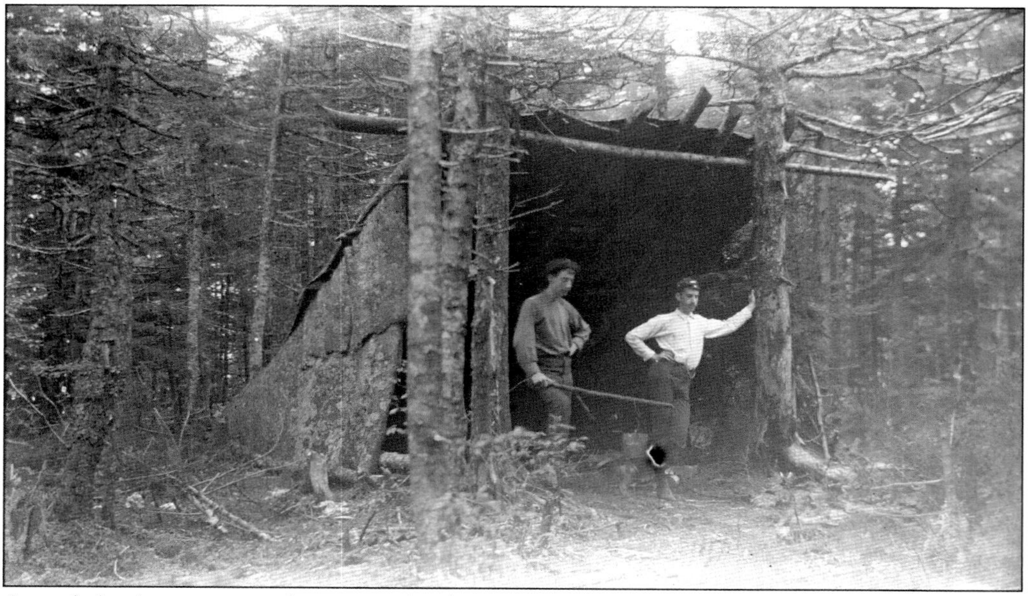

A crude log lean-to is a welcome rest for these campers on Wittenberg Mountain.

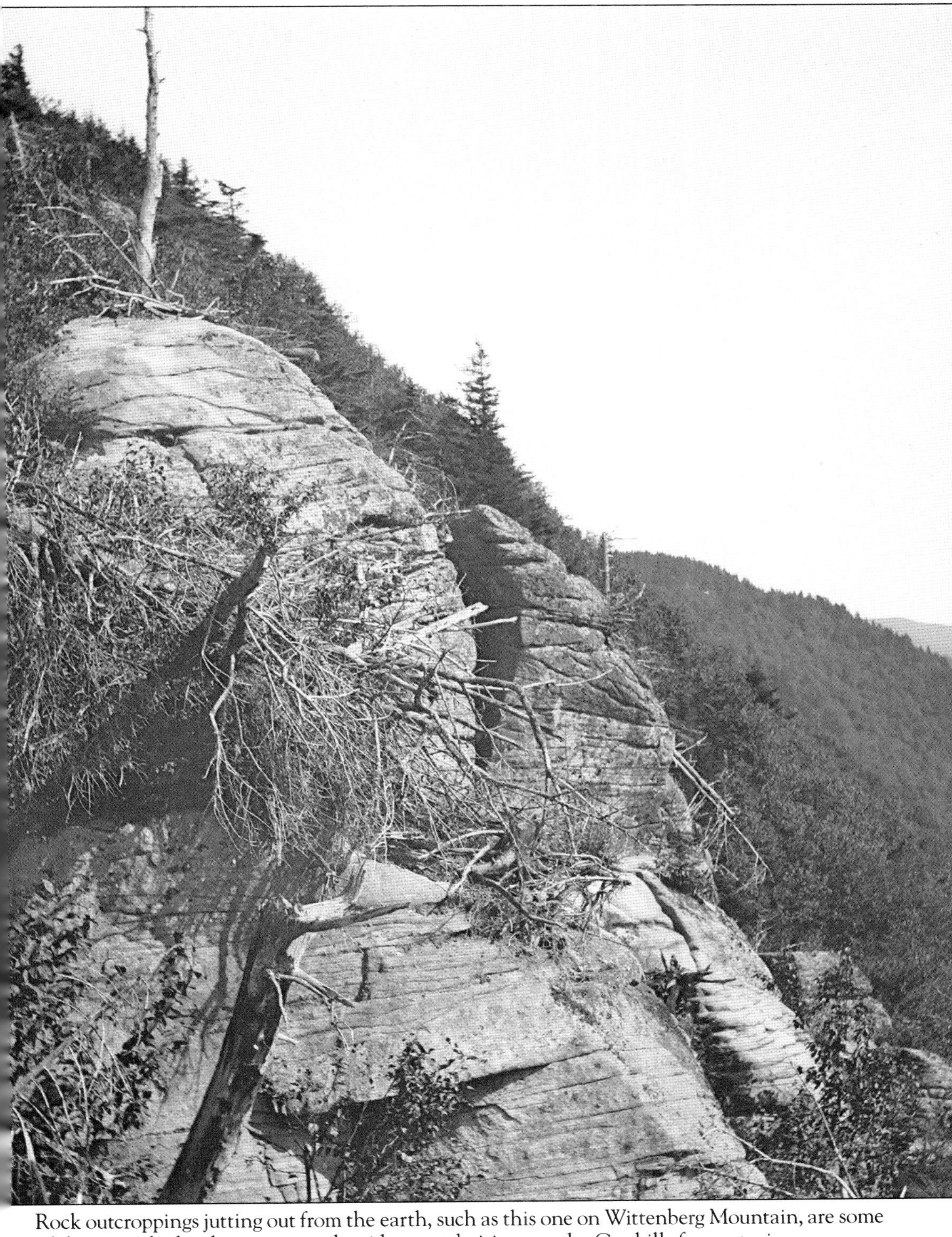

Rock outcroppings jutting out from the earth, such as this one on Wittenberg Mountain, are some of the marvels that have attracted residents and visitors to the Catskills for centuries.

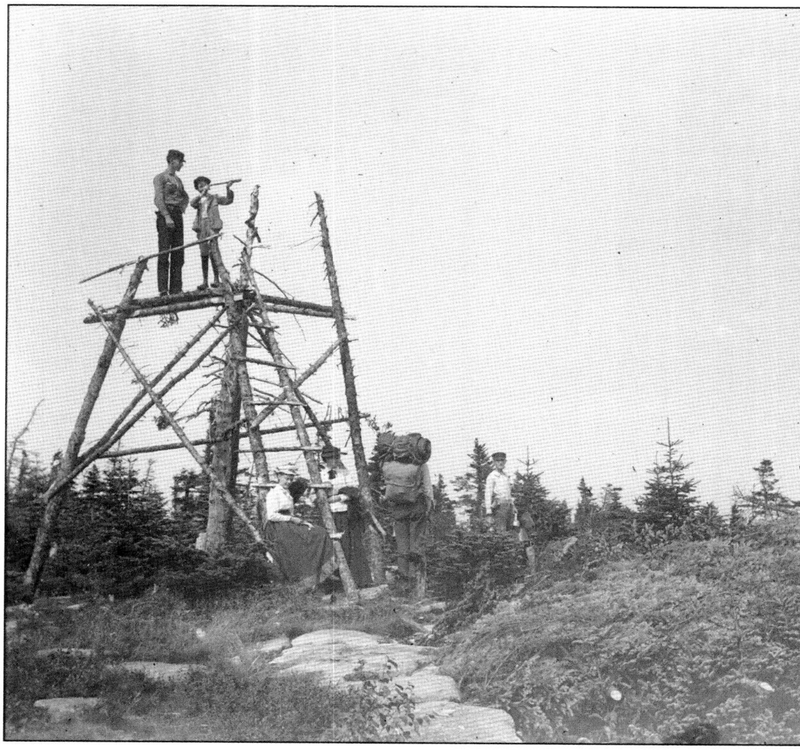

A group of hikers arrive at the observatory on Wittenberg Mountain, a favorite destination of tourists back then and still today. James Dutcher of Oliverea was a pioneering mountain guide who encouraged all his guests to hike Slide Mountain and even built up the trails to ease their journey.

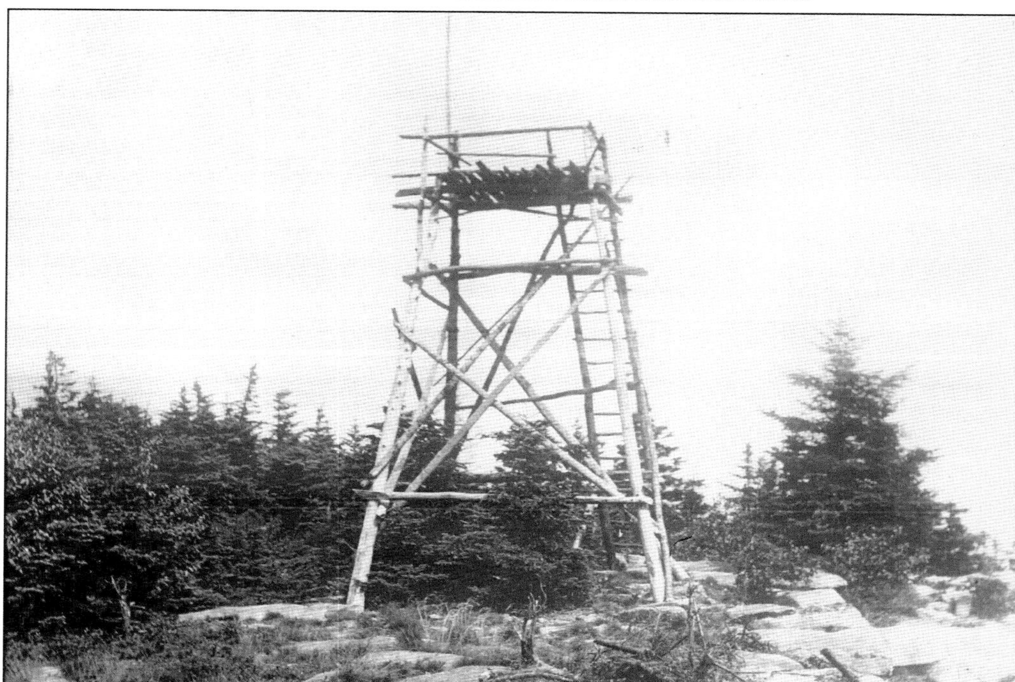

Crude observatories like this one were predecessors of the fire towers that were built on the mountains for the forest rangers of the New York City Conservation Council to monitor the wilderness.

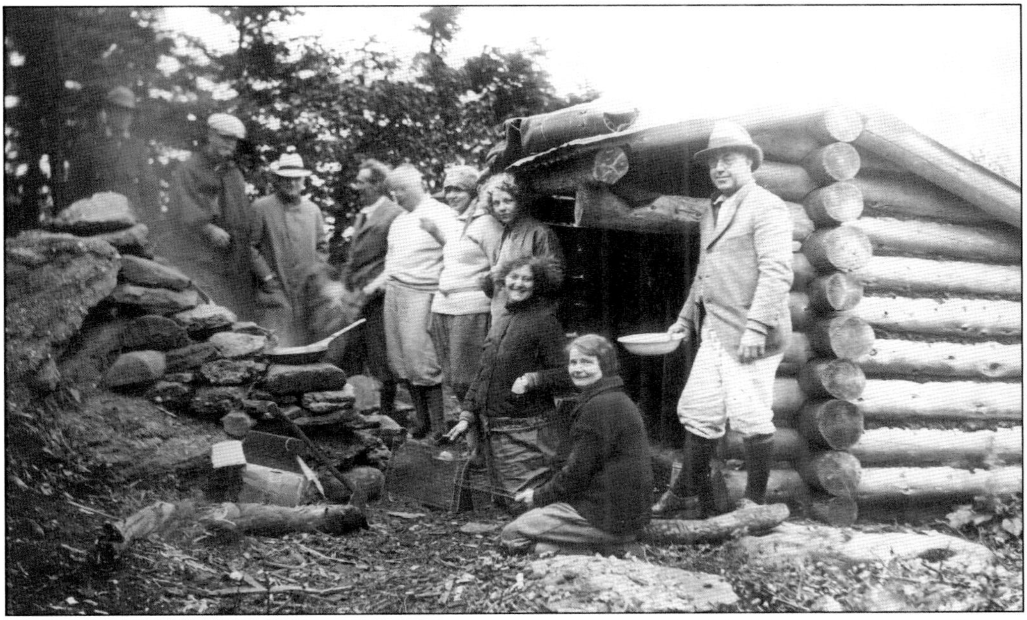

In 1929, professors from a New York City university conquered Slide Mountain in an effort to view and study a forecasted meteor shower. On the far left is Fred Andrews, forest ranger for New York State Conservation Commission. Sixth from left is Norma Andrews Burgin, seventh from left is Mrs. Fred Andrews, and eighth from left is Mrs. William Cruickshank Sr. (Photograph by William Cruickshank Sr.; courtesy of Bryan Burgin.)

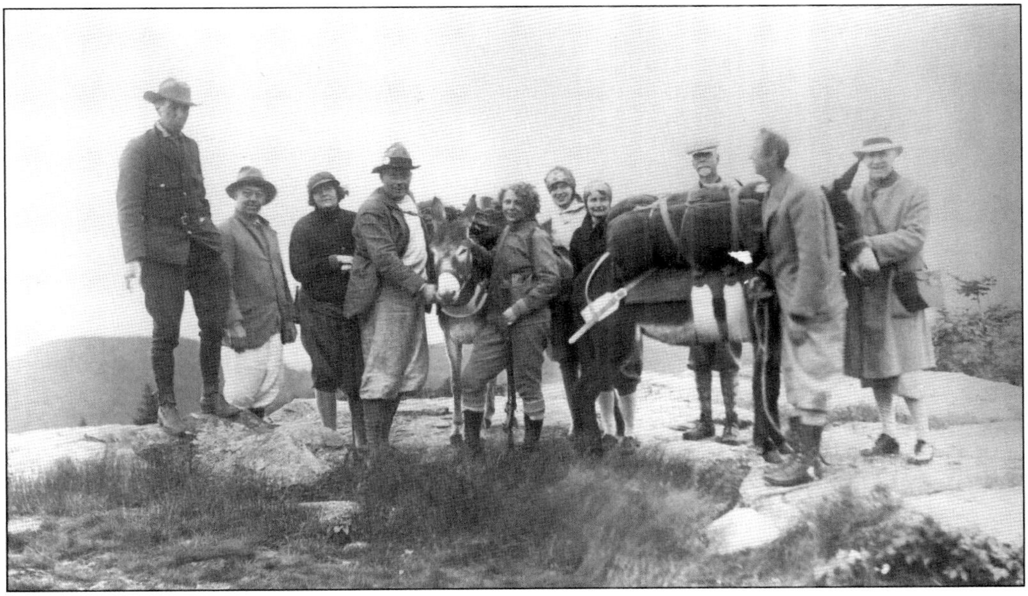

Little did these hikers know they would be adjacent to Panther Mountain, which would be proven to have been created by a meteor strike some 375 million years before. On the far left is Fred Andrews, forest ranger for New York State Conservation Commission. Third from the left is Mrs. William Cruickshank Sr. Sixth from left is Norma Andrews Burgin, and seventh from left is Mrs. Fred Andrews. (Photograph by William Cruickshank Sr.; courtesy of Bryan Burgin.)

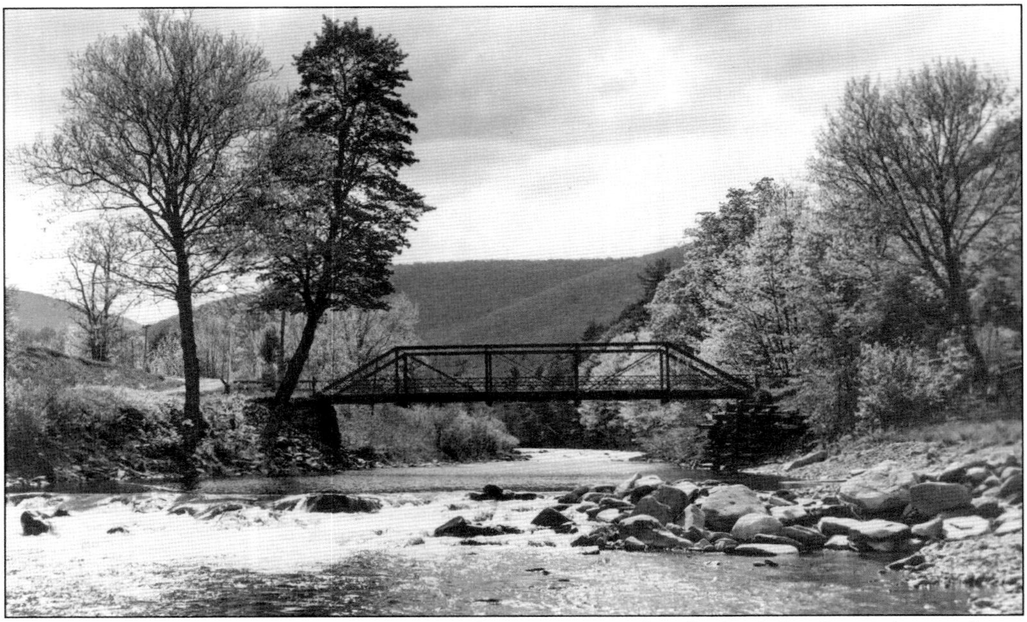

This picture postcard shows a bridge over the Esopus Creek. The high banks of the creek are deceptive, as it is not uncommon for the creek to swell over the edge during a storm.

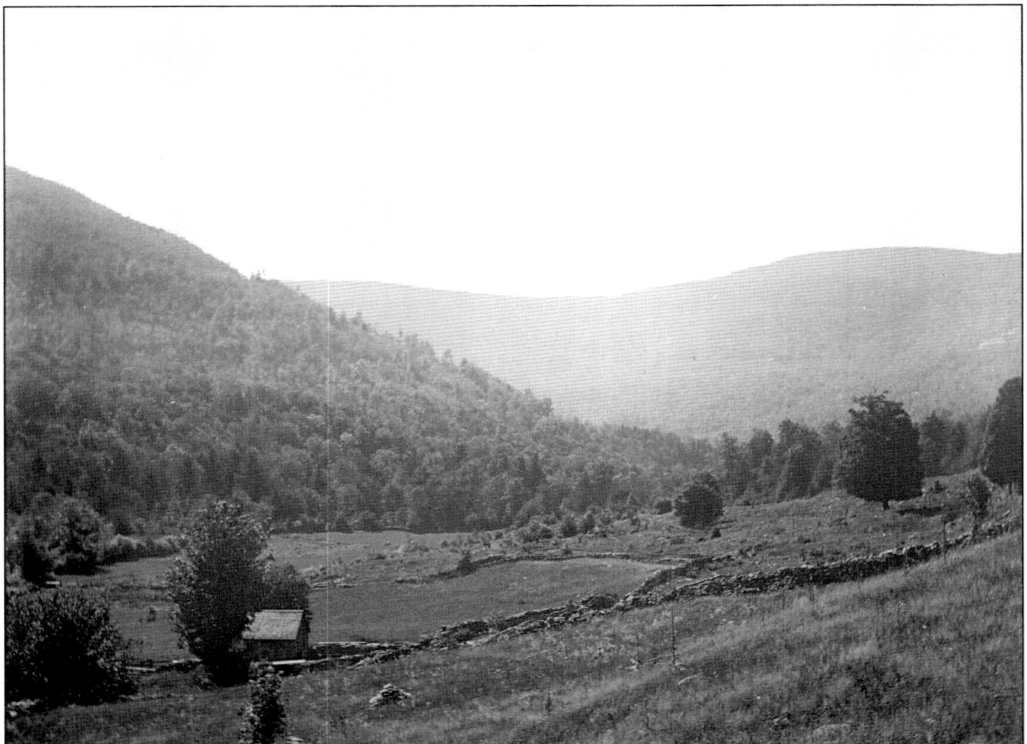

Stone walls, assembled to mark property boundaries and contain livestock, lend a picturesque quality to this mountain meadow.

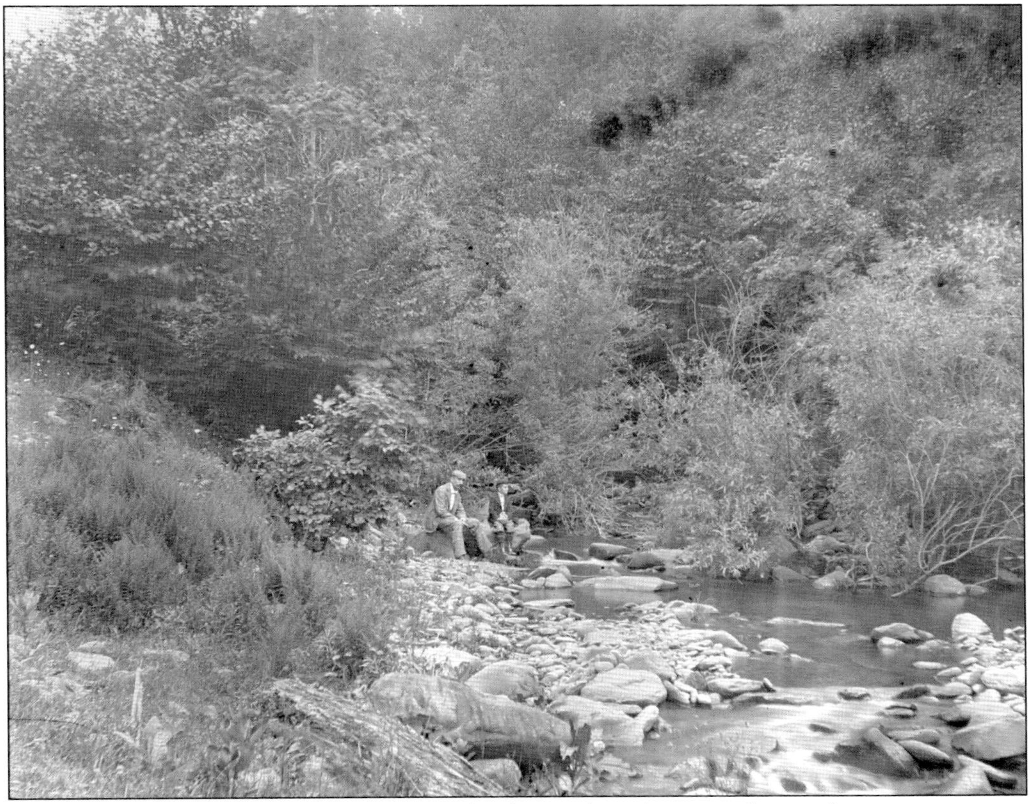

An unidentified man and boy are relaxing by the creek in this print from a glass negative.

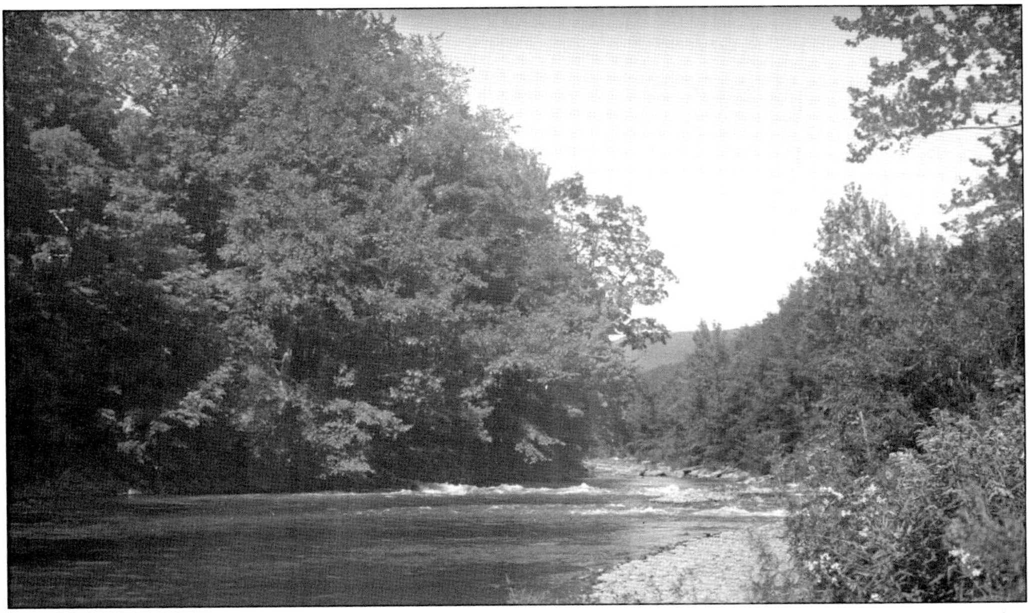

This photograph, reprinted from a glass negative, shows another magnificent view of the Esopus Creek.

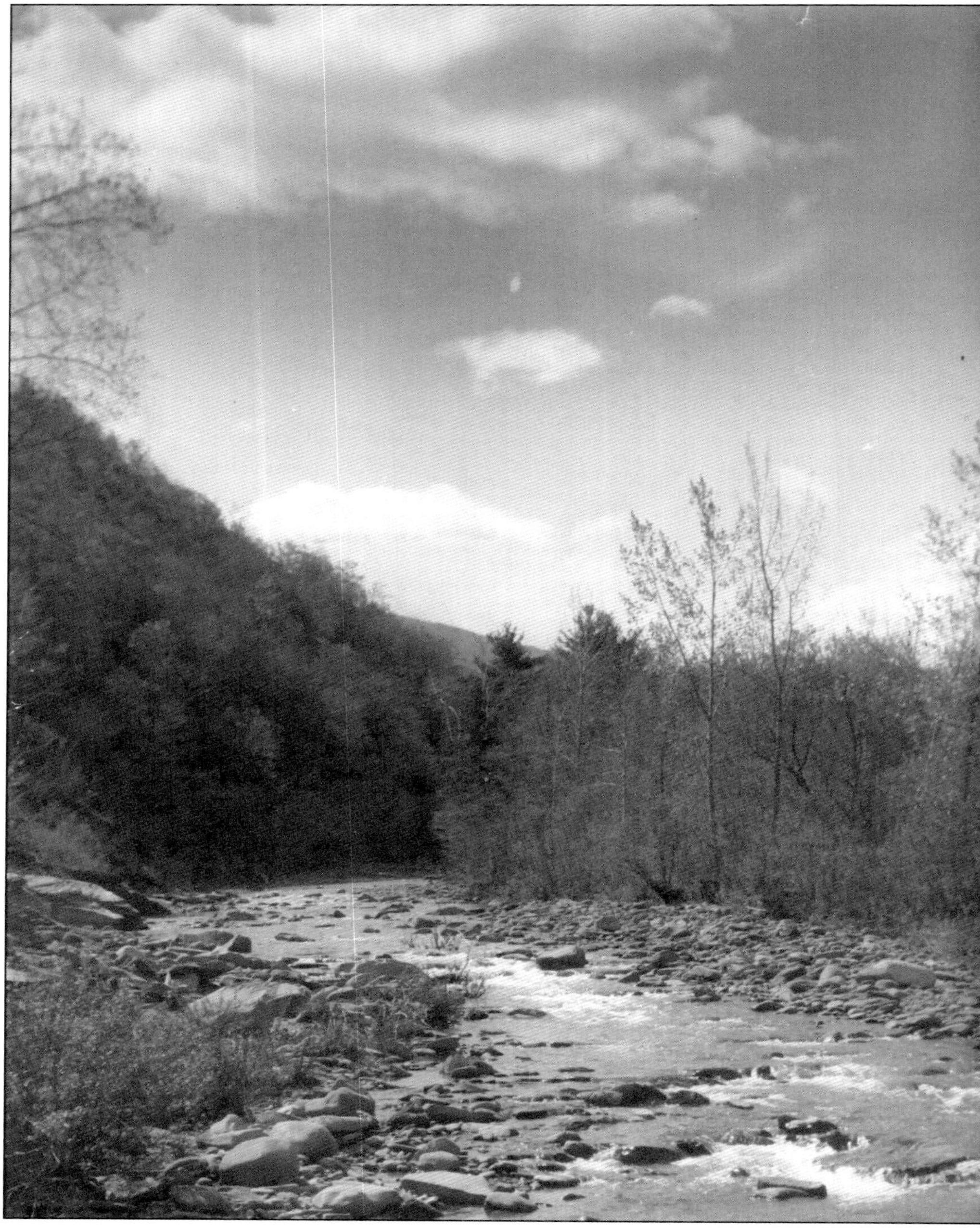

Art prints like this one of the Esopus were among the many souvenirs produced for the "board trade," as tourists were referred to in the early years of development.

About the Town of Shandaken Historical Museum

The Town of Shandaken Historical Museum is housed in the District Number 14 Schoolhouse on 26 Academy Street in Pine Hill, New York, in the Town of Shandaken. The schoolhouse building, erected in 1925, was listed on the National Register of Historic Places in 1997. The museum was established in 1988 to document the history of the Town of Shandaken in oral, written and physical forms. A fascinating collection of 19th and 20th century tools, books, machinery, clothing, letters, postcards, photographs, maps, and other artifacts relating to the 200-year-plus history of the town are on display.

For over 20 years, the museum board and staff have sought to research, document, and disseminate information on the Town of Shandaken and the Catskill Mountains. Operating on a nonprofit basis and relying on volunteer efforts, donations, and assistance from the town government for operating expenses, the board has assembled an impressive collection and institution that will serve the public for many generations.